One of the moving accounts in the a of two security-masked band of commandos. Launched from Australia across two thousand miles of enemy-controlled water they wreaked havoc amongst shipping in Japanese-held Singapore.

"Has all the qualities of a top-class thriller . . . will stand out amongst the war books of all time."

Australian Press Services

"Yet another example of fact outrivalling fiction in thrills and chills."

Adelaide News

"A story that sets the blood coursing."

Sunday Times, Singapore

The Heroes

by
Ronald McKie

ANGUS & ROBERTSON PUBLISHERS

*Unit 4, Eden Park, 31 Waterloo Road,
North Ryde, NSW, Australia 2113, and
16 Golden Square, London W1R 4BN,
United Kingdom*

*This book is copyright.
Apart from any fair dealing for the
purposes of private study, research,
criticism or review, as permitted
under the Copyright Act, no part may
be reproduced by any process without
written permission. Inquiries should
be addressed to the publishers.*

*First published in Australia
by Angus & Robertson Publishers in 1960
First Arkon paperback edition 1973
Reprinted 1975
A&R Non-fiction Classics edition 1977
Reprinted 1980
Second Arkon paperback edition 1983
Reprinted 1986*

Copyright Ronald McKie 1960

ISBN 0 207 13470 7

*Printed in Australia by
The Dominion Press–Hedges & Bell*

AUTHOR'S NOTE

THIS book is completely factual. The dialogue is based on records and the memory of men who survived. It is as close to the original, in fact and spirit, as is possible after a lapse of many years since the Pacific War.

The first part of the book could not have been written without the long co-operation and technical advice of Hubert Edward Carse particularly, but also of Arthur Jones and Horace Young—three shipmates who survived.

Much of the second part could not have been told in detail without the generous help of Hiroyuki Furuta, who befriended "The Heroes".

INTRODUCTION

AHEAD are extracts from the secret war planned in shadow and fought in silence—a war without names or names that were meaningless in which men served and died without even the cold acknowledgment of a casualty list.

In the Australian springs of 1943 and 1944 two marine raids were fired into Japanese-held territory from secret headquarters and bases in Australia by men whose unit, "Z", even to this day, is known only to the few.

Operation "Jaywick", the first, was perhaps the greatest sea-raid of World War II, a raid extraordinary in a war which spawned so many examples of brave eccentric virtuosity.

But Operation "Rimau"—"The Tiger"—which few people have ever heard of—was the raid whose story vanished behind the crying of the monsoon only now to emerge, for the first time, as a requiem for lost men.

Special long-range operations like these, and all they involved, could have come out of no other except the war against Japan, for they were part of the first major war to stain the Pacific and her islands.

But the all-embracing characteristic of that war, which dominated minds and bodies and everything that moved, was distance—distance almost incomprehensible to Europeans conditioned to frontiers a hop-step-jump apart.

Distance, not in hundreds of miles but thousands, helped defeat Japan, and distance made her defeat long and difficult, for distance was an invitation and a deterrent, a protection and a danger, a warning and a challenge. It forced leaders to revolutionize their thinking and men to fight in new ways. It made it inevitable that the secret war would be more arduous, more dangerous, and more likely to fail, for added to distance and little-known geography and disease and tropical heat and rain were white skins and fair hair and blue eyes against brown and black, and languages little understood.

It is important to realize that the white raiders of Jaywick were not in enemy-held seas and territory for a few hours or days, but for more than a month, nearly two thousand miles from their base and far beyond all hope of rescue, and of life, if their raid went wrong.

Their achievement was incomparable, though bravery alone was not enough to make it so, for any men who raided in the Western Desert or among the pink Greek islands or along the spiked coast of Hitler's Europe, were brave.

But it was Rimau, the raid which failed and disappeared, which cries the timelessness of courage—of men who knew capture meant death and who were ready to die, and to laugh as they died, under the sweep of a medieval sword.

These were the men whom even their enemies called "The Heroes", and this is their epitaph.

CONTENTS

OPERATION JAYWICK	viii
OPERATION RIMAU	153
AUTHOR'S NOTES	228

MAPS

The attack route of Operation Jaywick	76
Route of Operation Jaywick's three-canoe attack from Pandjang Island through Bulan Strait to Singapore	107
The attack route of Operation Rimau	156
Route of the junk *Mustika* from Merapas Island through Temiang and Suji straits to near Singapore	187

OPERATION JAYWICK

Major Ivan Lyon, M.B.E., D.S.O., the Gordon Highlanders
Lieutenant D. M. N. Davidson, D.S.O., R.N.V.R.
Lieutenant R. C. Page, D.S.O., A.I.F.
Lieutenant H. E. Carse, R.A.N.V.R., mention in dispatches
Leading Stoker J. P. McDowell, D.S.M., R.N.
**Leading Telegraphist H. S. Young, R.A.N.,
   mention in dispatches**
**Acting Leading Seaman K. P. Cain, R.A.N.,
   mention in dispatches**
Acting Able Seaman W. G. Falls, D.S.M., R.A.N.
Acting Able Seaman A. M. W. Jones, D.S.M., R.A.N.
Acting Able Seaman A. W. Huston, D.S.M., R.A.N.
**Acting Able Seaman F. W. Marsh, R.A.N.,
   mention in dispatches**
**Acting Able Seaman M. M. Berryman, R.A.N.,
   mention in dispatches**
Corporal R. G. Morris, B.E.M., M.,M., R.A.M.C.
Corporal A. Crilley, M.M., A.I.F.

1

ACROSS THE STREET, beyond the brooding shade of the big fig tree, the sunlight lapped the gates of the hidden Gardens as Ted Carse left the bar of the Botanical and began to walk up Domain Road.

At the corner he stopped for a tram to swing, then went on under the dappled leaves, up the sloping street, past houses and flats squat and ugly, past Marne Street and a flickering memory of other battles long ago, until he reached the crest and realized that the even numbers were on the other side.

He crossed, skirted a wall, and came to double iron gates between high columns topped with old broken wrought-iron lamp standards. The gates were faded green, diseased with rust scabs, and backed with rusty sheets of galvanized iron. And beyond the gates was a tall chimney grey and cold against the warm sky.

Then he saw the single iron gate, also backed with iron, let into the long red brick wall, and above the gate the name "Airlie" chiselled years before into stone, and beside the gate the number "260".

He reached for his cigarette pack and checked the address scribbled inside the flap—"260 Domain Road, South Yarra, Melbourne", beside the date, "12th January, 1943".

So this is it, he thought, excited now but not sure why, yet knowing that some part of his life was ending here, beside this wall, in this splinter of time.

He glanced up and down the road and saw a sparrow watching him with bright eyes from a smoking heap of fresh dung. He glanced at his watch. He approached the small gate. It was locked.

His hollow loose knock had hardly time to hide behind the wall before a pigeonhole opened and eyes studied him.

"Who are you and what do you want?"

The voice was crude, demanding.

"My name's Carse. I have a letter from Commander Long."

"Wait."

The eyes slipped away, the pigeonhole closed. He waited, probably a minute though it seemed much longer. Then a chain scraped across metal, and the gate opened inward.

"Come in," the voice said, and spat.

A soldier, with rifle at the on-guard, watched Carse from beside a small guardhouse, while the other soldier shut the gate, pulled a chain across and snapped a padlock.

The armed man flicked his bayonet point at the gravel drive.

"Go ahead," he said, and followed.

Carse saw that he was in a large garden with shaggy lawns

and rose bushes to the right and a long flower-bed lost under weeds to the left. The house was grey Victorian with a colonnaded veranda and an entrance covering, which reached across the drive, like an ornate shell topped with a miniature pagoda.

The guard pushed a bell, and they waited on the tile veranda as the sound echoed inside. At last the door opened and a buxom unsmiling three-stripe A.W.A.S. looked Carse up and down.

"What do you want?" she asked.

"My name's Carse. I have a letter from Commander Long." He was getting tired of his little speech.

"Wait," she said, and went away.

Carse and the guard stared at each other, but without communion. After a long time the A.W.A.S. returned.

"Follow me."

They crossed an entrance hall, heels like castanets on inlaid wood, and climbed wide curving stairs below a domed skylight of stained glass which drenched the stairwell with amber light. And as they climbed Carse noticed, too, that the guard watched him from the foot of the stairs.

At the top the A.W.A.S. stopped at a door to the left of two narrow archways and knocked. Then she opened the door and beckoned.

Now he was in a long room where all sound died in the thickness of the grey carpet or was captured by the heavy claret curtains. A British Army colonel was at an almost bare desk in the centre of a deep bay window. The room had no other furniture—not even a second chair. The walls were vacant.

The colonel had greying hair, a black bushy moustache, tanned skin. He looked up.

"Who are you?"

Carse noticed his teeth, big teeth; that his voice, though precise, was heavy, close, as though it had been thickened with flour; that the words were cold, impersonal. A seal—an angry seal—he thought, but said. "My name is Carse. I have a letter from the D.N.I." He took it from his jacket pocket. "Are you Colonel Mott?"

"Yes."

He ignored the offered letter. His eyes flicked at the one ring on Carse's naval jacket.

"I was expecting Lieutenant Carse. Are you Lieutenant Carse?"

Carse had just been promoted, but didn't know it at that time. He said, "As far as I know I'm Sub-Lieutenant Carse."

The colonel motioned to the A.W.A.S. "You can go."

The door closed and for a minute or more, while he played with a pencil, his eyes never left his visitor. At last: "I understand you know the islands and can navigate. Is that true?"

2

"Yes, sir."

Carse didn't like the man behind the desk. Or his cold appraisal. Or being forced to stand. He waited.

"Have you any guts?"

The word was like ripping cloth in the still room.

Carse didn't answer. He stared into the other's eyes, knowing that the man was deliberately probing, goading, and not knowing why. It's your move, he thought.

The colonel picked up a sheet of paper and began to read, and behind him, through a parting in the curtains, Carse could see a grey balcony and trees washed in summer haze. On the railing a dove, puffed with the conceit of love, was making pompous noises, and the urgent yet strangely peaceful sounds reminded Carse for a moment of years back in the Victorian snow country, up along the Indi, the hills and wind in his face, of the silence and peace of hills. And then he was back in the room, telling himself, "Keep your temper."

Now the colonel was bending forward, speaking urgently.

"We're running a dangerous organization and we want a navigator. That's why I asked to see you. If you were selected for the job could you take a ship from Melbourne to San Francisco?"

"I could take her anywhere," Carse said.

The colonel's stiffness relaxed. He showed his teeth.

"I like you. Would you care to join our organization?"

It was so sudden, so out of character, that Carse wanted to laugh. Instead, he shrugged.

"That depends. I don't know what it is or anything about it."

"It might lead to operations behind the enemy lines. It could be most dangerous. But until you join us I can't tell you more—and not much even then."

Now we're moving, Carse thought, wondering where, but knowing that this was an opportunity at last to get out of the rut, that almost anything would be better than the futile job he was doing.

"All right—I'll join—if you think my qualifications are good enough." And added, his deep brown eyes probing the other man's: "And particularly as you like me so much."

The colonel's mouth tightened, just a little, though Carse couldn't tell whether in anger or amusement.

All the colonel said was, "Good. When can you join us?"

"I have seven days' leave due. . . . I'd like to take that first."

"Right. I would like you to be in a position where you have no leave due for a full year. Now—where do you live?"

"Sydney."

"You'll need a movement order. Sergeant Samson—the A.W.A.S. you saw—will show you where to get it. Although you are Navy it will be an Army movement order and all your movements will be through Army. I won't explain. You will proceed to Cairns by air where you will be met at the airport and transported to Z.E.S. I can't tell you more, except that your number will be one one nine. That's all, except for one thing. I must impress upon you the need for the utmost security. Your life is unimportant—quite unimportant—but the security of the organization is vital."

He held out his hand.

"Thank you, Mr Carse."

Carse took the strong hand, dropped it, remembered he was still holding the letter.

"Destroy it," the colonel said, as he took papers from a drawer and began to read.

As Carse turned away he noticed the room had a white Italian ceiling decorated with leaf and fruit clusters, that a rolled chart—he knew it was a chart—was on the mantelshelf above the white marble fireplace. He was still staring at the chart, wondering if in some way it involved him, when Sergeant Samson, just inside the door, said, "Follow me."

She led downstairs to a big thinly furnished room and introduced him to two men. One, he was to discover later, was Lieutenant-Commander L. A. McGowan, the other Sergeant Roy Pegler, who months before had established the unit headquarters where he was to spend the following months.

McGowan gave him his leave pay and movement order, and then asked, "Have you a bank account in Sydney?"

"The Commonwealth."

"From now on your pay and your wife's allowance will be paid into that account—and into no other. I'm afraid that's all I can tell you."

Then he was outside and the waiting guard marched him in silence down the drive and the other guard, also without a word let him through.

As the gate rattled shut, and he again heard the scrape of chain on metal, Carse lit a cigarette, inhaled deeply, and let the smoke out in a long exhaust-like sigh. Then he grinned, settled his cap and walked slowly down Domain Road.

Ted Carse had been in curious situations in his life, had met some curious people, but the last half-hour was an entirely new experience. What had he joined? Who and what was Colonel Mott? What was this dangerous organization? What indeed was Z.E.S.? Above all, had he just made a goat of himself, done something foolish, something he would regret? The questions were all unanswerable. But one thing was positive. He was in something secret right up to the eyes.

As he went along the sloping pavement under the trees, the sunlight slapping his eyes through the leaves, he had no way of knowing that he would never see the fierce colonel again, never know more than a few details about him, never enter that secret headquarters again.

Nor was he to know for a long time, as he drank a badly needed beer at the bar of the Botanical and called for another, that the two men near him, the two civilians who argued racing, were to follow him all that afternoon, wherever he went in Melbourne, to keep a record of everyone he met, and to be at Spencer Street railway station that night just to make sure he caught the Sydney train.

As the Douglas turned over the shallows of Botany Bay and headed north, two American fighters like dirty green hawks slid across her wagging their wings and slid away.

Carse watched them go, down down and away, wondering as he lost them in the grey morning blueness around the Harbour Bridge whether they would buzz the city as he had seen them do in the last week, his last leave for a year, screaming below roof level along Elizabeth Street.

The Harbour . . . the pines along Manly beach . . . the sweep of headlands like dim battleships swinging east. . . . He dropped his seat-belt, and combed his fine black hair, which curled over his forehead, with long tobacco-stained fingers.

"You will report to Z.E.S. at Cairns. . . ."

Above the engines he could hear that unrelenting voice, but he was no longer interested in the stiff colonel behind the desk in that guarded house in South Yarra. What concerned him now was the organization he had joined, for his letter of appointment, which had only just reached him, told him virtually nothing—only a fraction more than he already knew when the gate at 260 Domain Road had slammed behind him.

At the naval base, where he had made discreet inquiries among the few friends who were not at sea, nobody had ever heard of the Inter-Allied Services Department,* or could guess what the vague name of this organization meant, and Z.E.S., his destination fifteen hundred miles north of Sydney, was still too meaningless even to be mysterious.

In one way he was glad of his ignorance. He had been able to answer the questions his wife Pat had pumped at him, and answer them with such ease that she knew he must be telling the truth. His destination was Cairns. That was all the information he could give her. He would know more when he got there.

Which was not strictly true, because he had already made a discovery which told him a lot—and still nothing—and only added to the enigma of his future. At Army Movements in Sydney a sergeant had almost sneered at the two rings on his sleeve until he had produced his movement order—and then a

*See Author's Notes, p. 277.

colonel's name had been crossed off and he was on the next morning's Australian National Airways flight to the north.

This didn't deceive Carse. It wouldn't have deceived a child. He knew there was no magic in his name or rank, and that his priority was not due to any special love for the Navy. There could be only one explanation—I.A.S.D.—and that meant that the Inter-Allied Services Department, which he already more than suspected was merely a cover-name, was not only secret but powerful.

As the Douglas drew north above the patched green coastal strip he knew that ahead at Cairns, or somewhere else beyond Capricorn, must be a ship that needed a navigator—a job on the sea now a backdrop of summer haze behind far glimpses of beach and surf beyond the starboard wingtip.

And for the first time since Melbourne he was glad, almost elated, not at the thought of the sea alone, which he had always loved and regretted leaving, but at the knowledge that he might be on his way at last to something useful and interesting, a job which promised skill and adventure after so many difficult, tedious, muddled and, yes, amusing years.

Like his parson grandfather from London, who had abandoned cloth and country to seek a fortune on the Victorian diggings during the gold rushes of the 1850s, Hubert Edward Carse had tossed away a career to go on a physical and spiritual walkabout which had taken him to strange places.

He was born at Rutherglen, Victoria. His father was a schoolteacher, his mother a Carmody of Carmodale, which is up where the Murray River is called the Indi, and his music teacher, when he was a skinny rat-faced brat living near Seymour, was a Miss Kelly who proudly claimed kinship with Ned and Dan and the last stand at Glenrowan, and who taught scales with a sharp-edged ruler.

At thirteen he became a naval cadet and one of thirty—Dowling, Rosenthal, Nisbet, Walker, Abbott, and many more—who survived the fourth cadet year of the Royal Australian Naval College at Jervis Bay. He passed out as midshipman in 1918 just in time to see, through the Orkney mists, Kaiser Wilhelm's High Seas Fleet scuttled at Scapa Flow.

And in time, too, to sail to the Arctic Circle in H.M.S. *Tiger* to transmit weather reports while the British dirigible R.34 flew to the United States and back, and, as the most junior officer in the battle cruiser *Renown,* to go on her post-World War I "glamour cruises"—with the President of Brazil to Lisbon, the Prince of Wales to the United States, the Prince to Australia when Edward's equerry was Lord Louis Mountbatten, a sublieutenant and at that time, despite his lineage, almost the lowest form of naval life.

At twenty-one, when Carse was a thin, big-nosed subbie, with a scorn for all authority and a tremendous capacity for beer, and after he had served in old H.M.A.S. *Australia,* on north Australia survey work in *Geranium,* and in submarines, he decided, in the gloom and disillusionment of the Mad Twenties, when any armed service seemed to offer little future, to leave the Navy.

He became a schoolteacher—an impulsive act he was soon to regret—though he lasted two years before the turbulent blood from his grandfather boiled over. He went around the world as an able seaman on a British merchant ship and was third mate on a Norwegian tramp to Rio de Janeiro. Then he bought a lugger at Thursday Island, sailed her to Darwin and fished for pearlshell and sea slug, and even ran one cargo of shell to the Indies. Eighteen months later he was a cleaner in a Sydney factory.

In the depression of the early 1930s he had a camel team around Tennant Creek in the Northern Territory, and scratched for elusive gold west of the Olgas. By the mid-thirties he was in Sydney again, this time running an S.P. shop in a Paddington backyard, and making money, until he was forced out of business, chased out by intimidation, because he refused to pay the regular police squeeze, which in those pre-inflation days was one pound on the last winner of the day, no matter what the price. He again turned to cleaning, with an artificial-jewellery firm, and had worked up to foreman by the time World War II began.

He volunteered almost on the first day, but back in 1919 the pneumonic influenza pandemic, which killed millions, had caught him at Portsmouth and left him with bronchial trouble; and when in 1939 the naval surgeons listened wisely, as surgeons appear to do, to his scraggy chest and eroded tubes, they shook their heads and, with regret, rejected him.

Later he tried again, and even had all his teeth out in the hope that this might encourage the Navy to accept him, but he didn't get in until 1942, when the Japanese held most of the Pacific and anyone who could breathe with difficulty was classed A1 and snatched by some Service.

Gratefully, the Navy made this Naval College graduate a sub-lieutenant and sent him to Townsville, under an old New Guinea hand, Commander Webb, to collect small boats for harbour defence and supply among the islands, and one of the first and best buys was a smuggler in good condition, but no longer in business, which anyone who had been in the North longer than a few weeks knew had been used a lot in the prosperous days before the war to pick up opium at sea from the incoming China ships.

In Townsville, months later, he met "Cockie" Long, then Director of Naval Intelligence, and an old colleague, who suggested, vaguely but unmistakably, that he might have more interesting work for a Jervis Bay graduate than messing around with old boats and getting drunk on rest days. And in a couple of weeks Carse was in Melbourne, walking away from 260 Domain Road, already a member of an organization so secret that nobody could tell him what it was, or what part he was to play in it, and so important that a week later, aged forty-two, with deep lines of dissipation on his lean sallow face, incipient bronchitis, and one more ring on his sleeve than he had worn in the R.A.N. twenty years before, he was on a top-priority flight, with islands now like water-beetles off the coast below, heading for a destination that was three letters, as picturesque but as meaningless as Japanese characters, on his movement order.

2

STRAY SQUALLS were chasing each other in from the sea when the driver who had picked him up at the airfield stopped beside a group outside the Cairns Returned Soldiers' Club.

"What delayed you?" a captain angrily demanded. "I told you to be here at. . . ."

"It was my fault," Carse said. "My plane was two hours late."

"Oh," the captain said. "Well—we'd better get cracking."

He climbed in beside Carse and the others got in the back.

"Step on it, Mick," one of them called.

The driver turned the truck and drove through the town and out along the road that led to Gordonvale. They drove in silence.

Carse wondered who they were. He knew that the lieutenant and the white sergeant in the back were Australian, but the other sergeant, the one with the wet towel round his neck, was Chinese, and the private could be almost any nationality, in South-east Asia—Malay, Filipino, even Burmese.

A queer bunch, he decided, wondering if they were to be dropped off along the road, and he would never see them again, or whether they were part of Z.E.S., and therefore linked with his own future.

The truck bounced in a rut, swerved to miss a car, and he grinned to himself at the thought that this drive was just like his own life—he had never known where it was taking him. But he had already made one decision; made it, he realized, the moment he left the house in Domain Road. He would ask no questions, but wait until he was told about the organization and what was expected from him. Instinct told him this would be the best attitude to adopt, for as a stranger in a secret unit he would undoubtedly be watched and reported on.

Outside Cairns, about two or three miles, they swung off the highway onto a dirt side road and came to a gate, with the letters Z.E.S. on it, in a wire fence. Sentries in jungle greens—Javanese, he decided—let them through and the truck growled uphill along a winding track between dripping poincianas and clumps of bamboo to the back of a sprawling bungalow he had noticed from the main road.

As they got out the captain said, "I'm Bill Jinkins. You'd better come and see the adjutant. Don't worry about your gear."

He led past an old stables, a splash of purple bougainvillea, through the heavy sweetness of frangipani, to the front of the bungalow and up typical Queensland steps to a wide veranda, partly enclosed with shutters, which circled the house.

"You've got a visitor," the captain shouted into one of the rooms.

"Give me a couple of minutes," someone called.

Pommy, Carse thought.

"Archie'll look after you," the captain said, and grinned. "See you later."

Carse tossed his cap on a canvas chair, lit a cigarette, and from the railings took his first look around his new home. North-east, through and above Moreton Bay fig and mango trees, were the roofs of Cairns and beyond them Trinity Bay, or just the Bay as he soon came to know it. East were blue mountains, bleached with cloud, their feet in the sea. South and far away down a long valley were canefields. And west he already knew were the purple-black peaks of the range staring seaward through splits in the cloud.

Below the house among the trees he counted a dozen tents, brown-heavy with rain, and among them several Australian soldiers and a bunch of dark-skinned troops in greens and with them a short, heavy-legged, cherry-faced officer, a Hollander with Indies soldiers.

Z.E.S., he thought, is certainly cosmopolitan.

Then, as another squall came in, the rain warm against his sweat-damp face, he turned quickly as a chair scraped on the board floor and a small bald man with grey at the temples came onto the veranda and held out his hand. He wore khaki shirt, shorts and old sandals. He had three cloth pips on his shoulders.

"I'm Ross," he said, and smiled. "But we expected a sub-lieutenant."

Again Carse noted that suspicious query.

"I was, a week or so ago."

The other nodded. "Many people on joining this unit have quite unknown to us gained seniority."

"My promotion was through before I joined," Carse said, curtly.

The adjutant didn't appear to notice. "We had a colonel joined us once. Nice chap. Then he turned out to be a lieutenant. Left soon afterwards."

Carse wondered when the adjutant would make sense, and what was coming next.

Captain Ross glanced at his watch. "The C.O.'s just back. While he's changing you might like to see our museum. In here."

Carse followed him into a room, bare except for a long table and glass cases against the walls. On the table, neatly laid out, were a Sten gun, an Owen, a stripped Tommy on oilcloth, a dozen Service revolvers and automatics. In one case were incendiaries, grenades, fuses, and two metal objects, like rusty chunks of iron, that Carse did not recognize, and in another case a collection of knives and stilettos, all shapes and sizes, including several kris and jungle parangs.

"Useful little objects," the adjutant said, pointing at the knives, "when you know how to use them. But hardly the Navy's weapons."

He opened the case and reached for a kris. "Javanese, I believe—a good one. The best come from near Jogjakarta, I'm told."

Slowly he sheathed the cruel wavy blade, returned the kris to the case and carefully shut the door.

"Know any Malay?" he asked.

The question was casual—too casual, Carse decided.

"A few words."

He had already noticed the blackboard, with what looked like Malay words chalked on it, propped against a wall.

"I can count to ten—satu, dua, tiga. . . ."

Ross laughed and turned off the light. "Traps should be ready by this. Come and get it over."

Two rooms along a young, good-looking major rose and held out his hand.

"I'm Trappes-Lomax. I heard you'd arrived."

And to the adjutant he added, "Would you mind telling Captain Wolfe I'd like to see him now?"

English, public school, regular soldier, Carse decided, and added to himself, Looks an eager type.

"Take a pew," the major said, "on the bunk there. You'll find that Z.E.S. has most things—except furniture."

"But a much higher movement priority than I'm used to."

"Quite. . . ."

A lanky captain drifted in. He had a vague surprised professorial expression, as though he had just got out of bed. He collapsed slowly onto the bunk beside Carse.

"Ah, there you are, Charles," the C.O. said, as though even he was a little astonished that the captain had arrived. "I think you had better take Lieutenant Carse under your wing and tell him about his duties—the bad ship he has and what he has to do when you've fixed it up for him."

He smiled. "And, Charles—he looks a little thirsty."

That was all. Carse following the gangling captain onto the veranda and along to a well-stocked ice-chest. Obviously Z.E.S. had no beer problem. He felt more cheerful.

The captain opened a bottle and reached for a glass.

"Your engine's all pulled down—hell of a mess."

"What sort of ship is it?"

"An ancient tub. I'll show you in the morning. You'll loathe her."

"Sounds promising. What's her name?"

"*Gnair*. . . . Forty feet long . . . diesel. Guinea Airways owned it. Why, I've never been able to discover."

"I suppose I'll live aboard," Carse said, taking the glass.

"Don't be a bloody fool. I've got a spare bunk in my room —at the back of this palace. Better living in the servant's quarters than feeding the mosquitoes down at the creek."

"Thanks very much. What else can you tell me?—about my duties, I mean."

The captain drank and smiled, a languid grin which seemed to get up and stretch. "You're in command of the *Gnair*, one naval whaler, one fourteen-foot dinghy, and six Folboats."

"What on earth are they?"

"Collapsible canoes. You have to teach people to paddle 'em—in all weather. And may the good Lord help you in your task."

"I'll need His help. I haven't been in a canoe for years."

"You'll learn."

Carse looked hard at his companion. He decided to break his rule. "Am I the only Navy man here?"

"That's right. They found they couldn't do without you."

"But what's my job? The major wasn't very specific."

The captain lifted his glass. "He seldom is, but you, my dear sir, are the admiral of the fleet and instructor of all sea-going operations."

"What operations?"

The captain raised both eyebrows, then slowly lowered one. "Don't ask silly questions. How should I know? I'm merely an engineer. . . . And now I think we might risk another before we see what Charlie—he's the cook—has concocted for us by intuition out of ignorance."

Later, as monsoon squalls drummed the iron roof and the

leaves of the fig tree clashed in the wind, Carse lay on his damp bunk, on a blanket sour with mildew, in the small, gear-littered room he now shared with Charlie Wolfe, and wondered if anything about this unit would ever make sense. Who was Trappes-Lomax? What was he supposed to do with his fantastic "fleet"? Who were all these people at Z.E.S. and what were they doing?

Kris, Tommy gun and Folboat . . . Dutchmen, Javanese and Chinese. Gathered by the winds and flung on the inexplicable heap of Z.E.S. they only added to his bewilderment and his curiosity, for everything he had seen and heard at this house on the hill pointed only one way—northward where the real war was going on.

He stared upwards through the dark, through the black ceiling into the squalls racing inland to the mountains, and felt the building tremble as a gust reached from the sea and slapped it. He was the only man who knew the sea, the only navigator, at this singular headquarters, and if he was going anywhere from Z.E.S. he looked like being the one to show the way.

He closed his eyes. Perhaps the strange colonel in Melbourne had not been talking nonsense after all.

When Ted Carse first saw his flagship, moored off the mangroves near the stinking tidal wasteland of Admiralty Island, south of the city between Alligator and Chinaman creeks, he knew that if he was to head north from Z.E.S., it would certainly not be in the *Gnair*.

"A beautiful craft, you must agree," Charlie Wolfe said. "She used to carry dredge buckets in New Guinea."

Carse was bitterly disappointed. He had expected a boat not a distorted harbour barge with a cabin tied on; had pictured a boat that could go anywhere.

"Is this a joke?"

Charlie smiled. "If you're referring to His Majesty's ship *Gnair*—yes. But you should see her engine—it's like a pakapoo ticket." He patted Carse's arm. "I wouldn't take her too seriously. I don't think anyone expects you to sail her to Tokyo."

He untied the dinghy and they paddled out from Smith's Landing, and as they climbed aboard a copper-skinned native boy grinned from the engine-room ladder behind the cabin.

"This is Saptu," Wolfe said. "He's a Torres Strait islander. . . . Saptu, this is Mr Carse, your new captain."

The boy touched his forehead. "Boss."

"Hello, Saptu. What do you do around here?"

"Clean boat . . . run engine, boss. Engine no bloody good."

Carse looked about him—at the rubbish, the oil patches, the

dirt, the rust. There would be plenty of cleaning to do.

Wolfe waved vaguely. "Saptu's your entire crew, Admiral. May I congratulate you."

"You can go to hell," Carse said.

Now his anger had faded and he felt better able to tackle whatever was ahead; felt, too, that he had known his lanky companion for years, a comforting thought after the negative nameless atmosphere at the headquarters on the hill.

Only an hour before he had driven into town with the same silent five as on the previous evening and, beyond a nod from Jinkins and the lieutenant, Ellis, whom he had met after dinner the night before, there was no contact.

"A mixed bag," he'd said, as the truck dropped the men at the baths.

Wolfe nodded. "Jinkins's party keep pretty much to themselves. The Chinese is Jack Wong Sue, God knows where from. The other sergeant is Jack Reedwick or Rudwick—I'm never sure—and the private answers to the name of Manaputa—from Balikpapan, I think. They swim every morning—an hour in the water at a stretch, and they spend the afternoons learning how to break each other's necks in the R.S.L. gym."

"If you asked them to do it in peacetime they'd tell you to jump in the lake," Carse said.

For once Wolfe was serious. "If you asked any of us. I've more than a suspicion that people like war. It's about the only time they feel they're functioning—feel alive."

"Even you and I."

"Yes, even you and I."

On the *Gnair* that morning they began by pulling off their shirts and rigging an awning to give some protection from the fierce sun and the glare from the narrow waterway where even the mangroves, lighter green than they are in the south, seemed to wilt above their beds of stinking black mud where crabs with scarlet nippers scuttled among the sharp roots. The rain had cleared, but cloud lay along the mountains and more cloud-drift roofed the sea. More squalls would beat inland before the North settled down after the monsoon.

Wolfe was below, just starting work on the dismantled diesel when the coughing explosions of a Bofors farther up the waterway sent the pelicans along Admiralty Island into sudden laboured flight.

"They're at it again."

"What's going on?" Carse demanded, watching upstream where spoonbills and ibis and gulls slashed the sky.

"It's the Yanks. They've got a couple of ack-ack guns up the creek and the boys are bored. They're shooting at the crocs on the mudbanks."

"But that was a Bofors."

"They'll use anything they've got. They peppered the crocs with a heavy machine-gun some time back, and once I'm told a field gun. There were enough ladies' handbags going on the ebb to start a shop."

Carse turned to the Torres islander. "How did you get aboard?"

"Swim, boss. Croc no catch Saptu's balls."

The Bofors opened up again and drowned Charlie Wolfe's hooting laughter.

Carse spent the first weeks, after the *Gnair's* engine had been repaired and his "fleet" and gear made "operational" (as Wolfe described it), teaching a dozen Javanese soldiers seacraft. They had never been in a boat. He had to teach them how to row, how to bring a boat ashore in surf in daylight and at night, how to sail, anchor, pick up a mooring: all the tricks he knew.

Then, before he could teach others, he had to learn all he could about the long, slim kayak-like Folboats—how to take them out of their waterproof bags—frame in one bag, rubber skin in the other—and assemble them in a few minutes, how to sit and paddle them in all types of water and weather in daylight and at night.

Although Carse enjoyed the active life, and, tanned near black, was soon healthier than he had been for months, he was far from satisfied at Z.E.S. He felt that canoeing round the bay, or watching his Javanese sail the whaler north to Yorkey's Knob, or taking the sluggish *Gnair* across to Green Island, was not very adventurous or even useful, and that his talents as a navigator, if indeed a navigator was wanted, were being wasted.

Week after week, at the baffling headquarters on the hill, the pattern of his first few hours there was repeated until he began to wonder if he had been a fool to leave Townsville and his small boats for a job as nebulous as this. Apart from his daily training schedules, posted on the notice-board outside the adjutant's office and as impersonal as a timetable at a bus stop, he was told nothing, given no instructions. His advice was never sought, his opinions were never asked. Navigation, secret operations, dangerous work—all those possibilities that the colonel in Melbourne had hinted at—were never mentioned by Major Trappes-Lomax, Captain Ross, or anyone else. He did not even know why he was teaching Indonesian soldiers, who spoke practically no English and who didn't know an oar from a cricket bat, how to handle boats.

But all the time he was sure of one thing: he was being watched. He had no evidence of any kind—not one word or sign that anyone was interested in him. But something warned him that everything he did and said was under scrutiny, that every time he drank too much in Cairns, or lost a chess game in the mess, or started an argument—and he was always arguing with someone—it was recorded in a little black book.

He began to be conscious, too, of undertones at Z.E.S., nameless stirrings like the rustling of leaves: a stray word, an unfinished sentence, a name, meaningless and out of context, conferences that went on half the night, censored glances, the presence of strangers who arrived, stayed an evening, and disappeared.

The regulars at Z.E.S. were absorbing enough. Men like chunky Van Aaron, who had escaped from German-occupied Holland; slim Van der Veen who, after Batavia had fallen, had sailed a small boat to Madagascar; little Tahija, an Ambonese who wore the orange and blue ribbon of the Military Cross of William, the Dutch Victoria Cross, for his work against the Japanese in Amboina; the Portuguese party who had escaped from Timor; M. de J. Pires who had been deputy Governor at Dilli, and whose cook, Pavlo da Silva, and butler, Cosme Soares, had come out with him, and the others, Fernandez and Cavalho and Zeka Rebelo; the brilliant English chemist Philip Monypenny, whose father was said to have produced the first stainless steel in England; Lloyd Wood the signals officer; Dick Noone of Z.E.S. Intelligence; Sergeant-Major Rex Harrison, Sergeant McLean, Corporal Ralph Shiress, and others.

Noone, he discovered, was a clever young anthropologist who had already distinguished himself in Malaya, where he had helped his even more brilliant brother, Pat, also an anthropologist, to watch Japanese activities across the Siamese border before Japan attacked in December 1941. Pat Noone during the Malaya campaign fought with the Argyll and Sutherland Highlanders and then returned to the jungle to organize guerrilla bands. He was never seen again. Dick Noone had got out.

But the men who interested Carse most were the "drift-ins"—shadowy fellows who disappeared into the C.O.'s office after dinner and apparently never emerged, for they would be gone next morning; or others who stayed a few days before moving on and whose brief passage seemed purposeless.

At first everything he heard or observed or sensed was fragmentary and without meaning. It was like being told some of the clues in a detective story without being allowed to read the opening chapters. Only gradually, after learning to associate what he heard and saw with individuals, time and other events, was he able to distinguish the first vague outlines of a developing pattern, a pattern with some apparent meaning and purpose which seemed to be leading—somewhere.

He had been weeks at Z.E.S. before he heard by accident

that the letters stood for Z Experimental Station, which told him no more than a later chance discovery that he was a member of Z Special Unit, which had been formed originally, though nobody knew when or where, as a unit for all Army personnel who joined the Inter-Allied Services Department. He was also to learn, again only casually, that the training by the silent five led by Captain Jinkins had to do with Borneo, though that was all he knew for a long time.

As his knowledge expanded, so did his awareness of unspoken unseen secret things around him—of movements and decisions and orders in which he had no part, or men who stayed for a time and went away and were never heard of again, of names that cried for explanation but remained just names like words in clear among a jumble of code. To the rustling of leaves was added the snapping of twigs among the undergrowth of fact and rumour and imagination.

In time, too, he realized that the atmosphere at Z.E.S., its negativeness, its lack of urgency, was far too casual to be unplanned; that although Z.E.S. was clearly an assembly point, a training centre, for secret work, its security system was so designed that no man could see more than a few of the brushmarks on the total canvas.

But this did not make his work seem any less futile, or his position in the unit any less drone-like, and he began to feel that he had been recruited under false pretences, false promises, and to consider applying for a transfer. What he did not know was that he was slowly moving towards a point where at least some of his doubts would be explained.

One evening he was so depressed that he had refused an invitation to go with Charlie Wolfe and several others to a film in town and had stayed on the veranda alone, watching the fireflies like tiny swaying lamps among the bushes and listening to the flying foxes. The foxes were thick that night. Before dusk they were over in black slow-moving flights which pulsed the stagnant air. Soon they were clipped to the fig trees, squabbling like pups as they fought for the clusters of brown fruit and splashed the leathery leaves and the ground with their seed-laced droppings.

Behind the house the Javanese were hunting them. The soldiers skinned their verminous brown fur and curried their little bodies. Carse could hear the crack of .22's as the men shot along torch beams, and their shrill yells as the foxes flew into the home-made nets which the Javanese slung in the trees across areas where the smaller branches had been lopped. As the men fired the foxes whirred from the figs in panic leaving some of their numbers dead on the ground or helpless with bullet-split wings, but still snapping as they were killed with sticks.

The hunt faltered and stopped. Soon the soldiers, chattering and laughing, were filtering through the bushes beside the house and back to their tents. The flying foxes returned in nervous ones and twos, and then in dozens, to swish again into the fig trees now their enemies had gone.

Carse was glad he had not gone into town, glad for once of the rare chance to relax, to be alone. But now the hunt was over he was suddenly weary. He tossed his cigarette over the railings, watched it flare as it hit a bush, and was walking along the veranda, making for his room, when a quiet voice said, "Come and have a nightcap. I've something that will interest you."

He jumped. He hadn't realized the C.O. was in his room. Or had he just come in the back way? He went in and sat on the bed.

"All the others out?" Trappes-Lomax asked as he opened a bottle of beer.

"Or in bed."

Carse took the glass.

"I wonder how long this war will last," the C.O. said.

"Probably a decade, the way it's going."

He wondered when the C.O. would get to the point.

"I can't see us beating the Japs except in China," Trappes-Lomax said.

"Why China? They own half the Pacific."

"Because when they're beaten in the Pacific, even in their own islands, they'll make their last stand on the plains of China. I've always felt that's where the final mass battles will be fought."

He reached across and topped-up Carse's glass.

Here it comes, Carse thought. And waited.

"But that's not what I wanted to talk to you about. I'll have a special job for you soon. We're getting a new party up here—all Aussies. I believe most of them have been in the Middle East. I hear they're rugged and may take a little handling."

"Sounds like a lively bunch," Carse said, still wondering.

"Quite. That's why they've been chosen. I'll get Monypenny to handle Folboat and sabotage instructions. But I want you to look after their sea training."

"Anything special?"

"Plenty of hard work in the whaler, and report to me if you have any trouble with them. They'll also get a lot of other toughening up, though that's not your problem—it's Carey's job. He's leader of Scorpion."

"Scorpion?" Carse hardly concealed his surprise. The word alone was menacing.

"Yes. For your own information, as you'll be watching their training, they're going to raid Rabaul."

3

SCORPION PARTY, which was to attack the key Japanese base of Rabaul on New Britain, was the idea of one man, a university graduate who looked more like a back-room boy than a Commando. Today he is Professor of Geology at the University of Tasmania, but then he was Captain Sam Carey, who for years before the Pacific war had worked as an oil geologist in Papua-New Guinea. He knew the natives, knew the territory's climate and topography. Above all, he knew Rabaul.

At the beginning of 1943 the battle for Papua, which was to end with the fall of Sanananda, a few weeks later, was virtually over. Names like Milne Bay, Kokoda, Buna, were already part of Australian military history. The battle for New Guinea was about to begin. Around this time Sam Carey, who had joined Z Special Unit in May 1942, was serving in a dual job—one open, one secret. His surface job was G.S.I.(T.), or General Staff Intelligence (Topographical), compiling topographical intelligence at New Guinea Force Headquarters in Port Moresby. His secret job, known only to top staff men, was liaison officer for Z Special Unit to the Commander-in-Chief, New Guinea Force (Lieutenant-General Herring) and to the Commander-in-Chief, Australian Military Forces (General Sir Thomas Blamey).

Carey had long believed that an attack on enemy ship concentrations at Rabaul would be an important contribution to the war in New Guinea and the war against the Japanese-held islands south-east of Rabaul. He drafted a plan, based on the use of submarine-launched canoes manned by old New Guinea hands like himself who knew Rabaul and its harbour intimately, and took it to General Blamey.

The white-haired, red-faced general was in a good mood that day. He was interested and sympathetic, but sceptical. He admitted he would like to see an attack on shipping at Rabaul, but didn't think Carey's plan had a chance of success.

"All right," he said, studying the draft, "you're dropped by submarine ten miles off Rabaul and you paddle in at night."

"Correct, sir," said Carey.

"Now, assuming you get into the harbour without being spotted—what then?"

"We avoid naval ships. They're generally better guarded,

and because of their construction harder to damage than other ships. Limpets will hurt them, but won't kill them unless you're lucky. My aim is to concentrate on big transports and cargo carriers."

"And how do you propose to get out of the harbour?" the general asked.

"We don't," Carey said.

"You don't." Blamey stared at him.

"At least not immediately. The plan is to hide out on Vulcan Island for about a week until the Japanese flap and search subsides. Then we paddle out at night and rendezvous with the sub. Vulcan—the island that rose in the harbour in the 1937 eruption—is heavily waterworn and covered in deep crevasses with caves in them. You could hide a division and they wouldn't be seen. Vulcan's the last place the Japs would look— and even if they did they'd have a job finding us."

General Blamey thought for a moment. Then he said, "If you want my candid opinion, you'll all be bloody well shot."

But Carey, who had fanatical faith in his idea, continued to argue. He urged that an attack would have more than an even chance because of its unconventional approach and surprise and because the canoe leaders would know the geography of their objective better than the Japanese. Desperately, he kept talking.

At last Blamey said, "I still don't think you would get away with it. But if you're confident you can make the raid, then go ahead. I'll give you all the help I can."

He sat back. "How soon can you leave to prepare the operation? Your boys will have to be tough."

"Tomorrow, sir."

"Good. I'll order a passage on a flying-boat going south in forty-eight hours. You will receive a letter this afternoon, and you will hold it at all times to show that you are operating under my orders."

The orders were terse. They were in an unsealed envelope to be presented to the Deputy Chief of the General Staff (Major-General Frank Berryman). They said: "Captain Carey is proceeding to Australia with instructions which I have given him personally. You will assist him in any way you can."

That was the origin of the party which Sam Carey secretly recruited and assembled at Z.E.S., Cairns. By the end of March 1943 they were ready to begin training as a unit.

Scorpion, the code-name of the party and of the projected operation, consisted of ten men—four captains, Sam Carey, leader, Tony Gluth, Dick Cardew, and Desmond McNamara; three lieutenants, Bob Page, Jack Grimson and Jim Downey, and Company Sergeant-Major Tom Barnes, Sergeant "Henry" Ford, and Corporal Gilbert MacKenzie. Four of these men,

Cardew, Gluth, Downey and Barnes, had been together in the same A.I.F. unit, the 2/8th Battalion, in the Middle East; and four, Carey, Cardew, Page and Grimson, were old New Guinea hands who knew Rabaul Harbour. It was these four, when training began at Z.E.S., who drilled the others, with maps and aerials of Rabaul, until they knew the harbour as though they had been born on its shores. But the real concentration was on physical perfection, for Sam Carey knew that success or failure would depend on the toughness of his team.

Day after day, first under Carey, and then Monypenny and Carse, they hardened their bodies. They began their course by swimming, before breakfast, one hundred yards backstroke, breaststroke and freestyle, and gradually doubled the distance until they could swim, every day, a mile at each stroke, and then run two miles in bare feet.

While working up to these distances they also spent long hours pulling and sailing the heavy whaler off Machans, San Remo and the other beaches which swing north to Palm, or paddling, often at night, the back-breaking Folboats in the great silent curve of Mission Bay. When Folboat training began they first had to learn to sit and paddle them, and then to cover a longer distance each day. An early target was a mile a day, but as skill and condition improved this was rapidly increased. In time they were able to canoe the length of the Barron River, with a portage round the falls, and return—the whole distance on hard rations and little sleep. And in one final exercise, part of the distance in a freak storm which almost froze their burnt and tortured bodies, they paddled 128 miles in the open sea.

But this was only part of their training, since they also had to master the new technique of limpeting—handling and fixing, at night from Folboats, the new and secret explosives called Limpets. The limpets, which looked like rectangular chunks of rusty iron, measured 11 x 8 x 3 inches. They weighed fourteen pounds loaded and contained a powerful horseshoe magnet and ten pounds of P.E. (plastic explosive) which was enough to blow a hole about five feet square in the plates of a ship. Limpets had two holes at the top. The instantaneous fuse and time pencil, which could be set for explosion any time up to six hours, went into one hole. One end of a five-foot wooden pole, like a broomstick, fitted into the other.

The technique of fixing limpets was simple. As a two-man Folboat came alongside a ship at night, the bowman clamped a small magnetic "holdfast", with a line attached to it, to the ship's side, and held the "anchored" canoe steady. The other canoeman, his limpet fused and timed, then fitted his "broomstick" into the other hole and lowered the limpet into the water between canoe and ship, getting it as deep as possible before carefully easing it onto the ship's plates. Limpets could be fixed without noise, but if carelessly applied they gripped too quickly and clanged against the plates, a sound that could easily be heard inside the ship and lead to discovery. Once the limpet was applied, the canoeman worked the stick out of the hole, the bowman released the hold-fast, and the canoe was paddled or allowed to drift to the next limpet position.

To get simultaneous maximum destructive force on vital parts of a ship, three limpets were generally applied, linked by instantaneous cordtex fuse. When possible the three connected limpets were sited on the engine-room, stokehold and one hold, or the engine-room and two holds, care being taken to fix them away from strengthening bulkheads, which involved knowledge of ship construction and ship types. Other limpet patterns. depending on circumstances, were also developed and applied.

In those first few weeks, as Scorpion party settled in and increased the pressure of their training, Ted Carse began to feel that at last he was a functioning member of Z.E.S. Although he was not one of the attack party, his almost daily association with them made him feel that he was at least contributing to an operation, and the more he listened to discussions and absorbed the detailed planning the more convinced he became that the operation would succeed.

He also felt that, from the moment Trappes-Lomax had confided to him the secret of Scorpion and its objective, he had passed some invisible test at Z.E.S. and that his frustrating novitiate, the long tyranny of silence and evasion, was over. He now knew what for so long he could not prove—that Z.E.S. was an advance training camp, perhaps one of many, for secret and highly specialized operations against the Japanese, and even far behind their lines. And for the first time he suspected that somewhere ahead, perhaps not far ahead, was an operation that would make even an attack like Scorpion seem insignificant, though he could not know how correct his theory was and that, already and unsuspecting, he was part of a slowly evolving pattern which included a ship he was ever to think of with a sailor's grudging affection, and a man he was to admire and love. Slowly and inevitably, as though in the past this had been decreed, he was drawn into the secret web that would hold him all his days.

It began this way:

During Scorpion's early training period Carse arrived at Smith's Landing one morning to find an ugly craft tied to the *Gnair*. She was about twice the length of the *Gnair*, with a tall mast forward and a wheelhouse, which reminded him of a typically Australian outside privy, near her covered stern. On her deck a scraggy, balding old fellow with a lined brown face, and wearing only ragged shorts, was squatting sipping tea from a stained enamel mug and picking at his toes.

"That's a beaut ship you've got there," the old fellow called.

The words were Australian. The accent was unmistakably Irish.

"May I return the compliment," Carse said. "What do you call yours?"

The old boy spat. "A real bastard. Her engine conked out ten times when me an' the other blokes were bringing her up from Sydney. If I'd been a mule I'd 've kicked her to death."

"Has she got a name?"

"Plenty. . . . *Krait*, that's what she's called—after that little bugger of a snake you find in India. But if you asked me I'd spell the bastard C-R-A-T-E."

Carse laughed. "What's she for? She doesn't look up to much to me."

The old boy winked.

"Search me, but Paddy McDowell'd know where to put her—and sideways—if he could catch the Nip who made her."

"She's Japanese?"

"And could anyone but a muckin' Nip make a crate like this?" He waved an arm along her length. "When she put her head under off Coff's Harbour, I reckoned she'd never lift her eyes an' look at God's sun again. Skipper—old bloke of the name of Reynolds—got off at Townsville to go to some other job. Can't say I blame him—half his bloody luck. She broke down again off Lindeman an' I brought her on at the end of a towline. Like a captain of a bloody hearse, I was."

He tossed the dregs over and pointed at the battered tin teapot. "Like a cuppa?"

"Thanks."

Ted Carse was to learn many things about Paddy McDowell, but never was he to know anyone more imperturbable than this man in the tattered shorts above knees like old roots, who was now coming out of the wheelhouse with a mug in his hand.

Paddy was fifty-six and had risen to petty officer in the Royal Navy—more than once. He had served in World War I with the famous Commander Gordon Campbell, V.C., in those decoy craft, the Q-ships, whose role was to lure German U-boats within range of their concealed guns, and even allow themselves to be torpedoed to encourage the enemy submarine to surface.

"A wonderful bloke," Paddy once said, "but mad as a meat-axe. He issued an order once that said, 'Should the officer of the watch see a torpedo approaching the ship he is to increase or decrease speed as necessary to ensure it hitting her.' But it's blokes like that who win wars."

Paddy had settled in Australia in the 1920s, never to return to his native Belfast, and, still R.N. Reserve when World War II began, had joined up with the Royal Australian Navy as a leading stoker.

But Paddy McDowell and his crate were only part of the web that was to enmesh Carse, for among Scorpion party was another personality to whom he was to be linked—a tall, lean, thin-faced youngster with brown hair, the bluest of eyes and a smile that seemed to splash his face. Carse had noticed Lieutenant Bob Page the first day he met the members of Scorpion, and during training he found himself watching the young man, listening to his soft, pleasant voice, encouraging him to talk. Then one morning at Smith's Landing, when the men were putting the oars into the whaler, someone told a dirty story and he saw Page blush and turn away. Carse, who hadn't blushed since birth, felt a sudden sympathy, a protective warmth, and all that morning he thought about the young man who had turned his head, and wanted to know more about him. He wondered why men went to war, why this man, so young, so immature, so sensitive, so enthusiastic about everything he did, had volunteered for work like this, and how he would react to war. And the more he observed Page the more he was attracted to him. He had charm—charm close to an old-world form of gallantry. He had intelligence, humour, warmth, a strong code of behaviour. And his perception, his understanding, was at times far beyond his years.

As their friendship developed Carse came to know and understand Bob Page—not only his background but what he thought and felt and what impulses drove him on.

He was a son of Harold Hillis Page and a nephew of Sir Earle Page, M.P. He had been a schoolboy at Sydney High School during the rise of Hitler and had just completed his second year as a medical student at Sydney University when World War II began. He had joined the A.I.F. and was with the 2/4th Pioneer Battalion on his way from Darwin to Dutch Timor when the Japanese struck at northern Australia. Heavily attacked by bombers in the Timor Sea the convoy put back to Darwin, where on 19th February 1942 Australians in their homeland came under attack for the first time. Page, then only twenty-one and one of the few in his group to escape injury, was bitterly disappointed that the Japanese had moved so fast since Pearl Harbour that he had not been able to fight them.

"A man must be ready not only to fight," he said to Carse one day, "but to give his life and give it gladly."

Yet, as Carse discovered, he was not an aggressive man with

any desire to dominate others. He had conviction. His loyalty was a deep personal thing, like religious faith. He believed that an individual had a responsibility to his country, a duty to serve it and to protect it. But deeper still, Carse sensed, was an idea in the young man's mind about his father, a wild, romantic, yet understandable idea, part of youth, part of growing up, part of war.

Harold Page, who had won the D.S.O. and M.C. and three Mentions in Dispatches in World War I, was both a fine soldier and a fine man, and to the boy he was a composite of all those things a boy wants his father to be. But while Japanese bombs were falling on Darwin, Harold Page, who was Deputy Administrator of New Guinea, was already a prisoner of the Japanese at Rabaul, and was to die (it is generally believed) when the Japanese prison ship *Montevideo Maru* was torpedoed by the American submarine *Sturgeon* off Luzon, in the Philippines, on 1st July 1942, when more than a thousand soldiers and civilians from Rabaul were drowned.

Bob Page knew of his father's capture—but never of his death—and from that moment all his thoughts and acts were channelled towards one objective. Carse, to whom he often talked of his father, sensed what this objective was, sensed that to the young man not long out of school and in many ways still emotionally a boy, war had a different meaning and significance from what it had to others. To Bob Page the war against Japan was a war of personal revenge. It was, Carse felt, even a war of dedicated romantic hope, vague, unformed yet constant, that he might be able to rescue his father, somewhere, some day.

On a rare off-duty evening at the end of May 1943, when Scorpion was nearing the end of its preparation, some of the party were arguing security in Philip Monypenny's room—an argument that had started with an "innocent" question from Tony Gluth whether anyone had heard that the Japanese had given the correct location of Z.E.S. over Tokyo Radio. This latest among a war of furphies was greeted with jeers, and Jack Grimson, sitting on the floor eating an apple, said, "That's almost as good as the one that General MacArthur prays only when facing a mirror."

But it was Page who asked, above the laughter, "Do you think anyone in town suspects what we're doing?"

"Why should they?" Cardew said. "Troops are everywhere and we're a small unit. Because we tear around so much most people seem to think we're part of the Commandos. Everyone knows they're on the Tableland."

Grimson chuckled. "A bloke the other day asked me straight out what we did. I told him we tested equipment before it was issued to the troops—even the food. I think the poor cow believed me."

"But what about the canoes?" someone suggested. "Don't they draw attention to us. What do you think, Ted?"

Carse shook his head. "Early in the piece perhaps they did—but not now. People don't associate canoes with anything more serious than keeping fit." He recalled for a moment how long it had taken him to know even a little about Z.E.S. "If security in this port was as good as our security everything would be fine."

"What do you mean?" Page asked.

"For months I've been getting in and out of this harbour at night in the *Gnair*, and I've been challenged exactly once by naval patrol. I'd like to bet it's possible to get into another port too—any port you like to mention."

"Could you get into Townsville?" Grimson asked. "It's a convoy assembly point—you know what that means."

"It's mined, too," Gluth said, "like this place."

"If it can be done here it can be done in other places," Carse argued.

"What about a Japanese port?" said Page.

"I don't know, but if you could get into Townsville or Brisbane or Sydney you could probably get into Tokyo Bay."

"Balls," someone shouted, and it was on.

As the argument became a free-for-all Sam Carey, listening near the door, smiled to himself. He had not yet told his party, but he had decided that, although Scorpion was ready to attack Rabaul, a full-dress rehearsal was necessary.

He smiled again as he left the arguing group and went to bed. He had selected Scorpion's target.

4

THE DRIVER STOPPED the southbound train just before the bridge over the Black River north of Townsville. That was his instruction before leaving Cairns. The station master had not explained.

Ten soldiers jumped from the last carriage, dropped their gear, and climbed back for heavier packs. The last men out slammed the doors and the guard waved his lamp and called good night. The train went on, across the bridge.

The time was 11 p.m. on 19th June 1943.

Scorpion was moving south to raid Townsville.

Sam Carey had considered warning the naval authorities that a raid would be made on the port, but his 2 I.C., Dick

Cardew, argued that with Townsville alerted the raid would be valueless as a true test of Scorpion's efficiency and of security in the port, and Carey had agreed. He then decided not to tell anyone in authority and to make the raid a full-scale war operation, even though the party knew, before they left Carins, that all or some of them could be killed or wounded.

Carey's first idea had been to go south by sea in the *Gnair*, but this was abandoned because of the danger of detection by naval patrol, and replaced by a safer plan to get near Townsville by train and then to use the canoes.

But because he had decided that the raid was not to be fully operational until the canoes were at sea and approaching the Townsville area, Carey had accepted information given him in Cairns that the Black River was tidal and that his party would have no difficulty paddling down it to the sea. He got his first shock, after leaving the train, when he slid down the river-bank near the bridge and found that he could walk across on dry sand. And even though he located water downstream, more than a hundred yards below the bridge, and called to the others, Scorpion's troubles were just beginning.

Scorpion men were a Bohemian-looking lot as they carried the heavy packs along the river-bed and began to assemble the Folboats. They wore khaki berets, jungle greens, American olive-green wind-cheaters, American gaiters and rubber boots, plus their individual armament of a Sten, pistol and Commando knife, plus binoculars, waterbottle and torch.

In addition to their canoes, which were in ten green bags, they had with them three days' supplies of dehydrated rations in waterproof containers and forty-five limpets fully charged with a total of 450 pounds of plastic explosive. They did not carry fuses, so that the limpets were harmless, and instead of instantaneous cordtex fuse to link the limpets they had white parachute cord.

Around midnight, when they had launched the canoes and loaded them, Cardew and Barnes were the first to start downstream, but they had paddled not more than fifty yards before they grounded and discovered that ahead was another long stretch of dry sand. Ahead, too, although the cursing men did not know it, was a slow and exhausting journey down a river of scattered pools, a journey made more difficult, frustrating and uncomfortable by the dark and the whine and sting of mosquitoes.

Half-carrying, half-dragging the canoes they moved downriver, splashing through shallow pools, stumbling into others, paddling a few yards across deceptive water only to ground again. At times they moved no more than a few hundred yards in an hour. At daybreak, still among a wasteland of pools, they stopped to eat and rest, and although they were all in superb condition every man was exhausted. But worse was ahead.

By 11 a.m., after covering less than three miles since midnight, they reached what looked like a tributary branching south, but as it was salt and as they had found that the river pools were fresh, and still fresh at the branch, they decided that the tributary was probably the main river which would take them to the sea. Instead it led them into a mangrove swamp—and it was mid afternoon before they got back to the main dry sand stream, dusk before they reached the mouth of the Black River and Halifax Bay, and early the next morning before they had paddled at least fifteen miles to land on Magnetic Island off Townsville.

Scorpion party, after dismantling the canoes on the beach at Picnic Bay, carried them and their supplies up to Nobby Head where, just before dawn, and among rocks and scrub, they established a fully operational camp. They lit no fires. They made no noise. They stayed under cover. And two men were always on guard as the others slept.

Townsville, with its crag of Castle Hill, its wharves and war shipping, was not six miles away.

By next morning, 22nd June, the men had recovered from their journey, and all day took turns to watch the shipping across Cleveland Bay and to map where the ships lay. Two ships were in the roadstead, and two more anchored there in the late afternoon; but the harbour itself, inside the breakwater which reached out from the southern end of the city, was packed.

Sam Carey, who had brought a small but powerful American telescope, plotted more than a dozen ships inside, including the big steamer *Katoomba* he knew well, and two destroyers and a smaller naval vessel. He could see a clock on No. 1 Pier and ordered everyone to synchronize their watches on Townsville time.

Carey decided that four canoes—Carey-MacKenzie, Gluth-Page, McNamara-Ford, Cardew-Barnes—would make for the harbour, while Downey-Grimson in the fifth canoe would attack the ships in the roadstead before following the other raiders. He also warned his party of the dangers ahead. "The most difficult and dangerous part," he told them, "will be getting through the narrow harbour entrance. You all know the approaches are mined and that there's a mine-control point at the extreme end of the southern breakwater. I don't have to tell you what that means. They're not expecting us—so we're Japs as far as they're concerned. We must get in unnoticed. If we're spotted, the mine-control boys will almost certainly blow the mines—and us with them."

At 11 p.m. that night Scorpion raid began. The night was cloudless, still and cool as the five canoes headed across the bay in broad arrowhead; but a three-quarter moon gave too much light for safety and the canoes trailed phosphorescent wakes which sparkled and writhed like watersnakes. Near midnight, when they were less than a mile from the port, they broke arrowhead and moved independently. Downey-Grimson dropped behind and swung towards the ships in the roadstead, while the other four canoes made for the long breakwater. They reached it without incident and edged against its shadowy bulk towards the harbour entrance. While still out at sea they had heard the faint chattering of winches, but now the noise of working ships was loud beyond the breakwater and the sky from distant wharf floodlights glowed faintly above them.

Carey-MacKenzie reached the end first and turned the corner, and now, hugging the inner wall of the breakwater, they edged through the entrance past the mine-control point. Crouching forward to reduce silhouette, and hardly moving their paddles, they drifted through, followed at intervals by the other three canoes.

Inside at last they moved along the breakwater until well away from the dreaded mine-control. Then they headed cautiously across harbour to the attack points they had mapped from Nobby Head and knew by heart—moved to the long line of berthed ships until the hulls were high above them like black walls between them and the floodlit wharves.

Because of the noise—chatter of winches, thump of cargo, calls and cries of men—the raiders had not to be over-careful about the noise they made, except when pushing the limpets down with their broomsticks between the canoes and the ships' sides and allowing the magnets to grip the plates.

Cardew-Barnes limpeted two destroyers and the *Katoomba*. Carey-MacKenzie attacked a Dutch ship and two American Liberty ships. Gluth-Page were the only raiders to have trouble at the wharves, but not from the "enemy". A barge, moored alongside a ship named the *Akaba*, left them no space to put their three limpets along the engine-room. Instead, Gluth fixed the limpets under the counter, but because space there was restricted by the barge he had to tighten the white cord instead of allowing it to trail slack in the water between each limpet.

While the harbour raiders were completing their work, Downey-Grimson had limpeted three ships in the open roadstead before paddling in to rejoin the others. But one ship had challenged them—if challenge it could be called. They had just attacked their third freighter when a sailor, lounging against the rails, saw them. "What are youse blokes doin' down there?" he asked..

"Just paddling around," Grimson said.

The sailor tossed a cigarette end towards them.

"Good night, mate," he said.

With forty-five limpets on fifteen ships Scorpion party moved independently up harbour and into Ross Creek to pull inshore and land near a bridge just before 7 a.m. And there, in the sight of early morning workers crossing the bridge, they dismantled their Folboats, packed them in their green bags, and had breakfast.

The freighter *Akaba* was high in the water, and still unloading, as her bell hammered 10 a.m., and along the dockside other bells answered her. As her cargo booms swung lazily in and out, spilling crates and bags on the heap already on the wharf, Army trucks backed whining into position and nibbled like cockroaches at the pile before scuttling away.

Her last slings were coming out when an officer from the ship astern, who was examining the headlines, noticed a white streak under the *Akaba's* counter. He was about to turn away, thinking it was floating rubbish, when an impulse made him look again.

Peering down from the wharf he saw that the white line looked like thin rope or cord strung between chunks of rusty iron attached to the ship's plates. On his knees, and shading his eyes from the morning glitter, he took a closer look. The objects, so far as he could see, were partly submerged and the cord between them was just clear of the water.

Just clear of the water, he thought. Then how long had these things been on her? *Akaba* had been unloading for hours and had risen in the water, so that the objects must have risen with her.

Suddenly he realized that if they had been on the ship when she reached Townsville they must have been well below the waterline. But how could she have picked them up?

As he walked along the wharf he saw the second mate of the *Akaba* coming down the gangway. He called and pointed.

"You seem to have picked up something."

"What's that?" the mate called.

"Something on your stern."

The mate grinned as he came up. "April's over."

"Maybe, but you'd better take a look."

They went to the stern. The mate whistled.

"What are they?"

"Damned if I know. You must have had them on when you made port. They must have been below waterline before you started unloading."

"By heavens, you're right."

"I know what I'd do."

When the captain came he didn't waste time. "I don't like the look of them. They could be mines we've picked up," he said to the mate. "Get along to the destroyer—quick, while I call Naval Control."

As news of the discovery flicked from ship to ship all work ceased. Men streamed off the *Akaba* and adjoining ships. Soon other ships were emptying as urgent calls to Naval Control reported mines stuck to their sides.

Soon the rumours spread to the town itself—raced in with the speed of a bushfire. The Japs have raided Townsville.... All ships in harbour have been mined.... They were about to blow up and the town with them.... Rumour jumped on the back of rumour. There was talk of Japanese midget submarines, of the capture of saboteurs, of invasion.

Townsville flapped—a near-panic which in its own way more than rivalled Sydney's a year before when Japanese midgets had raided the harbour.

The Navy acted. They cancelled the sailing of the convoy. They ordered captains of ships at the wharves or at anchor to stay where they were and under no circumstances to move their propeller shafts because of the danger that revolving propellers might detonate the mines.

Wharves were cleared, gates were locked, and the area nearby was evacuated. Harassed sentries swore that no unauthorized persons had got on to the wharves. Mine-Control insisted that not even a fish could have entered harbour. Coastal batteries reported nothing suspicious during the night.

From naval headquarters telephone calls went through to mine and scientific experts in Melbourne, reporting the limpet attack and imploring advice. And top priority signals reported the raid to all headquarters in Australia, to General Blamey, and to General MacArthur

But when word reached Colonel Allison, W.Ind. at General MacArthur's Allied Intelligence Bureau (under which Z Special Unit operated) in Brisbane, he thought for a moment and said, "Find Sam Carey."

At this moment, while Townsville expected every ship in harbour to blow up, Scorpion's leader, and his six officers were asleep at the Officers' Club. And Carey was still asleep at 3 p.m. when hammering woke him.

He stumbled to the door. "What do you want?"

"Captain Carey?" an Army captain asked.

"Yes."

"Regard yourself as under arrest."

As he dressed, Carey knew for certain that the raid had been more successful than he had expected.

At Navy nobody would believe him when he described Scorpion raid and explained that the limpets were harmless.

He had to produce General Blamey's letter, which he always carried, to convince them that he knew what he was talking about—and to be released from arrest.

The great flap was over—though not quite.

When Carey and Cardew were taken to the wharves, the captain of the *Katoomba*, the first man they saw, was in an ugly mood.

"But I tell you the limpets are harmless," Carey tried to explain. "I ought to know—I put them there and I can take them off for you."

"You won't touch anything," the captain roared. "If I let you near her I'll have a hole in my ship."

"But they can't hurt your ship."

"You keep away. You've done enough harm already."

The Navy men thought the whole affair was a great joke—until they, too, found that their ships were limpeted.

Scorpion raid, which panicked a port, delayed a convoy, and was regarded, with reason, as a Japanese attack, was hushed up. Even after the war practically nothing was known about it, except in the far north. This is the reason why the few reports that have been published about it since the war, in newspapers and at least one official publication, are either inaccurate or imaginative, or both. Writers of these reports knew nothing about Scorpion party or its objective—the harbour of Rabaul—and all guessed, wrongly, that the raid was a dress rehearsal by the men who were later to raid Singapore. If such confusion could exist long after the war, it is not hard to understand why Scorpion raid was one of the best-kept secrets of the war in the South-west Pacific.

The real Scorpion raid never took place. It was delayed for months and finally cancelled. There were two reasons for this: an American submarine was to drop Scorpion party ten miles off Rabaul, but the U.S. Navy lost a submarine by enemy action off New Britain shortly before the raid was to take place and decided not to risk another. About the same time, the capture of Huon Peninsula by the Australians gave General MacArthur control of the western side of Vitiaz Strait, between New Guinea and the western end of New Britain, and this was followed by the American landings at Arawe and Cape Gloucester on New Britain. Control of Vitiaz Strait was the prelude to the capture of the Admiralty Islands and the move north to the Philippines. Control meant that Rabaul, neutralized and no longer significant, was by-passed and left to rot.

But although Scorpion never stung Rabaul, the Townsville dress rehearsal was a valuable operation. It proved that a canoe raid could be deadly—that a defended port could be

penetrated and ships attacked. It proved that security was weak
—dangerously weak—and after the raid Sam Carey discovered
that the local naval authorities had long been trying, against
indifference and even opposition, to strengthen security in the
vulnerable port.

But the logic of Scorpion raid was that Japanese port security
was probably no better than Australian—logic which others
were quick to accept and apply as you will see.

5

WHEN SCORPION PARTY returned from Townsville they reached
Z.E.S. late at night. They evaded the sentries who patrolled the
fence, booby-trapped the latrines, entered the house through a
back window—across a room where two men were asleep—
found the correct key in the adjutant's office, burgled his safe
which contained highly secret information, fixed more booby-
traps, and went to bed.

Next morning the first man to lower a seat in the latrines
was almost blown into a mango-tree, and Charlie the cook,
when he opened the ice-chest, set off an explosion which
rocked the house and sprayed him with glass and butter.

But among the echoes of the booby-traps and the celebration
that night, when Scorpion raid was toasted in vermouth so
powerful that it skinned the varnish off a chair, Ted Carse
heard a whisper of a new name.

The name was "Jock Force".

A couple of months before a name like that would have
conveyed nothing to him in the vacuum-like atmosphere of
Z.E.S., but now he recognized it as a code-name, and almost
certainly the code-name of a new operation, and knew intui-
tively that in some way he would be part of it. He felt certain
that his long wait was ending, and this feeling of certainty
was strengthened a few days later when Bob Page told him he
had been transferred from Scorpion.

"Something to do with Borneo," Page said.

"Jock Force? I heard it mentioned the other night."

"Yes—but not a raid. An Intelligence job of sorts up a
river—a recce, with the oilfield near Balikpapan as a later
target."

"But what about Scorpion?"

"Delayed. That's all I know, Ted. But in the meantime I'm
seconded to Lyon's party."

"The pommy captain?"

"Yes—Houdini. The bloke who's always doing the disappearing trick."

"Know anything about him?"

"Not much—except that he's supposed to be a Bowes-Lyon, the Queen's cousin."

Carse chuckled. "Z.E.S.'ll have a coat-of-arms next."

That evening, while Carse was waiting for a poker game to start, Trappes-Lomax took him aside.

"There's a show coming along," he said, confidentially. "Would you like to make a trip away?"

"Would I? . . . Tell me more."

The major shook his head. "Sorry, old man, but I can't at this stage. I just wanted to know."

A week later Carse had heard no more, but he began to watch for the English captain, the man with the curly brown hair, the small clipped reddish moustache, the even closer-clipped voice. He had seen him a few times in the last month, had once sat beside him during dinner although they had not said more than a dozen words. Lyon was one of the Z.E.S. "drift ins"—here today, gone by midnight, back next week. Carse remembered, too, that although Lyon did not mix much with the other officers, and spent most of his time with the C.O., he seemed to be friendly with another casual visitor, the only other naval officer he had ever met at the unit, a big dour two-ringer R.N.V.R. type named Davidson.

But as Lyon did not appear and the C.O. never again mentioned the "trip away", Carse became more and more impatient.

Towards the end of his second week of waiting he returned to Z.E.S. late one night after being delayed by engine trouble on the crossing from Green Island. He was tired and sour, too tired to eat and disgusted with Z.E.S. and everything about it. He decided to get drunk. The idea appealed to him. It would break the monotony of useless work, stagnation among the stinking mangroves of Smith's Landing, the futile waiting for something to happen.

He was at the ice-chest, with a bottle in his hand, when Trappes-Lomax put his head out of his room.

"I've been looking for you everywhere, Ted. What happened!"

"The blasted engine conked out."

"Well, bring the bottle—and another with it. I've got news for you."

Carse slammed the ice-chest door. News. What in hell did it matter? He'd ask for a transfer. Anything would be better than this place. News. He was wasting his time here.

At the C.O.'s door he propped. Captain Lyon, the man he had been waiting for, was sitting on the camp bed. He had an empty glass in his hand.

"Just what the doctor ordered," Lyon said, smiling.

33

Carse noticed, as he put the bottles on the table, how Lyon showed his top teeth, how extraordinarily bright were his eyes, how boyish he looked in the hushed light from the shaded bulb.

He filled the three glasses, no longer tired now, but tense, watchful.

"I mentioned the possibility of a trip away," Trappes-Lomax said immediately. "We want you to navigate the *Krait*."

"The *Krait*? . . . But she's a tub with a worn-out engine."

"She was a Japanese fishing boat," Lyon said: "That's why she's important."

His voice was small in the still room.

"That may be," Carse said, wrinkling his big nose, "but everyone here calls her H.M.A.S. Mystery Ship—and it's not a compliment." He stared at Lyon. "If I have to navigate a tub like that, where are we heading—Borneo?"

Trappes-Lomax answered. "We're getting another engine for her, and because of the delay"—he glanced at Lyon—"the general idea of the trip has been altered."

"I would like you to go over the *Krait* carefully and report to me what you need," Lyon said.

"That'll depend on where we're going and how far," Carse replied. "What navigational aids has she got? What's her space like? I've seen her—who hasn't—but I haven't been all over her."

Lyon bent forward. "It's our intention to take fuel for thirteen thousand miles."

Carse whistled. "That's a damned lot of fuel—here to England."

For the first time he realized that Lyon reminded him of a sparrow. Perhaps it was his eyes or his almost pert habit of turning his head to listen, to watch, and holding it a little to one side. But the man lacked the compact sturdiness of a sparrow. Lyon had a curious physical frailty about him, something you sensed rather than saw.

Then Lyon was speaking. "With her old engine and fuel capacity she had a range of only eight hundred miles. That's no good to us. We're at present converting one of her holds into a fuel tank—yes, diesel—and we propose to carry another four hundred and forty gallons in drums on deck."

"A lot'll depend," Carse reminded him, "on the speed and fuel consumption of the new engine. What make is it?"

Lyon pulled on his cigarette. "It's a brand-new six cylinder Gardner-diesel—the only one in Australia. We pulled a string or two to get it. It's in Hobart, but we expect it here in about a fortnight."

Carse said, "A new engine will mean a new propeller."

The captain looked surprised. "I hadn't thought of that."

"The old prop. wouldn't do. Her pitch wouldn't suit the new engine."

"Right. We'll have to see to that. McDowell assures me that if we get the new engine in a fortnight—and we'll get it—that will be in plenty of time. He should know. It's his baby."

So Paddy McDowell's in this, too, Carse thought, and was glad.

Then Page and Davidson, the big English lieutenant Carse had met a few times but hardly knew, were in the doorway.

"About time, too," the C.O. said.

Davidson grinned. "We had to break up a poker game to get here—so make it snappy."

He sat on the floor. Page squatted.

Now what? Carse thought. Life at Z.E.S. was getting interesting.

Everyone waited as Lyon, expressionless, still, stared through the open door, through the veranda railings, at the distant lights of Cairns. He seemed to have forgotten the others in the room, and Carse was conscious of the tenseness of the man, a nervous tightness which seemed to be concentrated somewhere between his alert intelligent eyes.

Then Lyon turned his head and looked direct at Carse, as though he had read his thoughts.

"Now we're all here, and for the benefit of Lieutenant Page and Lieutenant Carse, I'd better explain. We propose to attack Japanese shipping in Singapore Harbour and to get there and back in the *Krait*. If we can't return to Australia we may have to head for Africa or even Pearl Harbour. That's why we must have long range."

His eyes flicked the listening officers. "I shall be in command and Lieutenant Davidson will be my 2 I.C. He will also command all operatives in the actual limpet attack. We will use canoes. The name of the operation was originally Jock Force, but for special reasons we have decided to change that. The new name is Jaywick. There will be other conferences as we work out details."

Again he looked around. "I don't think there is any need to remind you that from now on secrecy is vital. Thank you, gentlemen."

"And now," Trappes-Lomax said, "I think the mess, if we nudge it slightly, will stand another couple of bottles."

When Carse first examined the *Krait* she was on the slips at Stratford Bridge up the Barron River just north of Cairns, and when he had crawled all over her, from forward hold to the deck hole in her overhung stern which the Japanese had used as their heads—latrine—Lyon's plan to take her to Singapore seemed more insane than ever.

"She scares me stiff," he told Paddy McDowell.

"Gave me a touch of 'em first time I clapped eyes on her," Paddy admitted, "but you'll find she grows on yer."

He looked up from the cigarette he was rolling with fingers like charred sticks.

"We wouldn't be goin' too far in her, I hope?"

"I wouldn't take her across to Green."

"A bit further maybe—by the look of the fuel we'll be carryin'."

He stared unblinking at Carse as he slid the paper along his tongue.

The old devil knows, Carse thought. You can't bluff a sailor of his vintage.

"Could be," he said, and changed the subject. "Let's take another look at the storage space in your department."

Paddy grinned as they went below.

The *Krait* was originally black but looked as if she hadn't been painted for twenty years. She was 78 feet long with a beam of only 10 feet 6 inches, and was built of two-inch teak planking copper sheathed. Between her mast, which was forward, and her high bow was No. 1 hold, which contained six tons of concrete ballast, and between mast and wheelhouse were Nos. 2, 3 and 4 holds. No. 4 was the hold being converted for fuel. The holds, which were insulated with 9 inches of cork, were 8 feet 8 inches square, the coamings were 15 inches high, and the hatches were 4 feet square. The deck was covered with a 4-inch-thick bullet-proof composition like pitch which weighed more than two tons. It had only just been laid, at Lyon's orders.

The wheelhouse, which began almost two-thirds down her length, was raised 18 inches off the deck and was only 6 feet high and 6 feet wide. It was half-glassed front and sides, had a wood and canvas back, and port and starboard doors which opened back and clipped. The wheelhouse had an old binnacle and standard compass in front of the wooden wheel, one narrow bunk, a chart table which swung down over the bunk but had to be folded up and clipped to the bulkhead if you wanted to lie down, a bookshelf, and stowage space under the bunk which could be got at only by lifting the rubber mattress and a wooden cover.

The space aft of the wheelhouse near the stern was canvas-covered and fitted with canvas curtains which could be lowered to the bulwarks, and at the after starboard end of this covered area was the galley—nothing more than a small, partly protected deck compartment built round an oil stove. The ship's heads were also at the stern, but in place of the primitive Japanese lavatory—a hole punched through the deck—was an almost equally primitive cleat, with two arms, screwed on the rail right aft. You sat between the arms of the cleat, as lonely as a perching seagull, and could reach a roped bucket on the deck. It was simple, private, and uncomfortable, but, like the *Krait* herself, you became used to it.

The engine-room and a small hold for bosun's stores was below the covered stern area of the ship.

The *Krait* was like something you might find, in almost any world harbour, towing barges or tied to some rotting wharf. She was not only long and extremely narrow, but drab and uninspiring, the sort of craft no sober sailor would want to take beyond a harbour entrance swell.

And yet the appearance of the *Krait* was deceptive, in more ways than one, as her history shows.

Her original name was *Kofuku Maru*—a name which appealed on sight and sound to the intellectual instincts of sailors. She had been a fishing boat operated by a Japanese firm in Singapore, and she probably played her part in the "familiarization" training of Japanese naval officers in the waters off Malaya, long before Pearl Harbour, when the Japanese were already preparing for their Malaya campaign.

About six weeks before Singapore surrendered on 15th February 1942, Bill Reynolds, an Australian who had served in destroyers in World War I, who had lived in Malaya for years, and who was nearly sixty, offered his services to the Navy and was given command of the *Kofuku Maru*, which had been seized when the Pacific War began. And as Singapore was falling he took the old fishing boat south-east to the "Thousand Islands" of the Rhio Archipelago where, in those terrible days when at least fifty escaping ships were sunk by Japanese bombers and more than three thousand people killed, he used her as a ferry to pick up refugees from the islands, small craft and even rafts and wreckage, and to take them to Sumatra.

During this desperate period Reynolds and Captain Ivan Lyon met at the mouth of the Indragiri River, where Reynolds had just dropped a boatload of refugees combed from the islands around Linga. The two men had never seen each other before, but were temporarily in the same business—rescue and escape.

Captain Ivan Lyon, of the Gordon Highlanders, was an Intelligence officer at Army Headquarters in Singapore, and liaison officer with the Dutch, before being sent to Sumatra to help organize and supply an escape route—the "Tourist Route", as many remember it—across the island and onward to safety in Ceylon and Australia.

But what intrigued Lyon most, the day he and Bill Reynolds met, was the *Kofuku Maru*—a Japanese craft in British hands. He saw the boat as an invaluable aid to a plan, already evolving in his alert brain, to return to Singapore. The embryonic plan may have come first, or the *Kofuku Maru* may have given him the idea. It doesn't matter. The important thing is that during one of the worst defeats and panics in modern history this young officer was calmly planning, while on the run himself, how to return to Singapore to attack the Japanese. He was so sure that the boat would be useful to him in the future that he mentioned his plan to Reynolds, and they agreed that if they escaped they would find each other and see what they could do about it.

Old Bill Reynolds, with a load of Chinese refugees and an engine so old that copper wire held it together, sailed the *Kofuku Maru* up Malacca Strait, between Malaya and Sumatra, and across the Indian Ocean to Ceylon and eventually to Bombay. A Zero floatplane machine-gunned them in Malacca Strait, but missed and their engine broke down for five hours near the Nicobars.

Ivan Lyon, twenty-one days after Singapore had fallen, commandeered a big proa, the *Sederhana Johannes* at Padang, on Sumatra's Indian Ocean coast, and escaped with fifteen Europeans, a Chinese and a Malay. The Europeans included his own batman, Corporal Taffy Morris, Captain H. A. "Jock" Campbell, and Captain John Davis and Captain Richard Broome, both of whom had helped to organize the "Tourist Route" and who later landed secretly in Malaya to fight with the Chinese Communist guerrillas.

The *Sederhana Johannes* was old, sluggish and unseaworthy. She had no engine and her sails were rotten. But the party had plenty of food and water. Lyon, although an expert small-boat sailor—before the war he sailed alone in a small boat from Singapore to Saigon—knew nothing about proas or how to sail them, and was also no navigator, though this didn't matter since he had no instruments and his only chart was a page from a school atlas.

When Japanese aircraft machine-gunned them soon after leaving Sumatra and again farther out in the Indian Ocean, the Europeans covered themselves with bamboo matting while the Chinese and Malay waved hoping to deceive the Japanese pilots. The trick didn't work, for the Japanese were attacking everything that moved, but in time the proa moved out beyond range.

Thirty-eight days after leaving Padang, and still three miles south-east of Ceylon, a freighter picked them up, exhausted and covered in suppurating sores and boils, and took them to Colombo.

Ivan Lyon, who was awarded the M.B.E. for his work in Sumatra and his leadership during the escape, came from an Army family, though the popular belief among people in Australia who knew him during the war that he was a Bowes-Lyon, and a cousin of the Queen (now the Queen Mother) was wrong. Yet the belief persists. His father was Brigadier-

General Francis Lyon, C.B., C.M.G., C.V.O., D.S.O., a descendant of Thomas Lyon who left Scotland in the seventeenth century to settle first at Warrington in Lancashire.

Ivan Lyon, who went to Harrow in 1929-33, and to the Royal Military College, Sandhurst, and who was commissioned into the Gordon Highlanders in 1935, knew the right people or how to get to them, for immediately he reached India after his escape he began to use all his influence he could to win official backing for his return-to-Singapore plan. He had complete faith in himself and his idea, a personal ruthlessness which his rather spindly body, his habit of silence, and his nervous tenseness seemed to deny. Many people in India, when they heard his plan, thought he was crazy, but in New Delhi General Wavell became interested and passed him on to other top-ranking men in the British Services. One of these was Admiral Sir Geoffrey Layton, who was commanding in Ceylon. Another was Admiral Sir Geoffrey Arbuthnot, who was Commander-in-Chief of the East Indies station.

Lyon, who had discovered that Bill Reynolds had escaped and that the *Kofuku Maru* had reached Bombay, argued that she was the ideal ship for the operation he planned. She was Japanese-built, and boats of her type, common before the war in South-east Asian waters as genuine and also camouflaged fishing craft, would be accepted by the Japs as their own and would not arouse their suspicion. He also pointed out that the logical operation base was Australia, because the Singapore approaches from India and Ceylon would be more closely watched than the wider and more distant route from Australia.

In selecting Australia as a raiding base Lyon was not influenced by his family's presence there. His wife Gabrielle—a charming French girl—and their small son had been evacuated from Singapore to Perth before the surrender, and Lyon, posted to a staff job at New Delhi after his escape from Sumatra, had cabled her to join him when she could. But while she was waiting in Perth for a ship, his raid plans rapidly matured. He cabled her to stay in Australia and left for Melbourne, only to learn on arriving in July 1942, that she had already sailed for India; and not long afterwards he received news that her ship had been sunk and that she and the child had been landed at Singapore to become prisoners of the Japanese.

Lyon had reached Australia with British support and £30,000 worth of backing for his scheme, and he was followed by Captain (later Major) H. A. "Jock" Campbell, of the King's Own Scottish Borderers, who had been a rubber planter in Malaya, who had escaped with him in the *Seder-*

hana Johannes, and who was to become his administrative head and the behind-the-scenes organizer of Operation Jaywick.

Before Campbell arrived Lyon had difficulty getting active support in Australia. He had come at a bad time. The decisive Battle of the Coral Sea was over, and the immediate threat to Port Moresby and to Australia removed, but critical battles were soon to be fought in Papua, and Service indifference and even opposition to what must have appeared then as a mad and quite tertiary plan to raid far-off Singapore was understandable.

Lyon, however, was not an easy man to stop. Through family connections, he went direct to the Governor-General of Australia, Lord Gowrie, who played a never-publicized but important behind-the-scenes military role in Australia in World War II, and particularly in secret warfare. Lord Gowrie studied his "wild" plan, approved it, and began to use his great influence to help Lyon.

While this was going on, Lyon and the newly arrived Campbell outlined the plan to the Director of Naval Intelligence, Commander R. B. M. Long, who sent them on immediately to the First Naval Member, Admiral Sir Guy Royle. Admiral Royle, a friend of Lord Gowrie, gave Lyon his complete support, the Naval Board approved, and then General Sir Thomas Blamey and the Army came in behind the scheme.

And so Ivan Lyon's "Jock Force", to operate under the Inter-Allied Services Department, was born.

6

IVAN LYON had two immediate problems to solve once his raid was approved and every assistance guaranteed. He had to get his ship to Australia and he had to select his raiding party.

In Bombay the *Kofuku Maru* had been taken over by the Royal Navy and renamed *Krait* after the venomous little Indian snake which kills almost as many people each year as the better-known cobra. Her transfer was arranged and she was ordered to Australia; but Bill Reynolds, who still commanded her, had to abandon two attempts to sail her to Fremantle when her ancient four-cylinder Deutz diesel broke down, and she was eventually shipped on the deck of a British freighter and unloaded in Sydney Harbour in November 1942.

But long before this Ivan Lyon had already recruited some of his party for the raid, including his second-in-command and attack leader, a man of extraordinary character, courage and determination, and so temperamentally different from Lyon that they were almost direct opposites.

Lyon found his 2 I.C. under unusual and unhappy circumstances. One day in July 1942, an Intelligence officer, a woman who must remain nameless, received a telephone call from Government House, Melbourne. It was Lady Dugan, wife of the Governor of Victoria, Sir Winston Dugan, whom the officer knew.

"I would like you to come over and help us," Lady Dugan explained. "There's someone here whom you know. He's in terrible distress because of his wife. He has just heard she has been captured by the Japanese."

The Intelligence officer went to Government House and found that the guest Lady Dugan was so concerned about was Ivan Lyon, an acquaintance from Singapore days. He was close to tears. During the tense lunch which followed the guests tried to divert Lyon's attention from the news of his wife's capture, and afterwards the Intelligence officer took him aside.

"I know how bitter and fighting mad you must feel," she said, trying desperately to help. "Let's go over to my office and plan a raid on Singapore."

To her astonishment Lyon said, "That's just what I've come here to do."

He took a letter from his pocket and handed it to her. The letter was from General Sir Archibald Wavell. It concerned Lyon's raid.

"You see the irony of it," he said. "My wife's a prisoner in the very place I'm going to attack."

Later Lyon explained his plan and they even got out maps of Malaya and the Netherlands Indies, as Indonesia was then, and broadly worked out possible attack routes. Lyon told her that although he had considered a number of men for the job of second-in-command, he had not yet found anyone who combined the qualities and experience he needed.

"It's difficult," he explained. "He must be a man who knows canoes and who can train others how to use them, and he must be equally at home in jungle-type warfare."

"I know the very man you're looking for," she said. "He's on the staff at naval headquarters, and hates it. I saw him only a few days ago and he told me how much he loathed warming a chair during a war. He wants to get out and do something useful."

Lyon was immediately interested. He asked his name.

"Davidson."

"Not Donald Davidson—from Singapore?"

"Yes."

"I don't know him very well, but I met him and his wife several times. I even remember having a natter with him about canoes at a party we had in the mess. . . . That's right. He'd done a lot of canoeing in Burma, or was it Siam?"

"That's the man."

"Where can I find him?"

She reached for the phone.

Friends of Donald Davidson have often said that if Sir Edmund Hillary had not climbed Mount Everest, Donald would have tried.

He was a slim wiry six-footer with light-blue eyes, sandy-red hair already far back on his broad forehead, and the fair freckled tanless skin that often goes with that colouring. His normal expression was almost stern, and bearded he would have looked like one of those Presbyterian parsons who stare severely back from religious books and prints of the nineteenth century. He could be dour, too, and there were times when he seldom smiled for days, when he seemed to withdraw into a form of spiritual hibernation and shut himself in among secret things. But he could also be gay, with a careless disregard for time and a blunt satirical way of talking and telling stories which endeared him to many. At these times he could be an entertainer of almost professional standard, with a perfect sense of timing and an amusing charm which held and swayed an audience. He knew so many ballads and chanties, as well as more contemporary songs, that he had been known aboard ship to sing for hours, propped against the rail, strumming a mandolin or guitar and never repeating a tune.

Donald Davidson was the son of the Rev. Gerard Davidson, vicar of Woodford Kettering in Northamptonshire, and a relation of the late Sir Alfred Davidson, sometime general manager of the Bank of New South Wales in Sydney. Donald was educated at Cheltenham, and then came to Australia where he spent five years in Queensland, first as a jackeroo on Ooraine station in the Dirranbandi district in 1927, and later on Booka Booka station in the Charleville area, where for a couple of years he had a ring-barking contract.

Those who knew him in those days describe him as an indifferent rider and a maniac on physical fitness, a "powerful fearless bloke" who could put on the gloves with the best in a shearer's team.

But although he got on well with Australians, and liked the open country life, outback Queensland was too arid for him, too stark, and after five years he returned to England, joined the Bombay Burmah Trading Corporation, and went to work in the teak forests of northern Siam and later Burma.

From the start he felt at home among the black-green mountains and jungle. He was a natural adventurer, a born explorer, always wanting to go where no white man had been.

He would climb anything, go anywhere. He was a physical perfectionist and such a brilliant canoeist that he once canoed almost the full length of the long Chindwin River. The mountains and the jungle provided him with an outlet for these urges, forced him to toughen his wiry body, provided him, too, with a source of never-ending interest in everything that moved. He loved all natural things and trained himself to sit still for hours so that he could watch a bird building a nest, an animal in its natural surroundings. He taught himself to hunt, to recognize tracks and animal habits, to move silently among trees and rain forest, to learn nature's camouflage, to achieve an acutely developed sense of awareness of the differences and deviations and dangers in a jungle environment.

He preferred to observe and study and rarely killed on his hunting expeditions except for food or to protect himself, for he lived and worked in a land of tiger, of elephant, of cobra.

His preoccupation with nature, his love of animals and his gentle way with them, were strong traits that were reflected, too, in his love of children and his instinctive knowledge of how to approach them, how to win their trust, how to play with them.

But there was another side to him which was more difficult to understand—when he was not the gentle, almost introspective man he sounds. Danger to Donald Davidson was a necessity. He sought it, embraced it. He could not do without it. From it he seemed to absorb an ingredient vital to his spiritual survival. Love of danger, or what danger meant to him, was belly-deep, obsessional. To balance precariously between life and death was to function, to be alive.

In Burma he once tracked an old fellow tiger, a known man-eater. He followed it from the jungle into open country where there was little cover and no retreat. He walked up to that tiger and as it charged he killed it at point-blank range. But the significance of this story is that he knew, when he began to track the tiger, that the only ammunition he had was fine bird shot.

When World War II began, Davidson asked his company for permission to join the Army. This was refused, but he volunteered immediately anyway and was given a commission in the Burma Frontier Force. Soon afterwards the Burmese Government passed a law that no European could hold a commission in Burma unless he had a job to return to after the war, and this was too much for a man like Davidson. He decided to join the A.I.F., and was at Singapore waiting for a ship to Australia when he was offered a commission in the Royal Navy and decided to take it and stay.

His wife—they had married in Penang in 1935—and four-months-old daughter Caroline were evacuated to Australia in

December 1941, after Pearl Harbour, and Davidson left Singapore before the surrender with the Singapore Naval Base Staff and went to the Netherland Indies. He eventually escaped in a small boat from Sandakan in Borneo and rejoined his wife and child early in March 1942, in Melbourne, where he was given a post at the Navy Office.

It was towards the end of July 1942, after that telephone call from the Intelligence officer, that Davidson met Lyon and became his 2 I.C. in "Jock Force".

A week after this meeting Lyon and Davidson went to Flinders Naval Depot, near Melbourne, to select naval ratings for training. Volunteers had been called for "special service", and nearly forty men had offered. These men were told nothing, could be told nothing at this stage. Except for two of them, they were all about eighteen years old, had been in the Navy only a few months, and had never been to sea.

Lyon and Davidson interviewed every volunteer and selected seventeen. They warned them that only a few would be needed, that the selection of those few would depend on how well they handled their training, and that the service for which they had volunteered would be dangerous. Not one withdrew.

For the next six weeks Davidson trained with the volunteers at the Army Physical and Recreational Training School at Frankston, on the shores of Port Phillip. They wrestled, boxed, ran, climbed and learnt some of the tricks of unarmed combat. Then Davidson, who had carefully watched and assessed the men, dropped six who were physically weaker than the others and took eleven men early in September 1942 to a secret training camp—"Camp Z"—at Broken Bay, north of Sydney.

This camp was on a cliff-top at sheltered Refuge Bay, on Cowan Creek and about four miles west of Palm Beach, among the hungry Hawkesbury sandstone country—a lonely, secluded spot among rocks and twisted trees and silence.

From the start Davidson, who never gave an order he could not carry out himself, made a strict rule that the men must reach the beach below Camp Z by bosun's chair and must return by swing-climbing up the cliff-face on a rope—a Commando technique they soon mastered, though after a two-or-three-day exercise with little sleep and on basic raiding rations, the climb was almost impossible. Davidson also laid it down that a training day would be from daylight to lights-out at 10 p.m.—though trainees were often out of bed at midnight or later, or even all night—and he allowed practically no free time and totally prohibited smoking and drinking.

As one volunteer wrote afterwards, "We trained about eighteen hours a day for three months. We trained in strict secrecy, with no smokes, no beer, no women, no nothing. It was hell—the kind of life you like only when you look back at it when you're very old and want to impress your grandchildren."

Concentration at Camp Z was on physical fitness, canoeing, night movement, and the use of weapons and explosives. The men learnt to use and strip in the dark rifle, Owen, Sten, Bren and Lewis, to handle and apply explosives, to kill with hand, cord, knife, parang or blackjack. They learnt how to use a compass, read maps and charts, find their way by day or night on land or water, move silently, camouflage themselves and their equipment, stalk an enemy sentry or position, climb cliffs, go without food and water for long periods. They spent hours each day mastering the canvas canoes, learning how to sit, paddle, paddle silently, negotiate wave, rip and surf, right an upset canoe and change positions in the canoe, limit silhouette, approach a ship or land, use backgrounds, freeze at any time.

Davidson decided early that double-ended paddles, though they moved a canoe faster for a few miles, were less efficient for the job ahead than single-blade paddles. He claimed that all long-distance canoe races were won with single blades. Double blades, he said, were also more dangerous for the operator because they could be seen much farther away and because of the flash. His experiments in Broken Bay, and up the winding Hawkesbury River which flows into the bay, proved that flash from sun, moon or searchlight on a wet double paddle could be seen like a flash of a heliograph mirror several miles away, and more experiments showed that the single-blade paddle was easier to use, less tiring over long distances, and more silent, particularly when silence was most urgently needed on a final approach to an objective. He spent weary hours, including much time on the few rest days he allowed, testing paddles made from different woods and proving to himself, and then to others, that by giving the single blades almost knife edges he could eliminate the noise of a paddle in the water, and even the noise from paddle drips, almost entirely. He was so good that he could use a paddle at night and not be heard a yard or two away.

During the three months at Camp Z, while the volunteers were under constant pressure, Davidson watched more than the training efficiency of his group. Day after day he observed how the men worked and lived together, which men argued or complained or lost their tempers or sulked. Knowing a little of what was ahead, he looked for the men best suited temperamentally as well as physically for the exacting teamwork of living together under constant threat of danger and death.

Davidson did not make up his mind until a few days before Bill Reynolds brought the *Krait* up the coast from Sydney and anchored her off Camp Z at Refuge Bay. Then, from his eleven volunteers, he picked the five acting able seamen he felt were as near perfect as he could get for "Jock Force".

They were all young, strong, and balanced for their age, but in character they varied. There was Walter Gordon Falls, son of a dairy farmer in the Casino district of New South Wales, a man of twenty-three and the oldest of the volunteers; because of this he had been known from the start as "Poppa". He was fair, solidly built and of above-average intelligence, a man whose calmness and reliability strongly influenced others, particularly younger members like A. W. Huston. "Happy", as Huston was inevitably called, because he seldom smiled—although he was good natured and easy to live with—was a wiry olive-skinned boy who tanned almost black. He was only seventeen, and immature in many ways, but with a relentless type of determination to master what he was taught. He came from Brisbane, and the only work he had ever done was in a banana-ripening store. F. W. Marsh, also from Brisbane, where he had been a cabinet-maker's apprentice, was fair and broad-shouldered. He was the ideal Commando type—intelligent, quick to think and move, and good at all sports. As a fighter, with fists, gloves or knife, he was sudden and deadly, and seemed to know instinctively the right thing to do at the right moment. He was a formidable opponent, but never tried to dominate his fellows. His nickname was "Boof". M. M. Berryman's label of "Moss" came from his Christian name of Mostyn. He was a lively bright-eyed youngster who learnt quickly, and was adaptable, and exceptionally steady under any conditions. He had been an Adelaide shop assistant.

Of the five the only man with real Navy training and sea service was A. M. W. Jones, of Perth, whose great-grandfather had landed at Guildford on the Swan River with Captain Stirling when he began the settlement of Western Australia in 1829. "Joe", or sometimes "Arty", Jones had been to Perth Boys' High School and had been a grocer before he joined the Navy at nineteen in January 1941. He had trained at Flinders Naval Depot, and in November 1941 had seen overseas service in the Australian armed merchant cruiser *Manoora*. In June 1942 he had just completed a gunnery course at Flinders when he volunteered for "special service". This nuggety dark-haired man was the best educated of the five and extremely intelligent. Although outwardly the typical beer-loving, wench-chasing sailor, he was an extremely mature man of rare steadiness and courage. Joe Jones was an asset to any group.

These were the men who joined the *Krait* at Refuge Bay and went north in her, but there was another member of the crew, and he had been waiting at Camp Z even before it was a camp the day Davidson brought his eleven volunteers from Melbourne. This man was Corporal R. G. Morris—"Taffy" to everyone. He was a Welsh coalminer turned medical orderly in the Royal Army Medical Corps. He was Ivan Lyon's batman and had been with him in Sumatra and on the escape voyage from Padang in the *Sederhana Johannes*. Taffy, who wore the British Empire Medal for his work in Sumatra and on that voyage, sang at all hours, and in a Welsh accent nobody understood, songs which the others only occasionally recognized. He was slow, dour and unshakeable.

Early in his planning Ivan Lyon had fixed on 15th February, the anniversary of the surrender of Singapore, as the date for his raid, but early delays, the problem of moving the *Krait* from India, and the recruiting and training of his party had forced him to put back his striking date many months.

The *Krait*, with Reynolds, Davidson, Morris, Falls, Huston, Marsh, Berryman and Jones aboard, did not leave Refuge Bay for North Queensland until 18th January 1943, and even then she took nearly two months to reach Cairns. Her worn-out engine broke down first off Newcastle and then off Coff's Harbour, and she only just reached Brisbane under her own power. Captain F. G. L. ("Gort") Chester, British Army, was to have gone on the raid and travelled in the *Krait* from Broken Bay, but in the north his plans were changed and later he led secret parties landed in Borneo from submarines.

There, while the Navy repaired her engine, Leading Stoker Paddy McDowell joined her as engineer, and with him another experienced sailor. This was Acting Leading Seaman K. P. "Cobber" Cain, a thoughtful, handsome sixteen-stone Queenslander who had been in the merchant service, was a trained gunner, and who took a natural pride in keeping a ship clean and efficient. He had been all over the world and, apart from the sea, had worked at many jobs—as a market gardener, a boundary rider, and even a barman.

When the unreliable *Krait* headed north again from Brisbane she just managed to reach Fraser Island before her engine broke down for the fourth time in about six hundred miles. There, too, Donald Davidson developed an attack of malaria to remind him of Burma, and had to be ferried to the mainland and left behind in Maryborough Hospital while the *Krait* eventually limped on. She stopped again among the islands of the Great Barrier Reef, in Whitsunday Passage, and had to be towed, first to Townsville (where Davidson rejoined her and old Bill Reynolds left her to go to another job in New Guinea), and finally to Cairns to tie up alongside the *Gnair* at Smith's Landing that March morning during the early training of Scorpion's party when Ted Carse asked Paddy McDowell what he called his ship and Paddy replied disgustedly that she was nothing more than a "bloody crate".

7

FROM THE EVENING Ted Carse knew he was to navigate the *Krait* to Singapore, and perhaps to Honolulu or Durban on the return journey, he had difficulty visualizing the raid and his part in it. Even as he prepared the *Krait* and the almost endless lists of supplies and equipment, the work seemed to have no place in reality. Singapore was part of firmly held Japanese territory, so far away, so remote, that the thought of trying to reach even within a thousand miles of the little island at the foot of the Malay Peninsula, and to reach it in an old slow ship, seemed fantasy.

One day he spread out his maps and charts and made some calculations. He saw that the Pacific war was being decided in a gigantic square with its corners at Colombo, Tokyo, Honolulu and Sydney, but when he superimposed this square on the other war, the European war, he found that the corners there were Iceland, the Aral Sea in Russian Turkestan, St Helena off the west coast of Africa, and American Florida—almost all Europe except northern Scandinavia, a large part of western Asia, half Africa, and all the North Atlantic Ocean.

He grinned at the discovery, then reached again for his dividers. The raid he was going on was equivalent to an attack from Gibraltar on Oslo in Norway or on Scapa Flow in the Orkney Islands north of Scotland—and return. Or a similar two-way attack on Vera Cruz in Mexico launched from New York City. In addition, his theoretical attack parties would be in enemy territory for most of those distances there and back.

With these sobering statistics before him the more he thought of Singapore the more he became convinced that no member of the *Krait* party would ever see Singapore or survive the raid, and yet, day after day as he worked to get the *Krait* ready, he knew—and knew with a calmness which at times astonished him—that no matter what was ahead he had as a volunteer accepted all risks and must go on.

He did not realize until later that first Donald Davidson, and then Davidson and Bob Page, were to help him, in curious indirect ways, to bridge Australia and Singapore in his mind, and to make the impossible raid, with all its fantastic distances and dangers, seem possible.

Late one afternoon, after Carse had sat most of the day checking supply and other lists, he decided to go for a walk before dark, and was moving along one of the tracks in the rain-forest gully behind Z.E.S. when Davidson dropped out of a tree on top of him and had a knife at his throat as they hit the ground.

"Perfect . . . perfect," Davidson shouted, as he released Carse and bounced to his feet. "Got it right at last."

48

Carse lay dazed and winded, but he sat up at last and shook his head, and felt for the bump on the back of his skull.

"You thought you'd break my neck. . . . What in hell do you think you're doing?"

Davidson stopped grinning. "Sorry if I hurt you—but I couldn't resist it. I was expecting one of the Javanese—they often use this path—but when I saw you coming you were such a perfect victim—"

Davidson helped him up. "Sorry, old boy, if I hit you a bit hard."

Carse rubbed his head. "A bit hard. . . . What are you up to?"

"Somewhere on this raid we may have to kill," Davidson said, earnestly, "and I have to know how to kill in as many ways as possible. This is one of them. Properly handled it's all over in seconds."

Carse felt his neck. "It damned nearly was."

"Balance and timing—that's what's needed. Look, I'll show you."

He climbed the tree again and lay along a thick branch which curved over the track. He kept his balance with his left hand ahead of his body along the side of the branch, and his right hand back along the branch beside his body. From the ground, and among the leaves and vines hanging from above, he was almost invisible.

"This is how it works," he called. "Watch."

He half-rolled, half-slid off the branch and dropped, and as he fell about ten feet onto his hands he flipped onto one shoulder and rolled.

"Even if you make a slight noise as you drop it doesn't matter," he explained, as he got to his feet. "Your victim will look up—it's instinctive—but you're on him before he knows what's hit him and you've already cut his throat."

"You're a bloodthirsty bastard," Carse said. "Next time I take a stroll it'll be in the open."

"In a war you're in to kill, and when we go across the ditch to Singapore next month we may have to kill right on her front doormat."

"You think we'll get that far?" Carse asked, testing.

Davidson looked surprised. "Not a doubt."

"It's a long way in an old boat."

"A Jap boat, old boy, not one of ours. That's where the advantage is all on our side."

He snatched a knife from the sheath he was wearing and the next second it was twanging in the tree-trunk. The double movement, draw and throw, was so quick that Carse was amazed.

Davidson grinned as he pulled out the knife.

"I've put in a lot of practice, but I'd still like to be better at it. A good throw in the dark might get one out of real trouble."

He held out the knife. "Try it."

Carse tried, but the knife clattered against the trunk. He tried again, but although the point penetrated the bark it did not hold. A third time he missed the tree.

Davidson recovered the knife. "I'm no Itie on knives, but this is how I do it."

With his thumb he lightly held the handle of the knife along his palm, with the blade resting on his wrist and pointing up his arm. Then with a quick upward and downward flick of his wrist he put the knife into the tree. Carse couldn't even follow its flight.

"I can hit a six-inch target dead centre every time at fifteen to twenty feet," Davidson explained, "but beyond that I start to go adrift."

He paced five long yards out from the tree. Carse pointed. "That mark at nine o'clock the brown patch."

The knife quivered beside the mark.

Carse threw up his hands. "If you're not doing anything special after the war we'll join a circus. I'll be glad to manage you and rake in the dough."

Davidson tugged at the knife. "I might take you up on that."

As they walked back to the house Davidson explained that he and Bob Page were planning a practice canoe raid and asked Carse if he would help them.

"On one condition," Carse said. "No trees."

Davidson laughed. "I can promise you that—no trees."

Carse and Saptu, waiting in the *Gnair* off Smith's Landing, knew that the canoe with Davidson and Page would come in from the sea between 10 and 10.30 p.m. and up the creek against the tide. Carse, who had chosen Saptu because of his exceptional eyesight and hearing, knew that the raiders would have to use all their skill to escape detection by the Torres Strait islander, especially as moonlight, filtering through scattered cloud, gave just enough light to distinguish the waterway itself from its mangrove banks.

Stinking with mosquito repellent and wearing long greens and shirts with rolled-down sleeves, they waited. Saptu lay near the bows. Carse sat near the stern. The only sounds were the wet click-click of crabs in the mud, the ebb sucking gently at the mangrove roots, the rare far-off chill whistle of a curlew.

Carse shaded his torch, looked at his watch, and crept along to Saptu and touched him on the back—the signal that the exercise had begun. Then he returned to the stern and waited, staring into the dark until his eyes watered, watching where dark creek merged or seemed to merge with the slightly darker smudge of the mangrove banks, watching for a difference, a foreign shape or movement, a chance discovery of faint phosphorous swirl that might betray a paddle.

Ten, fifteen minutes passed. He stopped trying to locate the raiding canoe with his eyes and now depended on his ears, listened to every sound and for sounds among them that might be the slight creak of a canoeman shifting position or a paddle splash or drip. He held his breath and strained to hear, above the beating of his heart, the pulse, pulse in his ears.

"Man on boat," Saptu suddenly called.

Carse pressed his torch and split the dark. Davidson was crouching on the *Gnair's* port side. Page was half over the side.

"You little beaut," Bob Page called.

"Good work," Carse said, as he lit a lantern and Saptu pumped the primus to make tea, and while they waited they sat in the stern and discussed the raid.

"We were alongside for two or three minutes at least," Davidson said.

"I never heard a sound—not one," Carse said. "I'm damned if I know how you did it."

In the lantern light Page's teeth were brilliantly white against his blackened face.

"We came in along the mangroves and then cut across. We reached up-creek of you, then drifted down. We passed you within a few yards."

"It's hard to believe."

Davidson chuckled. "The Catalina boys won't be so polite when I phone their C.O. in the morning."

"Before we came in we raided every Cat in harbour," Page explained. "We left visiting cards on them saying we'd sunk them. They had a guard on each boat."

Davidson smacked at the whining mosquitoes. "All the advantages are with the canoe—and don't let anyone bluff you they're not. Canoes are almost impossible to see, even in a fair amount of light. And if they're properly handled"—he bowed low to Page—"you shouldn't be able to hear them. They're almost part of the water. They take what I call the shape of the water. But Bob and I thought you might pick us up in a narrow creek like this, didn't we, Bob?"

"That's right. We thought you'd spot us as we crossed from the mangroves."

They laughed about the Cats and talked of the land raid they planned for the following night on the planes at the airfield, while Saptu made the tea and brought each man a tin mug.

"I gave up trying to see you," Carse explained, as they sipped noisily. "But I thought I might be able to hear you."

"And you were waiting for us," Davidson put in. He lowered his voice so that Saptu couldn't hear. "It just goes to show what hope the Nips will have of picking us up in a harbour like Singapore. And they won't be expecting us."

"You drop us there, Ted, and we'll do the rest," Bob Page said quietly.

He raised his mug. "Here we come, Tojo, and if tonight's any indication we're already home and hosed."

Now preparations for the raid were almost complete and Carse could feel at Z.E.S., and within himself, a new tension, a sudden awareness of something that could not be defined except as a subdued voiceless excitement, a hidden undertone of increased activity and expectation.

Not a man at Z.E.S., except the few executive officers linked indirectly with Jaywick, knew anything about the operation, yet all except the latest arrivals understood in their own way that soon there would be empty chairs at the mess table.

Ivan Lyon had ceased to be a drift-in and was now permanently at Z.E.S.—training with Davidson, Page and the others in the canoes, conferring with Trappes-Lomax, listening to Paddy McDowell, dropping cigarette ash on Carse's charts, bending over lists with tubby Jock Campbell, whose unenviable job, which he handled effortlessly, was administration and supply.

Carse noticed that Lyon was never still, that he slept little and ate less, that although he gave the impression of talking a lot he in fact let others talk while he listened, or asked a brief question or merely said yes or no or quite so. The only time he appeared to relax was before dinner with a glass of beer—and he could drink beer for hours without showing any effect, except that his accent became more precise and his eyes, as Page once said, "a bit more thyroid".

Carse decided that Ivan Lyon, as man and leader, was, like Midshipman Easy, " all zeal", but, more than that, he was able to convey to others a feeling of confidence despite his distant impersonal attitude. Lyon, Carse felt, and others felt it, too, was not a man you would ever know well. He could be friendly, charming, and yet he lacked warmth, lacked those touches of personality which make others feel that here is a man who recognizes and understands them as feeling, suffering human beings. Lyon was always a little apart, and others were conscious of his aloneness and of the barrier he erected and stayed behind.

This, too, was the time, as training reached its peak, as conferences continued late at night, that supplies, equipment and arms poured in—supplies alone for a four months' voyage which would end no one knew where. Carse was busier than he had ever been. As captain of the *Krait*, he had to know every item she would carry—where to store it, how to get at it.

The basic food, except for flour, rice and prunes, was mostly tinned vegetables, fruit and fruit juices, and the only meat taken, apart from tinned bully beef, was finely powdered dehydrated mutton in cardboard cartons.

Operational supplies, for use by the actual raiding party, were in sealed tins—"Four by Fours"—which held food and canned heat for four men for four days. These supplies included tinned meat, condensed milk tablets, chocolate, biscuits, peanuts and glucose sweets, plus cigarettes, matches and even a paperback novel. Separate were one- and two-gallon tins of distilled water. All tins were sealed so that they could be buried or even anchored submerged off a beach at strategic points where they might be needed.

Medical stores included vitamins, atebrin, quinine, acriflavine, epsom salts, and a first-aid kit which contained sulpha drugs and morphia bottles with needles attached. Listed also under "medical" were a dozen each of Beenleigh rum, Dewar's whisky, Gordon's gin, and lime juice.

Ted Carse had to find space for fifty thousand cigarettes—English Capstans and American Camels—most of them intended as "trade" goods, or bribes for natives who might help them among the islands. And bribery, too, was the reason why £200 worth of Dutch guilders, all in gold, was taken in the *Krait*.

Arms, ammunition and explosives were among the heaviest and most space-filling items. The *Krait* carried two Lewis guns, two Brens, eight Stens, eight Owens and fourteen Smith and Weston revolvers, in addition to two hundred hand grenades, stabbing knives, ten-inch throwing stilettos, and jungle parangs. And explosives included forty-five limpets, enough to sink fifteen ships at three limpets to a ship, and 150 pounds of plastic explosive.

Care was taken that as many articles as possible of personal or common use were Japanese made. Sunglasses, for example, which might be recognized at a distance as Japanese by Japanese. Pencils, paper, cooking pots, even toothbrushes—all were "Made in Japan". The main reason for these precautions was that if any article accidentally went overboard any Japanese finding it would recognize its make and would not be suspicious.

Equipment also included the flags of all nations, in waterproof containers, and playing cards and sets of draughts and chessmen.

When most of the supplies, equipment and spares had been loaded, and while the new Gardner-diesel, which had been flown to Cairns from Hobart, was being installed and tested by naval engineers and Paddy McDowell, Carse was ordered to Melbourne to see the Director of Naval Intelligence, Commander Long, for a final briefing, and to collect the latest Dutch charts from the Dutch Admiral Konrad, who strongly advised that if the *Krait* party wanted to hide their ship while in Japanese waters they should sneak up one of the rivers in Sumatra and camouflage her among the overhanging Nipa palms along the banks, where there would be plenty of water to float the *Krait* even at low tide.

Carse was back at Z.E.S. at the end of July 1943, but only to learn from Ivan Lyon that Jaywick's complement was still not complete, although Leading Telegraphist H. S. Young, a Western Australian of twenty-two, had joined as the *Krait's* radio operator. Young was a tall, thin, grey-eyed, studious youngster, but behind his quiet, almost gentle nature and reserve were great stability and courage and a first-class brain. He had built his first radio set at eleven, had started his working life at fourteen as a telegraph messenger, and at sixteen had joined the Royal Australian Naval Reserve as a cadet wireless telegraphist. Mobilized immediately World War II began, he first served in small vessels and was at H.M.A.S. *Assault*, the Naval Combined Operations School at Nelson's Bay, north of Newcastle, when he met Lieutenant Donald Davidson and volunteered blind, in June 1943, for the *Krait* raid.

But, as Lyon explained to Carse, they still couldn't leave without a cook. A man who had volunteered for the voyage had decided to return to the Navy and a replacement had to be found.

Lyon acted quickly. He asked the Army to call for volunteers among the cooks of the Australian 7th Division then training on the Atherton Tableland behind Cairns, and a couple of days later, with Davidson and Carse, he drove to the Tableland where, at a parade, two men volunteered. Lyon, however, was reluctant to make a selection because both men were married with families, and he was discussing the problem with Davidson when a small, curly-haired corporal, who had not taken part in the parade, approached Carse.

"I hear you're looking for a cook."

"That's right. But I'd better warn you—it could be a tough job."

"I don't mind. I'd like to soldier-on a bit longer."

Carse took him across to the others.

"Are you married?"

"No, sir."

"I can't tell you at this stage what the job is," Lyon warned, "but it could be dangerous."

"That's O.K. by me, sir. I'd like to see some more active service."

"Can you cook?"

The corporal grinned. "I'm not much of a cook, but I'm a pretty good motor mechanic."

Everyone laughed. Lyon glanced at Davidson, at Carse. They nodded.

"Right. We'll sign you on. I'll arrange for your movement order."

"Thank you, sir," the corporal said.

And that was how Corporal A. Crilley, or "Pancake Andy" as this Queenslander came to be called, became cook, fourteenth and last man to join the *Krait* party, and, with Bob Page, the only other member of the A.I.F. to serve with Operation Jaywick. Not until later did Carse discover that Andy Crilley, because of ill health, was about to be boarded out of the Army.

Jaywick was at last ready to go.

8

NEAR MIDNIGHT on Monday, 9th August 1943, Ted Carse took the *Krait* out of Cairns to begin the 2400-mile journey from North Queensland to Exmouth Gulf, on the coast of Western Australia, the launching-point of Operation Jaywick.

It was eighteen months that night since Ivan Lyon had sailed the leaking *Sederhana Johannes* out of Padang in Sumatra on his desperate attempt to escape the Japanese and reach Ceylon, and eighteen months since Donald Davidson had escaped to Australia in a small boat from Sandakan in Borneo.

A year had dribbled away since the naval recruits had volunteered for "special service", and it was eight months since the strange colonel in Melbourne had asked Carse if he had any guts, if he thought he could navigate to San Francisco.

That night, as the *Krait* ruled a phosphorous wake on her journey north towards Cooktown and Cape Melville, towards where the rain-forest mountains of Cape York Peninsula are black-green walls behind thin yellow beaches, was the beginning of a great adventure of the sea, in one of its oddest ships, and with a crew more unconventional still. The fourteen men aboard were Lyon, Davidson, Page, Carse, McDowell, Morris, Cain, Falls, Jones, Young, Huston, Marsh, Berryman and Crilley—two public-school Englishmen with Scottish names and backgrounds, a Welsh coalminer, a Northern Irish-Australian, and ten Australians, one of whom, Page, was a medical student descendant of French Huguenots, and another, Carse, the grandson of an English clergyman who had renounced all to search for gold.

Of the fourteen, four were soldiers and ten sailors Lyon, the leader, was a professional soldier with plenty of experience in small boats but no deep-sea experience and no ability to navigate, and Davidson, although an expert canoeist, was a jungle-sailor who had never been to sea. Only four of the fourteen—Carse, McDowell, Cain and Jones—were real seamen, and of these Carse and McDowell were the only two with long sea training and experience who were capable of taking the *Krait* to Singapore or anywhere else. So that on these two, the only navigator and the only engineer among a group to whom the sea was largely a restless mystery, lay the responsibility of getting the *Krait* to its target and, what might be much more difficult, getting her home again.

This first stage of the journey into danger, as Jaywick moved to its launching-point, was important to all aboard, but especially to Carse who, as captain and navigator, was solely responsible for the running of the ship and for her safety and the safety of all on board. Where the ship herself was concerned his decisions were final and were obeyed by all, including the operational leader himself.

The long journey "over the top" of Australia, from the Pacific to the Indian Ocean, made it possible for Carse, or the "Admiral" as the others in Jaywick affectionately knew him, to study the ship, her behaviour, her stowage, and to teach his soldier-sailors not only their jobs but how to live together on what was little more than an unstable platform eighty-odd feet long and a standing-jump wide.

Although the *Krait* was fully operational, on this first phase of her journey she was within home waters, within cover from airfields in northern Australia, and able in an emergency to use her radio, so that all aboard could settle down without constant threat to a routine which had become familiar by the time the raid itself began.

Number One hold near the bows held the limpets and hand grenades. Food was in No. 2. Combined officers' quarters and the radio equipment was in No. 3. And No. 4 hold, almost under the wheelhouse, held enough diesel fuel, with the eight 44-gallon drums carried on deck, to give a cruising range of about 13,000 miles. On deck also were eight four-gallon drums of petrol to feed "Mickey Mouse", the small auxiliary engine which gave electric light and air pressure to start the 100-horse-power Gardner-diesel. All weapons and ammunition were carried, not in the holds, for guns had to be easy to get at, but in a big waterproof box on the engine-room hatch just aft of the wheelhouse.

Lyon, Davidson and Page used No. 3 hold, which was also Young's radio room; and, except for McDowell, who sometimes slept on the engine-room hatch, sometimes beside his engine if he was not satisfied with its performance, and Carse, who used the bunk in the wheelhouse, all others slept and ate in the covered curtained after section above the engine-room between the wheelhouse and the galley.

All except Crilley the cook, Young the radio operator, Morris the steward and Lyon's batman, and Marsh and Berryman, who assisted McDowell in the engine-room, were split into two four-hour watches. Lyon, Page, Huston and Jones kept one watch, and Carse, Davidson, Falls and Cain the other, though this pattern was varied at times during the voyage. An officer was always at the wheel—a rule from the start—with a stern lookout, a midships lookout who also relayed messages to the engine-room, and a man up the mast. This man, who had to climb the ratlines and stand on the yardarm holding onto the swaying mast, was relieved every hour by one of the others on watch. The masthead watch was extremely important because it extended vision for many miles and enabled the *Krait*, which was low on the water, to see most approaching craft long before she could herself be seen, and to take evasive action.

The *Krait* reached Thursday Island on Black Friday, 13th August, and although Carse wanted to leave the same day, after arranging with the R.A.A.F. for air cover across the top of the Gulf of Carpentaria, he was overruled.

"If we sailed today we couldn't have a successful journey," Lyon insisted. "I know for certain we would strike trouble."

Carse patiently explained how much the strong westward tide-set would help the slow *Krait* at the start of the voyage, but the leader was adamant.

"I'm sorry, Ted, but I won't leave until tomorrow."

This was not the first time Carse had noticed that Ivan Lyon was superstitious—and it was not to be the last. Coming up the coast from Cairns Lyon had been irritable, jumpy, when off Cooktown the *Krait* had nosed through blood and bloody froth as killer whales, running just below surface past the ship at an estimated thirty knots like white torpedoes, had attacked a huge whale. The whale, which was almost as long as the *Krait*, leapt again and again from the sea, up, up in a glistening, bleeding curve before falling back, with a crash of a 25-pounder gunburst, to lift a house-size splash of blood and foam.

And only a few weeks before this, when Carse and Davidson casually mentioned in the mess at Z.E.S. the small fortune they were about to win in a lottery, Lyon had gloomily shaken his head and come to them later, more worried than either had ever seen him, and said, "If you win anything in that lottery I'm not going on the raid. I'll pull out immediately and cancel the whole show. If you're lucky with money you can't be lucky in war. It just isn't possible."

When the *Krait* moved on from Thursday Island, westward now on her eighteen-day cruise from Cairns to Exmouth Gulf, even a Roman patrician would have been satisfied, or terrified, by the omens. Far west of Torres Strait, and approaching the Wessels, that long low island string north of Cape Arnhem, one of the lookouts spotted a brilliant light-flash high in the cloudless northern sky at 3.30 p.m.

"Enemy aircraft bearing green," he shouted

Carse hammered on the back of the wheelhouse.

"Action stations!"

Men on and off duty scrambled for the gun box. Cain and Falls set up the Bren and Lewis on air mountings, the barrels stabbing through flap openings in the canvas roof of the aft compartment. The others grabbed Owens and Stens, while in No. 3 hold Young, earphones clamped to his head, sat beside his set ready, if attack came, to call Spitfires from Millingimbi strip in eastern Arnhem Land.

The area they were crossing had an evil reputation, for Japanese bombers and flying-boats, operating regularly south from Amboina over the Arafura Sea, had killed a freighter there only a month or so before.

As Carse edged the *Krait* closer to the Wessels, the strange spot of light, about 45 degrees from the horizon, was as bright as a mirror reflecting the sun.

Davidson, sweeping with glasses, called, "Could be a Jap—but she's very high."

But Carse, watching the light through the starboard window of the wheelhouse, noticed that its bearing didn't change. He studied the light carefully just to make sure he wasn't wrong. Then suspicion became certainty.

"Relax," he called. "It's Venus."

"At this hour?" Lyon queried. "Are you sure?"

"Certain. Its bearing hasn't altered. The Dutch in Melbourne reminded me we might see it north of Australia."

"Thou in thy lake does see Thyself," Donald Davidson proclaimed, lifting the binocular strap over his head. "So she beholds her image in her eyes reflected. Thus did Venus rise from out of the sea."

"Struth," Carse said, and called, "Guns away."

Next morning, 17th August, and Ivan Lyon's twenty-eighth birthday, the crew were seated in a circle on the engine-room hatch cleaning and oiling the guns. This was their routine after-breakfast job. Plates and cups, waiting to be cleaned, were piled near the galley where Andy Crilley was scrubbing a dixie before trailing it in the sea.

Cobber Cain, sitting cross-legged like the Buddha he resembled, with a Lewis across his knees, was slowly turning the pan on the gun when a round went off with a shattering explosion in the enclosed deck space. The bullet hit a bottle of tomato sauce near the galley and whined out to sea, and glass and sauce sprayed everyone. A small piece cut Taffy Morris on the shin and a larger piece ploughed into his ankle and cut the artery. Blood spurted among sauce and glass splinters, as shouting men, thinking the ship was under attack, climbed up from below.

For the next two hours Bob Page worked to stop the bleeding and remove the glass. He probed and snipped and tied, then packed the wounds with sulpha. And for a week Taffy Morris could not walk, and for the rest of the trip he limped.

After the "Battle of the Wessels", as the men called it, Carse noticed that Lyon was more than usually silent, almost morose, though the leader made no comment until the day they sighted the cliffs of Melville Island, north of Darwin.

Lyon, who was steering, turned to Carse who had just awakened.

"I don't like the way things are going, Ted. Luck seems to be dead against us."

"I wouldn't say that," Carse mumbled, still half-asleep. "A few engine stoppages—nothing serious."

He raised himself on one elbow.

"We've had a pretty good run so far."

He disliked having to talk when he'd just woken up. He hoped Lyon would shut up. But he didn't.

"The things that have happened—Morris, the star, the whale. I don't like them. They're all against us." He looked over his shoulder. "I believe in luck. I believe it rules our lives from birth to death—decides our fortunes. Luck's as tangible as that land over there."

Carse sat up and looked south at the far-off cliffs.

Bull, he thought, and said, "Maybe", and Lyon didn't say any more.

But late that night Carse smiled in the dark when a shout from the bow lookout, followed by a grinding, sliding bump, woke him. Lyon, who was at the wheel, had grazed a sand-bar. Nor could Carse help being amused two days later when the sea a hundred miles from land rippled and squirmed for miles on either side of the *Krait* with small brown crabs, and among the crabs, like long mustard-coloured smears, lay the most evil-looking flat-headed, flat-tailed seasnakes he had ever seen.

Yet even Carse lost some of his scepticism when, at the wheel the next night, he knew, without question, that the ship was heading into danger. He had no evidence, only a sea-sense, an awareness that something was wrong. He didn't hesitate. He turned the ship and motored back along his course for several hours before turning and heading south again, though he was still so conscious of danger somewhere ahead that when Page came to relieve him he stayed at the wheel.

Anxiously they waited for daylight, and when it came the *Krait* was back in her original position and ahead, as the light hardened, were reefs, not shown on the chart, on which the sea was breaking not a mile ahead.

As they altered course the two men stared at each other.

"If you hadn't turned," Page said, "nothing could have saved us from piling up."

Carse nodded. "Work that one out if you can."

But what interested Carse most was Lyon's reaction when he heard how disaster had been avoided. "Good show, Ted," he said, cheerfully, "our luck's turning at last. Soon it will be on our side."

Then the gannet arrived. It slid in against the sunset to settle on the boom and be christened immediately by Falls "Lucky Joe." It left next morning, but returned before dark and spent each night on the *Krait* for the last week of the voyage. Lucky Joe was so amiable that he wouldn't move even if the men stood beside him. But coming in to land one evening he bombed the ship, and his direct hit on Happy Huston's head was regarded by all aboard, except Happy, as the most favourable omen of all, and especially by Lyon who, from that moment, never mentioned luck again.

Even when the *Krait* ran into heavy seas near the Monte Bello Islands, north of Exmouth Gulf, and began to bury her head dangerously and take in water, Lyon showed little concern. When Carse advised that the two and a half tons of bullet-proof material covering the deck should be jettisoned, Lyon, who vividly remembered being machine-gunned in the unprotected *Sederhana Johannes* and who had insisted that the bullet-proofing should be put on the *Krait*, agreed immediately, though Carse had felt sure he would refuse.

"Carse is right," he told the others. "It won't stop a bomb or a shell. It has no real value except perhaps to give Young an extra few seconds to get away a last message if we're attacked."

While the *Krait* ran before the sea he even helped prise the thick proofing off the deck and heave it overboard until the ship, free of the heavy top weight, was able to turn and resume her course.

Eighteen days after leaving Cairns the *Krait* reached Exmouth Gulf and anchored off "Potshot", code-name for the American Navy base behind the shoreline sandhills and spinifex twenty miles from the island- and reef-dotted entrance to the long, wide gulf. The first stage of Jaywick was over, but days of work were still ahead before the ship would be ready for sea again.

Admiral Christie, commander of the base, Captain Hawes of the submarine repair ship *Chanticleer*, whose father had been a sheriff in Texas in the bold bad days, and the other Americans entertained them, stocked the *Krait* with fresh supplies, and opened their workshops for repairs. They also asked no questions of their mixed guests of soldiers and sailors, though they would never believe that the *Krait* had come from Cairns.

"I'm an old sailor," Captain Hawes growled at Carse, "so don't expect me to swallow the yarn that you came right round in that scow. Why, I wouldn't take that thing to sea for a Texas oilwell."

At Potshot four new canoes, which had been flown at top priority from England to Exmouth Gulf, were waiting in their neat little bags. They were an improved type of Folboat to replace the old training canoes which had been brought from Cairns and were now put ashore. They were equipped with small masts and black silk sails. The new collapsible canoes were 17 feet long and 2 feet 6 inches wide, finely tapered at both ends, and their hulls, which pulled on to fit like skins, were seven-ply rubber and canvas and almost impossible to hole. The covering included top decking except for three manholes. Two of these were paddling positions and the other was for supplies, though they were really three-man canoes. Each hold had a flexible waterproof covering with an elastic aperture which fitted the paddler's waist. The covering on the stores hold could be tied.

While the attack "operatives", as they were called—Lyon, Davidson and Page, and Falls, Jones, Huston, Marsh and Berryman—practised with the new canoes, and competed against each other, in daylight and at night, to see how quickly they could assemble and dismantle them, Carse painted the *Krait's* deck flat grey to reduce her visibility from the air. And when he flew in an American two-seater from Potshot to check the result he found that in most lights at anything above three thousand feet the grey-decked ship was hardly visible on the deep blue sea.

During all this activity Donald Davidson arranged with Carse to clear the *Krait* of men for a morning while he prepared her for "blowing", for at this time only the officers knew of Lyon's plan to blow up the *Krait*, and everyone in her, if capture could not be avoided.

This morning Davidson opened No. 1 hold and carried the unmarked boxes, which held 150 pounds of plastic explosive, to No. 3 hold, where he stowed them behind Young's radio equipment. He wired the explosive and ran the cordtex fuse across one end of the radio table to a point under Ivan Lyon's bunk, and then fitted an instantaneous detonator to the hatch in such a way that any movement of the hatch would fire the detonator and the charge. All Lyon had to do was connect the fuse with the detonator—a few seconds' work—and the ship was ready to be blown up.

On 31st August, after four days at Potshot, Lyon decided, in a conference with the other officers, to fuel the next morning and sail immediately, but only if information he was expecting from Melbourne arrived. That night the Americans gave them a final party at the base, where an ice-box as big as a cottage contained everything from the finest Scotch to the best Kentucky Bourbon. And, in return, the *Krait* party presented the base with the training canoes and a heavy spare propeller, and the only thing of any real value in their possession. This was a compass, from the Sultan of Johore's yacht, which old Bill Reynolds, the original skipper of the *Krait*, had "liberated" during the fall of Singapore.

Next morning the *Krait* went alongside the *Ondina Star* to fuel, and the men lunched on fish fresh-caught in a net let down into a huge hole in the tanker's side below the waterline. The *Ondina Star* had been torpedoed in the Indian Ocean, where she had also sunk a submarine, and the hole in her side was as big as a large room—big enough to hold a twelve-foot shark, which had stopped all fishing for a day, while the *Krait* was at Exmouth.

While the *Krait* was completing her fuelling, Admiral Christie, Captain Hawes, Surgeon Commander Dennis, Captain Alan Grantham, who was in charge of A.I.F. workshops at Exmouth, and many others came aboard to say good-bye before the *Krait* anchored off Potshot to await the signal from Melbourne which Lyon was expecting.

For three hours they waited. Then near 5 p.m. an American signalman came out with two messages. Lyon read the first and put it in his pocket. Then he opened the second, smiled, and called, "Leading Telegraphist Young."

Horrie Young appeared from the aft compartment.

"Sir."

Lyon held out his hand. "This is what we've been waiting for. Our congratulations. It's a boy."

"Daddy!" everyone yelled, and gathered around Young to shake hands. (The baby, Young's first, was Brian Stewart Young, born in Sydney.)

"And now," Lyon said, "we can sail."

Slowly, as men waved from the shore and from the ships off Potshot, the *Krait* began to move, but she had gone less than a hundred yards when her engine stopped, and Paddy McDowell appeared on deck with gloomy news. The coupling key of the intermediate propeller shaft had sheared. They would not be able to move unless it could be repaired.

Lean old Captain Hawes took charge. He ordered the *Krait* to be towed to the *Chanticleer*, but when her engineers removed the shaft and examined it they shook their heads: the shaft would have to be brazed. Even when the job was completed that night and the shaft was back in the *Krait* by next morning, the engineers warned that the repair was only temporary and might break down again any moment.

"When you get to Fremantle—if she gets you that far," the senior engineer advised, "have the shaft properly repaired."

Paddy McDowell promised he would as soon as they reached "Fremantle", and thanked the Americans for the wonderful job they had done, but as the engineers departed he tipped his greasy cap off his forehead, looked at Carse and winked.

At 2 p.m. that day, 2nd September 1943, Paddy reported to Lyon and Carse that the shaft was cool.

"Time to go," was all the leader said.

Now the Blue Ensign was again raised at the *Krait's* stern, for Jaywick was an Army operation which came under General MacArthur's command, though the Army flag had been a source of speculation at Potshot. And now the Americans lined the rail and lowered gallon tins of pineapple juice to the men of the *Krait*, who drank a last toast to their friends of U.S.S. *Chanticleer*.

In the wheelhouse Ted Carse waited until the tins were empty. Then he called. "Cast off forward."

"Goodbye, boys," Captain Hawes shouted through a megaphone from the *Chanticleer's* bridge. "Goodbye, Long John Silver," he boomed at Carse. "We'll see you when you get back."

The *Krait* began to move, and as she edged away from the big ship a sailor called sadly. "Will you guys make the end of the gulf?"

Then everyone was waving and cheering, and as the *Krait* moved out the last words Carse heard were from the senior engineer: "Don't forget to get that shaft fixed when you reach Fremantle."

Operation Jaywick had begun.

As Australia deserted to the invading dusk the *Krait* began to dip her nose into the flooding tide-rips struggling in the arms of the southerly. The wind, funnelling up the gulf, wailed and sighed in the dark around the labouring little ship as she began to reach through the islands and reefs for the open sea, nosing deep and lifting with such a shuddering lurch that at times she was almost rail under with broken waves racing each other along her deck.

As a cross-wave smacked her bow and she corkscrewed, Carse spun the wheel to pick up the six-inch backlash before he felt the steering chains gripping and the ship responding, then gently he persuaded her back on course until the one brass-topped spoke was in line with the compass card floating on its soft glow in the binnacle, and as she steadied and rose and shook herself the sea, milky in the dark, hissed and boiled in the gaping freeing-ports along the streaming gunwale.

Before she could dip again Carse could just see someone scrambling out of No. 3 hold and swaying along the deck to the wheelhouse. With one hand he reached for the metal latch.

"A bit dirty," Ivan Lyon shouted as he slammed the door. "Will we get it like this further out?"

"The wind and the rips are in a clinch," Carse shouted back. "When they break we'll be right in the middle . . . but it won't last. We should be clear in half an hour."

The *Krait* began to nose under again. Lyon put his head out the port door and the wind snatched his vomit away, and as he pulled back a new sea came aboard to shatter like broken glass against the wheelhouse windows.

"Sorry," Lyon said, wiping his face with a handkerchief.

"Don't give it a thought," Carse said, blessing a stomach so mistreated for so many years that it would stand anything. "Some of the boys aft started much earlier."

Lyon was sick again—a dry stiff sound.

You've got guts, Carse thought, but he couldn't see the other man except as a blurred mass, though he knew how ill the uncomplaining captain—no, a major now—must look.

"What's your opinion of the old crate?" Lyon asked. "You should know her character by this."

"Character." Carse peered over the binnacle. "In a flat or following sea she's a lamb, but in a head sea like this she's a second-class trollop."

"Our lowness in the water doesn't help much."

Carse laughed. "That's an understatement if ever I heard one. We're more than six inches below Plimsoll line. No sane port authority would ever allow us to put to sea."

He paused. "I'm a bit worried about that shaft."

"Don't. Thinking about it is worse than being sick. . . . Should we have sailed?"

"We can always turn back."

"No." The small word was big and fierce in the dark. "We've been delayed too long already. We must take our chance."

"I agree. If you wait till everything is perfect in this life you never do anything. Paddy'll watch it. He knows what he's at."

Now Lyon's dry-retching was like the dark rubbing its hands together.

"The Japs have my wife and child," he said at last. "I suppose you know."

"Yes, it's tough. Where are they now?"

"Singapore—I think. . . . They could be dead."

Singapore, Carse thought, amazed how detached he could be about that name, how remote it seemed at this moment with an angry sea around them under a swaying sky.

Then up through the wheel he felt the *Krait's* movement begin to change—a change of mood, sensed through his fingertips, understood by his brain, as frail as a rumour, but strengthening and demanding recognition. He bent to starboard and could just see the mast like a thin shadow against the night sky and above the masthead a restless star, and above the bows the spray was white and beyond the bows was the white-splashed blackness of the sea.

"It's easing," he said at last, both hands on the wheel again. "She's not burying so much."

He turned. "How do you feel?"

"Better," Lyon said.

"A bugger of a sensation, I'm told."

The small hatch in the back of the wheelhouse squeaked open.

"Cocoa," a weak voice announced.

Lyon fumbled for the enamel mugs.

"Sorry it spilt a bit," the voice said.

"Thank you, Crilley."

"Andy, you're a genius," Carse yelled over his shoulder. "I'll get you a medal for this. . . . What's it like aft?"

"Wet. A wave nearly washed Marsh overboard."

"That'll teach him to hang on. . . . How do you feel yourself?"

"I'm all right, sir."

The words were frail as old lace.

"Get some of this inside you," Carse called. "And tell the boys it's easing. . . . We're through the worst."

The flap squeaked down. They sipped the inch of cocoa left in the mugs. It was warm, sweet, friendly. With their feet now they could feel the *Krait* still dipping, but not so deeply, and as the sea came aboard she was getting rid of it, tossing it off with a new and healthier petulance. Soon she began to lift and fall with more regularity and the sea no longer broke in high flying spray above the bow, half-way up the mast.

"We're through the rips," Carse at last announced. "It's open sea from now on."

"Time I took over," Lyon said. "You're an hour over your watch already."

"Feel up to it?"

"Yes."

"How are the guts shaping?"

"Better."

"O.K. Course is north. Call me if there's any trouble."

In the cramped space which smelt of salt and ancient paint and rusting metal he fumbled for the chart table, folded it up against the starboard side of the wheelhouse, and clamped it with an inch of wood which spun on a screw. But as he cautiously reached for the bunk with his backside and sat down he slammed his right elbow against the sharp edge of the now folded table. The pain flared like a little explosion. He cursed and rubbed his funny bone. Then he swung his legs on to the bunk and settled himself on the foam rubber mattress. He just fitted on the narrow bunk.

Lying there now he could still feel the pitching of the ship in his feet, his fingers, yet the movement under his body was steady as she rose and fell in the swell, running smoothly with the dying southerly behind her. Lying there, too, in his shirt and shorts wet with spray and sticky with the clamminess of salt, he was suddenly overwhelmingly glad to be where he was, to be on the way at last, to be at sea again. The future, with all its unknown unsolved problems and dangers was tomorrow and the next day and the next. For the moment the present was enough.

"All well?" he asked once, hearing the creaking of the wheelhouse and the grinding rattle of the wheel chain below.

"Yes," Lyon said.

He slept.

As Andy Crilley banged a dixie of porridge on the aft deck and Taffy Morris limped with another dixie to the officers sitting forward on No. 2 hold, Paddy McDowell gazed at the crew with disgust.

"A beautiful mornin'," he said, "with a sea like flat Guinness, an' all youse blokes can do is look like a bunch of cut cats."

He grunted. "Get it inside yer and you'll feel better."

He scratched under one arm. "Sailors an'—worse—soldiers."

Paddy had always been scornful that Jaywick was an Army-controlled operation, and never liked taking orders from landlubbers, particularly Army landlubbers.

He filled a plate, sucked a flick of porridge from a greasy thumb and covered the grey sticky mess with sugar.

"Hell," he shouted after the first mouthful, "rope-ends with no bloody salt."

The *Krait's* crew were indeed a frail-looking lot that first morning, and the cruel early light, bouncing from the shimmering sea, made them look paler than they were. Few had slept. All were red-eyed. Except for Carse, McDowell, Cain and Jones, all had been seasick, and their khaki shorts and shirts were still wet and streaked with salt. The only parts of the ship that were dry were the forward section of the engine-room and the area around Horrie Young's radio equipment, in No. 3 hold, which he had covered with a tarpaulin.

Breakfast was a gloomy meal, brightened only by Crilley's pancakes, which even Happy Hutson admitted were "not too lousy", though the sight of dust-dry bacon, curled like cedar-wood shavings, almost sent Falls and Morris to the side. But as the sun warmed the men and the ship dried, the crew began to enjoy their first day at sea.

It was not, however, until late in the forenoon watch, when Carse mustered everyone, including the lookouts, that the crew were told where they were going.

Carse took the wheel as Ivan Lyon stood on the hatch cover below the wheelhouse. The men waited, watching in that silent, expressionless, near-insolent way Australians reserve for officers; and only eyes flicking wordless messages into other eyes told that they knew they were about to hear confirmation or denial of months of rumours about their destination.

They had all long known it was outside Australia, for the specialized training and their knowledge of the equipment and arms carried had prepared them, even before they knew they would travel in the *Krait*, for a journey into Japanese territory. Borneo was the popular guess, though Falls had once heard Davidson mention Sumatra and from that moment was convinced the target was the oilwells near Palembang. Jones, however, had borrowed an atlas and studied the harbours between the Philippines and Malaya. Either Surabaya, the former Dutch naval base, or Singapore, he argued with Falls, his special friend since their Melbourne training days. He was convinced that all evidence pointed to a harbour attack.

"I know you have all been wondering where the *Krait* is taking us," Lyon began, "but for security reasons laid down by the organization to which you all belong it was not possible to tell you until our operation was at sea. . . . We're going in to attack the Japanese where they won't expect us. . . . Our objective is Singapore."

Excitement rippled among the men. They tossed glances at each other, changed positions, grinned.

"Told you so," Jones whispered to Falls.

"I wasn't far off the mark, mug."

But Paddy McDowell sadly shook his head.

"It's a sad disappointment to me. If I'd known it wasn't to be Tokyo I wouldn't have come."

"Good old Paddy," someone called, and the men cheered ironically.

"We propose to attack shipping in Singapore Harbour," Lyon went on. "Apart from the material damage we'll inflict—on merchant ships and possibly tankers—we feel that the raid, deep inside Japanese-held territory, will damage enemy morale and might even check the movement of their Navy into the Indian Ocean.

"Our plan is to enter the Java Sea through Lombok Strait and to sail to an island near Singapore. The operatives for the attack will be Lieutenant Davidson, Lieutenant Page and myself, and Able Seamen Jones, Falls and Huston."

Boof Marsh and Moss Berryman, the other two operatives, protested. "Aren't we taking part?" Berryman asked.

"I'm sorry," Lyon said, "but we've decided to attack with three canoes and to keep the other in reserve. During the attack itself the *Krait* will hide, probably in Sumatra."

He paused and gazed out to sea and Carse, watching, felt that Lyon had forgotten them, that probably in his mind he was in Singapore, with his wife and child, if that was where they were. Carse felt again the strange rigidity of this man, the same near-fanaticism he had noticed that night at Z.E.S. when he had learnt of the coming raid. And the others, he noticed, seemed to feel this, too, for eyes sought eyes as the men waited —restless, almost uneasy.

If he could only relax, Carse thought. We're all in this up to the necks. And for the first time he felt that a force beyond Lyon's control was driving him, compelling him towards Singapore, and that nothing the man could do would prevent this inexorable movement; and then a stray idea came to him, and in this fleeting moment he felt that the whole operation had been planned long ago, in the distant past, and that whatever was to happen, even their deaths, had already been decided.

A gull slipped across the wind. Carse looked at Page and Page winked—a small sly wink just big enough to see—and then Lyon began to speak again, but stopped and waited as Paddy rolled back after taking a quick look at his beloved engine.

"The holiday is over," he said. "From now on discipline will be strict, lookouts must be doubly alert and all rules must be obeyed. Your lives will depend on it. We are a Japanese fishing boat and we will be flying the Japanese flag. You know what that means. . . . "

Someone whistled softly. The sound seemed to slide over the rail into the sea.

"We are a type of ship well known in the waters ahead and we must be recognizable as such—in every way. Nothing we do must destroy or help destroy that illusion. As we will be under observation at times we will continue to live only if those observing us find nothing to arouse their suspicions and therefore do not challenge us."

He paused. "I repeat. We are a Japanese fishing boat and it is therefore most important that we conform in appearance and behaviour. In a day or two we will all wear sarongs and stain our faces and bodies. We will not even comb our hair any more. But if you don't intend to grow a beard, as Lieutenant Carse has done, you will shave—daily.

"In enemy waters and under observation, we must never show more than the man at the wheel and one lookout forward—and there's good reason for this. In the waters ahead you seldom see on any craft more than one man steering and one lookout in the bows or up the mast if the waters are shallow or otherwise dangerous. Also, if there is any possibility or suspicion that we are being watched at any time the doors of the wheelhouse must be closed and kept closed and the man at the wheel will remain at the wheel and will not be relieved until we are out of range."

For such a reticent man Lyon talked quickly now, as the men listened, still and serious-faced. Even Carse, as he kept the gently vibrating, slow-moving *Krait* on her northward course, and occasionally shifted his eyes from Lyon to sweep the horizon and the cloudless sky, was conscious that his fingers had tensed on the wheel as he listened and realized more fully than ever before that his life and the lives of the thirteen others largely depended on his own accuracy and judgment.

"This will be a dry ship for everyone," Lyon was saying, "and there will be no smoking from now on except by special permission from me."

He held up his cigarette butt. "This is my last until this operation is completed and we are safely back in Australia."

He flicked the butt overboard.

"From now on nothing—I repeat, nothing—will be thrown overboard. Rubbish of any kind might give us away—even matches. McDowell here, who as you probably know served in Q-ships in the Great War, agrees that this is a good rule, and so does Lieutenant Carse. They are both experienced sailors. McDowell had personal experience of a German submarine being tracked and sunk because her crew dropped matches overboard at night when the U-boat was on the surface charging her batteries. . . . Papers, packs, scraps—everything will be collected, put in tins and the tins dropped overboard only when they have been holed so that they will rapidly sink. Lavatory paper must not be used. You will have to accustom yourselves to sea water. You will also not shave in the open and will keep shaving mirrors under cover. The flash of a mirror might be picked up miles away. We will show no lights, except in the engine-room, No. 3 hold for the radio, and in the binnacle, and torches, if they are needed, will be used only under cover and shaded."

He glanced around. "Any questions?"

He waited, then added: "I don't need to warn you that your lives may depend on your strict observance of these rules. The man who forgets once could destroy us all. Another thing. Lieutenant Carse is in charge of the navigation and safety of the ship. You will therefore obey him at all times—implicitly.

"There is one more thing. Because our job is primarily sabotage, and also Intelligence, we will not go looking for trouble. On the contrary, we will try to avoid it wherever possible. But if we are attacked we will, of course, fight."

As he stared down into the set faces the only sounds were the mutter of the exhaust, the hushing of the sea, the wind in their ears.

"Right. Dismiss."

Ted Carse was sitting on No. 2 hatch next morning, about to go on watch, when Paddy McDowell beckoned.

"Come aft, skipper, there's somethin' I want to show yer."

"What's wrong?"

"Come an' look," Paddy said mysteriously.

As he led aft he said: "I was sittin' on the throne, contented like, thinkin' of Belfast, when somethin' warns me. I turn aft an' look. . . . "

They reached the stern and Paddy pointed.

"You'll notice, skipper, we've got somethin' in our wake that shouldn't be there—a bit of a bend. I'd call it."

Carse saw the curve in the wake. He looked for the sun.

"We seem to be going almost due south."

"It occurred to me," Paddy said.

Carse hurried back to the wheelhouse.

"Take a look at your wake," he said to Davidson.

"Why—what's wrong?"

Davidson stepped outside, looked astern, and returned.

"Looks all right to me."

"Right, my arse. We're moving in a great circle—going south at this very moment and only just starting to come round. . . . Look at the compass."

Davidson looked, frowned. "Well, I'm damned. I could have sworn. . . . " He grinned. "I was thinking about. . . . "

"I know—working out some more devilry. On the way round from Cairns I watched you one day actually looking at the compass and not even seeing it. You were points off course. . . . Here, I'll bring her back."

He took the wheel. "Now—what were you thinking about this time?"

Davidson leant against the side of the cramped wheelhouse. "I still think I could handle a Jap destroyer if one bailed us up."

Carse slapped the wheel. "So we're on that again." He pointed to the dinghy lashed across No. 2 hatch. "There she is with the tubes in her bottom—like a bloody enema. You tried her out at Exmouth and it worked. I know that. You could stay under her and breathe through the tubes. But that was calm water—mighty different to the open sea."

"Look," Davidson argued. "A destroyer stops us. We launch the dinghy with one man to row her. I get underneath her with two limpets strapped to me. We row to the destroyer, muff the approach, and I put the limpets on her near the bows where the flare is so great not a soul on board would be able to see us. With instantaneous fuse we'd blow half her bows off."

"And what happens to you?"

"Me? Oh, I'd be killed in the water, but the man in the dinghy would probably get away in the panic, and the *Krait* would almost certainly escape as the destroyer filled. They wouldn't be able to bring any but small weapons against her."

Carse knew that the big freckled man meant every word. He remembered, too, hearing Joe Jones say, during the crossing from Cairns. "Some of Davo's ideas are bloody well harebrained."

He patted Davidson's shoulder. "You go and have a good sleep. You'll be better by next watch."

"It could be done," Davidson insisted. And then he smiled. "Sorry about the bent wake, Ted, but when I get an idea into my head. . . . " He looked at his watch. "Time I sorted those sarongs before I turn in. It's changing day tomorrow."

When tomorrow came and Exmouth Gulf was three hundred miles astern, the day was warmer, almost hot, first hint of the monotonous crowding heat of the tropics. A few clouds sat along the northern horizon, and the sea was so clean that the men, kneeling at the side like Moslems facing Mecca, brushing their teeth and gargling—fresh water was already rationed— saw that it contained not a trace of debris.

Davidson distributed the sarongs that morning and everyone stripped and put them on. The crew were in checks, the officers in stripes and checks. Lyon's was red and blue, Davidson's red, white and black, Page's green and white, Carse's mustard, black and white.

When Moss Berryman put his on he wriggled his hips and Boof Marsh pounced on him and growled, but big Cobber Cain, who almost needed a brassiere, was voted, without question, Dorothy Lamour. It was, however, the big snarling tiger's head on Lyon's chest which attracted almost as much attention as the new sarongs. The tiger was blue, with touches of red, and it "snarled" when Lyon, for once relaxing his rigid officer-man relationship with the crew, moved his arms in and out across his body. Only the canoe operatives, who had trained with Lyon, and Morris, had seen the tattooed tiger before.

Then Davidson opened the make-up box, specially prepared by Max Factor, and handed out bottles of dark brown dye.

"Rub it all over," he advised, "and I mean all over."

For the next hour they rubbed and spread the stain. On fair-skinned men like Davidson it dried in long uneven streaks and blotches, but on olive skin the colour spread more easily and dried more uniformly. Sarongs and deck were soon spotted and streaked with the stain, and fingers printed and smeared everything they touched, so that, no matter how careful the men were, fingertips jutted from brown hands like pink nipples.

"It wouldn't bluff a King's Cross landlady at three yards," Bob Page decided, after studying the disguises.

"If we get as close as that to a half-witted Jap we'll be fighting, not bluffing," Davidson replied.

"It's nothing more than a long-range disguise," Carse explained to the men. "Through glasses it should be pretty convincing."

Of them all, the solidly built, dark-haired Jones looked most authentic. On his olive skin, already dark-tanned, the dye was even, and because he now looked like a dark Japanese he was given the job of appearing on deck and waving if Japanese aircraft became inquisitive. Page, too, once he had rubbed his hands through his brown hair, and particularly when he smiled and showed his teeth, could almost have been a Tamil priest from Madras—except for the now accentuated blueness of his eyes. Carse, with his black hair, lined satanic face and twisted smile became a Buginese pirate from the inland seas they were about to invade, and Paddy McDowell resembled an aged Ceylonese fisherman who would sell you a bad fish at a huge profit, while Cain ceased to be Miss Lamour and became a rather sooty version of the Laughing Buddha.

But Lyon and Davidson, even after two coats of the dye, looked ridiculously unconvincing. Lyon particularly never succeeded in appearing more genuine than an amateurishly stained public-school Englishman in fancy dress, and Davidson never more than a music-hall darkie who had forgotten to put on half his make-up. His fair skin almost flamed in patches through the dye, and even the reddish hair on his arms and the backs of his hands would not hold the stain.

When the staining ceremony was over, and Davidson had taken a photograph, Carse fetched the Japanese flag, the "Poached Egg", from under his bunk and unfurled it, and Paddy McDowell brought up a quart of dieseline and poured it on the deck.

"Now for the final ritual," Carse said. "I'd better explain that where we're heading flags, if you see them at all, are generally filthy—and that goes for Nip flags, too. At least, that's been my experience. So get this one dirty and we'll put her up."

He dropped the new flag on top of the oil and the men stamped on it, rubbed it on the deck, wiped their hands on it. When it was almost unrecognizable, Cain bent to pick it up and the sight of his unstained backside, white under his short sarong, brought a roar from Paddy, who slapped both hands over his eyes and shouted, "An' if the Nips see what I can see, Cobber, then we've all had it."

The laughing men crowded aft and then, in silence, for every man was suddenly aware of the significance of the act about to be performed, Horrie Young lowered the Blue Ensign and ran up the crumpled, oil-stained flag of the enemy.

10

STEADILY THE *Krait* climbed towards the Indies, her wake a white, slowly healing scar. The sea was blue-black, without a stain of wind, but quilted here and there with the yellow, indolent backs of turtles. And each day was hotter, and each day the clouds collected in the east and scattered and drifted away like torn decorations.

Even as she closed with the Indies the low thick haze, which the Navy weather men in Melbourne had promised Carse would help shroud the *Krait's* approach to the Lombok area, never materialized, so that the horizon remained, hour upon hour, a hard clear line ruled just beyond the little ship's questing bows.

Ivan Lyon's original plan was to approach Nusa Besar, the high fortress-like island at the southern entrance to Lombok Strait, at night, to lie-up against the island's thousand-foot cliffs all day, and to go through the strait after dark. But Carse had never liked the plan because of the risk of being seen from Nusa Besar itself, although the island was supposed to be uninhabited, or of being sighted from the air during daylight, for the *Krait* would be within minutes' flight of two main airfields, one at Den Pasir on Bali, the other at Malang on Lombok. He also knew that, in twelve hundred feet of water right up to the island's cliffs, the *Krait* would not be able to anchor and would have to steam at reduced speed all day among little known and probably dangerous currents.

But Lyon had argued that the ship, if close to the perpendicular cliffs of Nusa Besar, would have little chance of being discovered, and had insisted that his plan stand. Under protest, Carse had agreed, and when the time came, in the late afternoon of 7th September, he began his approach.

Lyon's plan was never carried out because the *Krait's* low speed was so reduced by the current sweeping from Lombok Strait that by 11 p.m. on 7th September it was obvious that the ship would not be able to reach the doubtful safety of the cliffs until after daylight, and so Carse was forced to turn south with the current to get out of sight of land by morning.

Although Lyon favoured another attempt to reach Nusa Besar the next night, both Davidson and Page supported Carse's argument that the safest thing would be a bold natural approach to the strait in daylight and a direct night passage through it, and Lyon finally agreed. So that after breakfast on 8th September they turned north again to make the second attempt, after dropping overboard the last empty drum of their deck-carried fuel and sinking it with Bren fire.

This morning, when the *Krait* was seven hundred miles north of Australia, was brilliantly clear, with only towards noon a thin ribbon of grey-white cloud far ahead like a copy of the true horizon. Carse, who worked almost entirely on star sights for his navigation, knew from his position—about fifty miles south of Lombok and a divider point on the chart pinned to the table—that they should soon make a sighting, and so he began to watch the distant cloud-line.

The *Krait* was strangely quiet, and even the sea seemed hushed as it curled away from her bows. The evening before Paddy had fitted a silencer to the exhaust, which poked an inquisitive nose through the covering of the aft compartment a few feet behind the wheelhouse. The silencer had eliminated sparks and a pinkish night glow above the exhaust, and had reduced the steady engine thump to little more than a monotonous comforting vibration—a pleasant soundless sound which had such a hypnotic effect upon the crew that they all agreed they slept almost from the moment they went off duty.

At noon, when Lyon took the wheel, Crilley opened the

Attack Route of Operation Jaywick.

The map on the next pages shows the route taken by the *Krait* from Cairns, in North Queensland, to the American Navy base of "Potshot" on Exmouth Gulf, Western Australia, and then north through Lombok Strait across the Japanese-controlled Java and South China seas to the Rhio Archipelago and Singapore.

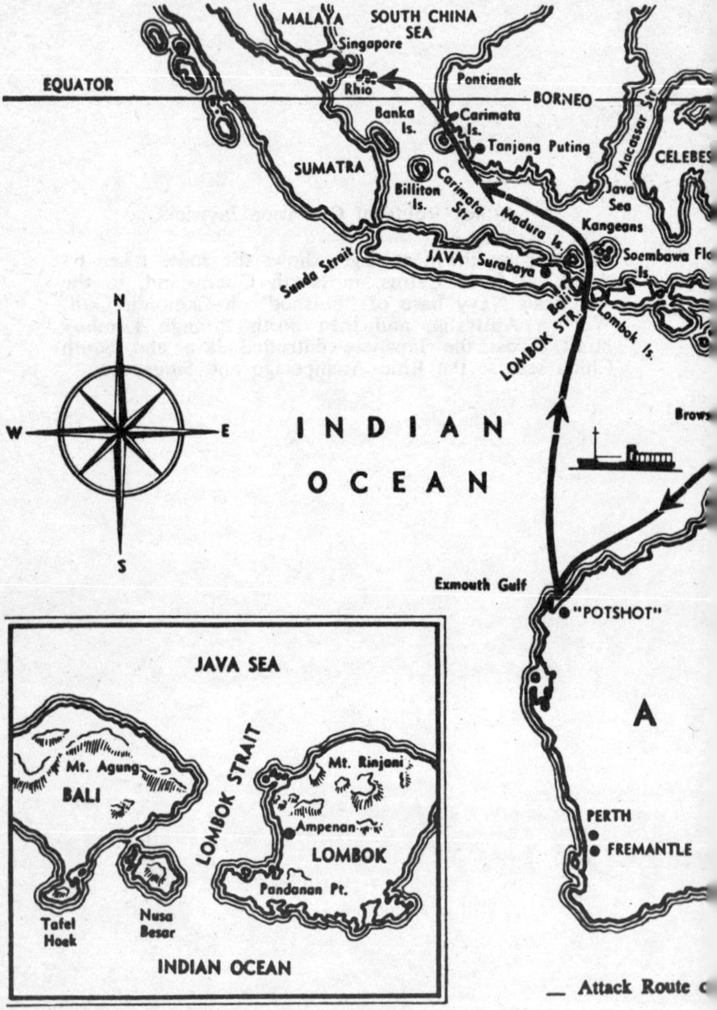

ENLARGED SECTION OF LOMBOK STRAIT

ration Jaywick.

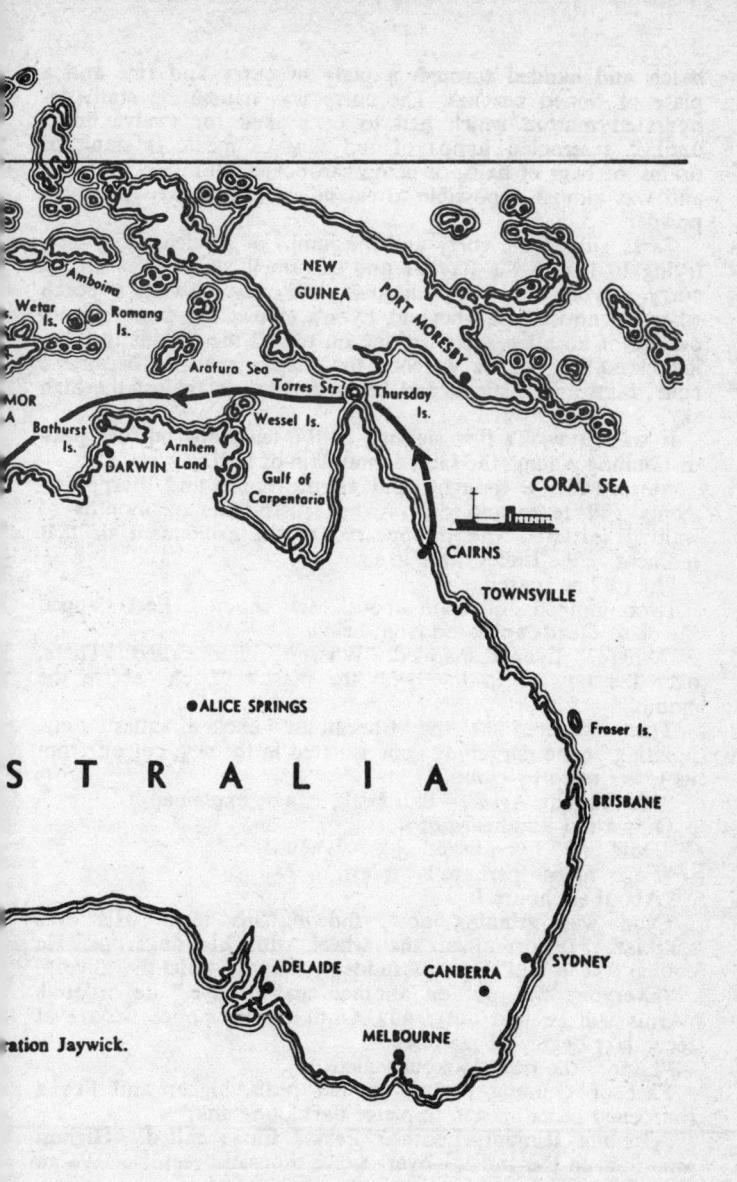

hatch and handed through a plate of curry and rice and a plate of tinned peaches. The curry was nauseating stuff, dehydrated mutton which had to be soaked for twelve hours until it resembled lumps of red sausage meat. It stank of drains, of bags of nails, of damp cardboard, all mixed together, and was almost impossible to eat unless suffocated with curry powder.

Carse gulped the curry and the lumps of sodden sticky rice, trying to ignore the flavour and the smell which even strong curry powder could not disguise, and was chewing a peach when he noticed, far beyond Lyon's elbow, the faint blurred outline of an alien shape resting on top of the distant thickening cloud-line. As he watched the shape gradually became a cone, faint and distinct, and began to darken against the high sky.

It was Jaywick's first sighting of the ten-thousand-foot peak of Gunung Agung, the sacred mountain of Bali.

At last! Carse thought, and all the hopes and disappointments and fears and delays and frustrations of months of waiting scattered and disappeared in the excitement of that moment as the Indies came in sight.

"Land!" he roared.

Lyon jumped and spun about. Men shouted. Feet slapped the deck. Heads appeared from below.

"Where?" Lyon demanded. "Where?" others called. "There, over the bow." "In line with the mast." "Look—above the cloud."

They gathered at the wheelhouse—excited, questioning, pointing at the darkening cone isolated in the sky, cut off from its lower mass by cloud.

"It's Gunung Agung—Bali Peak," Carse explained.

Only a few had heard of it.

"How far?" Lyon asked.

"Forty miles—perhaps a bit less."

"About six hours."

Lyon was grinning now, showing his teeth. His eyes sparkled. He drummed the wheel with his fingertips. He couldn't keep still. He was suddenly, almost violently, alive.

"Everyone will put on another coat of dye," he ordered. "Arms will be laid out ready. Until further notice we are at secondary degree of readiness."

"Land!" the mast lookout yelled.

East of Gunung Agung another peak, higher and like a sharpened pencil, began to pierce the cloud-bank.

"Gunung Rinjani—Lombok Peak," Carse called. "Highest mountain in the Indies—over twelve thousand feet. . . . We go right between them."

Little Bali, east of the long island of Java, is shaped like Aladdin's lamp, and the still smaller island of Lombok, just to the east, looks a little like a skull in profile.

In between them is the twenty-five-mile Lombok Strait—the Strait of the Red Peppers—where pirates from the Celebes and farther east boarded ships, slit throats, and plundered even into the twentieth century.

But Lombok, which has a southern entrance about twelve miles wide but broadens to thirty miles in the middle, is more than a strait, four thousand feet deep in parts, linking the Indian Ocean with the landlocked Java Sea. It is the edge of the continental shelf of Asia—actual frontier between Asia and the Australian regions of the south-west Pacific, the line where one geographical zone ends and another begins. Bali Island, still Hindu in a predominantly Moslem Indonesia, is Asia. Lombok Island, where Sasaks were dominated and enslaved by the Balinese until modern times, has different trees and growth, different animals and birds. Lombok is a transitional area, as scientists call it, where Asiatic forms of life, as you move eastward, begin to be replaced by Australian forms.

It was along this dividing line, through the Strait of the Red Peppers, that the planners of Jaywick had decided to penetrate the Java Sea and beyond. They reasoned that Sunda Strait, between Java and Sumatra, would be much used by the Japanese and was likely to be patrolled, and that the other straits east of Lombok were too far away from Jaywick's target. Lombok was the logical, the audacious, choice, for, once through, a ship might disappear for weeks among the islands and wide spaces of the Java and South China seas.

The planners, however, couldn't answer the most difficult question of all: was Lombok patrolled and, if so, would even an innocent Japanese fishing boat, flying the Japanese marine flag, be allowed to pass without a challenge?

This was the gamble the planners, and especially the operatives, of Jaywick had to take.

With the peaks of Agung and Rinjani rising ahead, the officers gathered at the wheelhouse to discuss the passage. They all agreed that the total lack of air activity was the best indication that the Japanese were not deeply concerned with the southern approaches to the Indies.

As Page said, "Why should they be worried? When they raided Exmouth a few months ago they found no sign of a build-up along the Western Australian coast. They probably feel pretty secure from this direction."

"There's still time for them to get inquisitive," Carse reminded him.

Davidson nodded. "True—but if we're seen between now

and dark, what are we?—a Jap fishing boat, with the Poached Egg up, making for either Bali or Lombok."

But Lyon, who had been studying the chart, said, "The thing I'm worried about is the current. Look what it did to us last night."

"Me, too," Carse said. "When I was in Melbourne not a soul seemed to know much about it—even the Dutch. Although there's always a southward set from the Java Sea through Lombok—during the equinoxes, with the trade winds along the equator—the set is less now than during the monsoons. The Dutch reckoned the current at this time shouldn't be more than four knots inside the strait and a bit more in the narrows between Nusa Besar and Lombok. But even four is some current."

He reached for his *Sailing Directions* among the navigation books and found a page he had already marked.

"Listen to this. 'In 1928 the *War Krishna* hit heavy tide-rips and whirling eddies and swung three to four points off course.'" He looked up. "That's about forty-five degrees—a hell of a lot." He continued: "Here's a couple more. 'H.M.S. *Falmouth* in 1939, with calm wind and sea, hit a heavy breaking swell, enough to broach-to a ship of a thousand tons.' And this: 'In 1932, in the vicinity of Gili Sound, under the Bali shore on the west side of the north entrance, the *Franconia* hit heavy tide-rips and eddies. At a speed of fifteen knots the ship was swung more than a point off her course.'"

"So even if the Nips leave us alone," Davidson said, "we look like taking a pasting from old mum nature."

But it was Carse who asked the question all wanted answered—a question avoided until this moment.

"What do you all honestly think of our chances of getting through, making the raid and getting back again? What's the betting?"

"One chance in three," Lyon said, without hesitation.

Davidson chewed his thumb nail. "One in two."

"I give us one in ten," Carse said.

Page shook his head. "I won't bet on it. But I'm sure of one thing—we'll get back."

The mast lookout called—called again and pointed. Ahead and to port the dark sea was streaked with white, and slicing the streaks were the black evil fins of sharks.

Carse grabbed his glasses. "It's a log . . . they seem to be attacking it . . . must be a dozen of them." He handed the glasses to Lyon.

As the *Krait* closed the men could see the white belly-flashes as the sharks dived at the log and bumped it with their snouts. Then one big fellow, nearly twenty feet long, his fin almost clear of the water, attacked. The log rolled as he hit it, and Lyon called excitedly, "Look—look at the gull."

The gull was on one end of the almost submerged log, so that it was nearly standing in the sea. It stood there, indifferent to the circling, diving, splashing sharks, and only its pink feet moved, padding against the roll, keeping time with the log's slow revolution in the white-streaked sea as the *Krait* swept past not twenty feet away.

The episode fascinated Lyon. With glasses he followed the log and gull, gently rocking in the wash, until they were out of sight, and when he lowered the glasses at last and saw that Carse had been watching him he smiled, and Carse, in that fleeting moment of communion, knew why.

Again the lookout called, and far ahead, between the dark cone of Agung and the pencil point of Rinjani, a lump of misty blue land floated in the sea.

Nusa Besar was in sight.

The light was spilling from the day when the *Krait* began her direct approach to Lombok Strait.

Nusa Besar, now a black box ahead, with the last of the sun splashing its high rock face, was ten miles ahead and to port, and away to starboard was Pandanan Point on Lombok Island, low in the sea-dusk and wooded green.

Officers and men finished their supper of bully beef and Crilley's pancakes, and stared at the slowly approaching land as they drank their tea. They stared mutely now as night swept the land away and then the sea and left them isolated in the dark, each one alone with his thoughts of tonight and tomorrow. This was the beginning and in a few hours they might be dead. Even the youngsters were aware that beginning and end might be close, even men like Huston and Marsh who only an hour before had been wrestling like a couple of pups on the after deck, for ahead was twenty-five miles of enemy water, a funnel leading to the Java Sea, or a trap and extinction under the winking guns of a Japanese patrol.

A full moon, a moon near perigee, lifted to starboard, and from the west a searchlight answered, an angry probing light which seemed to splash across them as it swung out to sea and left a murmur of excitement and of fear in the little ship.

But in the wheelhouse Lyon said clamly, "That fellow won't worry us. We're way below his horizon."

"Must be on Bali," Carse said. "Probably way south on Tafel Hoek."

Lyon called to the crew. "We're out of range of that light."

They muttered among themselves, not sure whether Lyon was telling them the truth. And now they kept their voices down as though they feared the Japs might hear.

Twenty minutes later the distant searchlight swept again and gave enough reflected light to show white water ahead, squirming like seasnakes among the moonstreak, and then the *Krait's* bow began to rise and dip into the first of Lombok's rips, and then they were among angry water and aft in the galley a plate crashed to the deck and went overboard in pieces as the ship rolled and pitched and the spray sang above the wheelhouse.

At 8 p.m., when Lyon took the wheel, they were almost abeam of Nusa Besar, and in the middle of the narrows—and then began a struggle, with the black unfelt current pouring south from the Java Sea, for every yard.

At 10 p.m., when they could see a fixed light on top of Nusa Besar sixteen hundred feet above them to port, they were still only abeam of the island, though thankful now that Lyon's plan to spend the day there had been abandoned, for the general opinion was that the light was a Japanese observation post.

By 11 p.m. they had drifted backwards a few hundred yards, a dismal fact which told them that the current was a little faster than their own top speed of 6¼ knots.

By midnight, when Carse began his watch, they had moved up and were again just abeam the island, but for the next two hours they never advanced a yard.

Not a man slept that night.

Paddy McDowell sat beside his engine—nursing, coaxing, listening for the slightest variation in its accent, talking to it, even gently cursing it.

"Me lovely bastard," Marsh heard him mutter once, "if yer don't behave yerself I'll kick yer bloody guts in."

Even those off duty lay on their bunks or in their hammocks, wide-eyed in the dark, waiting and wondering how long the battle between the *Krait* and the current could continue. Defeat, after coming eight hundred miles from Exmouth alone, was unthinkable. And yet....

"I don't like the look of things," Lyon said.

"Neither do I," Carse agreed. "It's nearly 0200 and we haven't made more than half a mile in the last six hours."

Only his dark hands on the wheel, the dye patchy as a quilt, were dimly visible in the glow from the binnacle, the fading moonlight.

"We can't go back now," Page said from the deck outside

It was almost a plea, and Carse guessed that he was thinking of his father.

"If this keeps up," Lyon said, "we might have to.... Look, there's another light on Nusa."

The light moved. It disappeared.

"The Nips are there, all right," Davidson growled.

But Carse broke in. "That light didn't move. It was us. We're going ahead."

It was true. The *Krait* was moving, slowly at first, then a little faster as they began to clear the rips.

"Tide must be changing," someone said.

By 4 a.m., when Page took over, Nusa Besar was six miles astern. But by first light, when they hoped to be through to the Java Sea, they were still in the middle of the enemy strait, right in the centre of the trap.

As the light hardened, Carse, on his bunk behind Page, could clearly see the Bali coast, solid green to the water, and ten thousand feet above the shoreline, with its rock facets shimmering and flashing like windows facing the rising sun, was the lovely dark cone of Agung.

Page bowed three times to the sacred mountain and said over his shoulder, "I'm a good Anglican, Ted, but if we need help—it's now."

Carse grinned wearily. "My grandfather was an English vicar—perhaps we could call on him as well. . . . But take a look across the way. That's where trouble's coming from if she comes."

On the Lombok side of the strait towering Rinjani hid behind morning mist thick as smoke, but above the shore they could see the tents and huts of a Japanese camp near the tree-covered homes of Ampenan.

"This is it," Page said quietly.

Carse felt his mouth go dry.

"I wish we had more power," Davidson called from behind the wheelhouse. From under cover he had just photographed Agung.

And Lyon, framing his face in the food hatch in the back of the wheelhouse, said, "If they spot us—it's now."

From then on, as the *Krait* moved forward, an awful brooding stillness wrapped the ship. Everyone seemed afraid to speak, even to move. Eyes stared at the Japanese camp and searched the sea in front of it for movement. Eyes watched other eyes.

At 8 a.m. Carse relieved Page who, not daring to leave the wheelhouse, lay down on the bunk. At 9 a.m. Rinjani poked her peak through the mist and then, miraculously, all three were in line—Rinjani, the *Krait* and Agung—a perfect line east and west.

Carse licked his lips and slid his tongue around his mouth, thinking: I'd like to clean my teeth.

He glanced at the chart. Bali was about twelve miles to port. Lombok was about eight to starboard.

At last, at 10 a.m. and sixteen hours after entering the twenty-five-mile strait, Carse wrote these brief details in his log:

"Thank Christ! We are just through Lombok steering for Sekala 68 miles distant. Barometer 29.9. Slightly higher. Wind SSE increasing to about Force 4. After a clear early morning the haze now is increasing. Although the island of Bali is still visible, Lombok is almost totally obscured. . . . This war is certainly hard on the nervous system."

He had just closed the log when Lyon called: "Crilley, we'd like some tea. Crilley—we're thirsty."

They were the first words spoken for nearly three hours.

11

As BALI FADED Ted Carse searched the locker under his bunk for the carton wedged between the first-aid kit—which only Page had authority to touch—and the canvas bag of gold guilders. At last he got to his feet and waved a packet of cigarettes.

Lyon smiled. "You've earned it—only, no smoking on deck after dark. That's all I ask."

"Funny thing," Carse said, as he opened the packet. "I'm a heavy smoker—fifty a day at least—but until this moment I haven't wanted a fag for a week. . . . Have one."

"I'd love to, but I can't. . . . I made a promise to the men. I can't go back on it."

Carse inhaled deeply and had to grab the side of the wheelhouse until the dizziness passed. He shook the blur out of his head.

"That hasn't happened to me since I was ten."

But now he was suddenly aware that his body seemed soaked in weariness, and that all he wanted was to sleep and sleep.

"An' would the engineer be included in this little ceremony?"

It was Paddy, on deck for the first time in hours, the white stubble showing like new weeds through the dye on his lined cheeks, his eyes watery red from lack of sleep.

"Yer see—I took the trouble to have one ready."

He winked as he plucked the rolled cigarette from behind his ear. Carse gave him a light.

"Thank you, McDowell, for keeping us moving," Lyon said.

Paddy blew smoke through his nose. "Think nothin' of it, Major." He hated saying sir to a soldier. "The bitch winked at me only once—an' then she behaved herself."

He sucked at the smoke. "This is good."

"And so's this open water," Carse said.

Paddy grunted. "Never was one meself fer bloody ditches. . . . Troublesome-like. Give me somethin' ye can move in."

Now they were in the eight-hundred-mile-long Java Sea, right inside the Japanese perimeter, and every sail and every island, every light and every human being was suspect. The enemy was all round them, unseen but there, a presence felt by all the senses, a brooding reality. Now it was his wits and skill and audacity against theirs.

They had decided that, once inside Japanese-controlled waters, with a Jap watching from every headland for all they knew, survival depended on the observance of certain simple rules: to avoid main shipping lanes whenever possible, and to cross them, when they must, at top speed and at right-angles; to turn away from all ships, even the smallest, and so reduce the chance of being challenged or reported; to keep as much as possible to shallow water, among reefs and islands where, if challenged by enemy craft, they would be fighting something their own size on reasonably equal terms; to shun human contact, even if friendly, for human eyes and ears, not only Japanese, were their greatest enemies.

These were the reasons why, once through Lombok Strait, they headed almost due north to lose themselves among the Kangean Group, whose isles and shoals lie like sprinkled seeds east of Madura. From the Kangeans they proposed to turn north-west for the long blunt headland of Tanjong-Puting on southern Borneo to miss shipping using Macassar Strait from the Celebes Sea and the Philippines to Surabaya in Java. And from there they would round southern Borneo and island-hop up busy Carimata Strait, between Borneo and Billiton Island, before hugging Borneo's western coast until just south of Pontianak, when they would swing north-west to cross the open South China Sea.

The cruel passage of Lombok was over; but in its place was a new tension to endure—quieter, more insidious—for although they were the hunters they were also the hunted, outcasts under an enemy flag who could expect no quarter. From now on everything in this sun-bruised world under its drained bloodless sky was enemy—islands, reefs, ships, gathering thunderheads, the sea itself, so alien to the ocean they had just left, a sea now edged with lime green, emerald, cobalt, on which patches of salmon scum drifted like stale soup.

Now, too, the landlocked heat, especially for men who had never known the tropics, was as thick and hairy as a Bedouin tent. The forward deck, above which the heat-waves danced, smouldered from early morning, so that the men could not stand on it in bare feet unless they almost continuously washed it down. Long after dark the planks were still hot, as hot as the covered stern decking during the day.

The men dipped canvas buckets into the sea and poured water over themselves and splashed it on the canvas sides of the aft compartment, and on its canvas roof, as they tried to keep cool and to ease the new burn and itch of prickly heat which flared in patches through the brown dye.

Despite the heat, the at times dreamlike indolence of helmsman and lookouts in the early days of the journey was replaced by an almost frenetic vigilance, for all knew their lives might depend on sighting first. Sea and sky had to be patterned and endlessly swept, fore and aft, port and starboard, in a flickering glare which bruised eyeballs and left eyes burnt and heads aching, and at night, running without lights, the helmsman and lookouts could never relax their alertness for a moment.

Shortage of water, for the *Krait* carried only four hundred gallons when she left Exmouth Gulf and had caught no rain, was a problem, particularly for men who sweated even as they slept, or tried to sleep. All were rationed to three cups of tea a day and a waterbottle every three days. No fresh water was available for washing and all except Carse, whose black beard was an inch long and beginning to curl at the ends, shaved dry or dipped brushes over the side and won an anaemic lather with saltwater soap.

To conserve water Crilley soaked the dehydrated mutton in sea water before cooking it in fresh, but when Cobber Cain discovered this above Lombok he was so horrified that he refused to eat anything but Bully for the next two days.

"Sea water," he shouted at Crilley. "But think what goes into the sea!"

"Oh, pull your head in, you mug sailor," Pancake Andy replied.

"Who said that?" yelled the Navy, rising and advancing on the cook.

"I did," Andy yelled back, "and it's an order. Corporals outrank able seamen."

"Get a load of that from a no-hoper two-striper," Joe Jones sneered.

This Army-Navy argument had been going on for days. Lombok had stopped it temporarily, but now it was on again—in the middle of the Java Sea with the enemy waiting for them perhaps on the next island. And the argument continued on and off for most of the voyage, even though Moss Berryman claimed that a corporal's pay was a few pence less than an able seaman's, and by unanimous vote the Navy—in a big majority, anyway—decided that in future the two corporals, Crilley and Taffy Morris, would take orders aboard the *Krait*.

During these days, as the *Krait* edged towards Singapore, no man worked harder than Bob Page, who, apart from his routine duties as helmsman and lookout, mothered and doctored the crew. Each morning he did "rounds" with iodine bottle, vitamin pills and salt tablets. No scratch or bruise escaped his iodine swab, and he personally distributed three Vitamin C tablets to each man each day and waited while they swallowed them. He also stood over Crilley at the galley to make sure that he produced a steady flow of stewed prunes to ease the reluctant bowels of men whose exercise was limited to physical jerks and wrestling, and whose liquid intake was so restricted.

"It won't matter a bit, Andy, if you overcook them," he advised. "They're stronger and do more good that way."

Bob Page was a born doctor of the old school—the school which treated bodies as suffering human beings. He was acutely conscious of discomfort in others, and aware that pain besets minds as well as bodies, and as he moved about the ship in his green and white sarong, observing, persuading, even bullying a little where necessary, everyone responded to this enthusiasm and his repeated warning that the efficiency of their operation and its success depended on the good health of every man.

"On a show like this," he told the crew one morning, "the man who gets sick is threatening the life of his cobbers."

It was good psychology—good medicine.

The *Krait's* first day inside the Japanese perimeter was uneventful, except for the sighting of an enemy plane, which looked like a "Betty", but far away, and a Macassar proa, a big two-master with curry-coloured sails, but miles to starboard and melting into the hurried dusk.

But next morning, 10th September, opened dramatically.

Men off duty were cleaning weapons after breakfast when Horrie Young's voice, stuttering with excitement, exploded among them from the small loudspeaker he had bought at Cairns with his own money and fitted behind the wheelhouse.

"Italy's surrendered, boys. The . . . the B.B.C.'s just announced it."

Guns clattered to the deck and the noise and gabble woke those who were asleep. There was a rush for No. 3 hatch where everyone, talking at once, demanded more details.

"There wasn't much," Young said, half-way up the ladder from the hold. "All it said was that the Italian armed forces have surrendered unconditionally. Fighting between the Italian Army and the Allies has ceased. The announcement was by General Eisenhower."

"We'll have old Andy Cunningham out here any moment with the Mediterranean Fleet," Carse pronounced.

"Better still," Lyon said, "we'll have cocoa all round to toast the surrender."

He looked about him. "Where's Crilley? . . . Oh, there you are. Suspend rationing and make cocoa."

"Coming up, sir."

But when the excitement had subsided someone said, "Oh, bugger the Ities. What's the news from home?"

"Something about paratroopers," Young muttered. "After landing in the Markham Valley they're advancing on Lae. But that wasn't from home. Australia faded just before Lombok—haven't heard her since. But London's strong—and so is Tokyo and Tokyo Rose."

"What's that syrupy bitch nattering about?" Joe Jones growled.

"The usual bull. Messages to the mothers of p.o.w.'s."

"'John is well and sends his love,'" Jones mimicked the well known voice. "Just dripping with friendliness."

"You know what you can do with her," Marsh said. "And Tojo."

As the men returned to duty or to try to sleep in the gathering heat, Horrie Young dropped below and settled himself on the hard stool beside his old Air Force transceiver, battery-operated from the engine-room. The hold smelt of damp and of cockroaches—big lean fellows which rustled like tissue paper when they came out at night. It was a gloomy place at any time, even though light speared it down the hatchway, and to work, to take notes. Young needed the added light of a low-powered bulb fixed on the bulkhead above the set.

This morning he lit a cigarette—Lyon had given him permission to smoke—and reached for the big pale-green volume, the Admiralty *Handbook of Wireless Telegraphy*, on top of the transceiver, for much of his spare time during Jaywick was spent calmly studying for examinations in radio telegraphy in the sweaty gloom of No. 3 hold.

He drew on his cigarette, balanced it on the treacle tin lid he used as an ashtray, opened the volume and began to read. "The arrangement of aerials in a warship presents problems not usually encountered elsewhere. With the exception of the layout lines, ships (and small shore stations) require to use one line of communication only. . . . "

He scanned this again and read on.

"It is obviously impossible to separate the transmitting and receiving aerial systems by any appreciable distance. There are, however, two methods of. . . . "

He sniffed—sniffed again. He looked up from the page and froze.

The white cordtex fuse, which trailed across his table from the 150 pounds of plastic explosive behind his radio, had somehow fallen across his ashtray and was charring. He grabbed the fuse, spat on his fingers, pinched the burnt section. Then he covered the area with fresh spit and watched the fuse, thinking desperately that the ship would blow up any moment.

But a minute passed and nothing happened, and at last he sighed with relief. He twisted the fuse so that the charred patch would not be so obvious and hoped the officers would not notice; but for days his guilt sat like a little brown man on his shoulder every time he looked at the fuse or an officer came into the hold.

Young didn't know then that the ship was never in any danger, because the cordtex did not burn, like a cracker fuse, but needed a detonator to flash and explode the charge.

Later that day Paddy came on deck to get some relief from the heat of the engine-room, and was leaning against the wheelhouse yarning to Carse, when Boof Marsh called from the engine-room ladder.

"D'you want me to check that petrol?"

"Aye," Paddy said, without looking round. "I don't like the look of that rusty tin."

Marsh came forward to where the round four-gallon tins of petrol for Mickey Mouse were stowed in the forepeak. He unscrewed the top of the doubtful tin and sniffed.

"Smells all right to me."

Paddy looked up and saw Marsh with his nose to the tin. "An' how in hell can yer tell by smellin' it?"

"I thought...." Boof began.

But Paddy stopped him. "Yer thought! When I joined the bloody Navy the chief asks me a question. 'I think it's all right,' I says. 'Yer do,' he says. 'Now look 'ere, son, in the Navy you're not allowed ter think till you're forty—an' then bloody little.'"

He leered at grinning Marsh. "Have yer got a rubber tube—don't tell me what I can do with it—I know. Well, git one an' bring it here."

In thirty seconds Marsh was back.

"Now," Paddy said, "we'll see."

He sucked a mouthful of petrol from the tin, rolled it round his mouth, rolled his eyes skyward, and spat it on the deck.

"Piss," he spluttered. "Don't yer know piss when yer taste it?"

Paddy was right—almost. Sea water, taken aboard when leaving Exmouth Gulf, had rusted the tin and contaminated the petrol.

"Yer thought!" Paddy sneered, and spat.

From aft where the men had been enjoying the entertainment, for they loved Paddy dearly, came the chant, "Piss, piss, piss", loud enough to be heard a mile away.

And that evening Lyon, after conferring with Carse, issued a new general order. "There is too much noise aboard," he told everyone. "We will soon be approaching the coast of Borneo. Sounds can be heard at long distances over water, so all noise from now on, including the radio, will be reduced to a minimum, particularly when we are anywhere near land, other shipping, and at night. From this point on one stray English word could betray us."

The heat, under a bleached sky, on a lifeless sea, was like a weight. It pressed down on them and seemed to squeeze all energy from their dehydrated bodies. They continued to sweat, but it was an event if anyone went to the side to dribble a little urine like dark sherry. Crilley cooked, but no man wanted food except a few mouthfuls of tinned fruit and men off watch lay open-eyed on the planks aft on the damp imprint of their own bodies.

Davidson and Page, who were drawn together by some personal chemistry, particularly during uneventful stretches of the long journey, sat on No. 4 hold in the wheelhouse shade and softly whistled a lament, a monotonous little tune which went on and on until Carse, at the wheel, could stand the concert no longer.

"Shut up."

The whistling stopped.

"What's biting the old Admiral?" he heard Bob Page say.

"What's the matter?" Davidson called.

"This is a ship," Carse barked, "even if it doesn't look like one. You can whistle in the dog watches—and that's an order."

For a few minutes they were quiet. Then, very softly, they sang "I'll go no more a roving with you, fair maid," until Carse snarled again.

They got up and stood on either side of the wheelhouse, leering at him.

He took off his Japanese sunglasses and cleaned them on his dank sarong. His eyes were scarlet and sore. They almost closed as he grinned at them.

"You're a couple of prize bastards."

That afternoon two other events helped to break the monotony of the crowding heat. A towel and a straw hat went overboard and the *Krait* had to go about to pick up the evidence of their presence.

And then the butterflies arrived. One minute the ship was alone, the next dozens of butterflies were following her and flying ahead like scraps of gaily coloured paper. They stayed with the ship for miles, then vanished as though a wind had scattered them, but one had settled near the mast and Davidson stalked and caught it. Its wings were polished black marked with scarlet and celestial blue, and as he held it gently, and men gathered round him, almost shyly, they all noticed a subtle perfume, an elusive scent of flowers, and in that moment the war receded, the harsh world of sky and water receded, the enemy was forgotten. And then he let the butterfly go, a splash of colour, and it was gone, and beauty and gentleness had gone.

By late faternoon the *Krait* had run out of the oily scum which stained the sea and by dark she was among the islands near Borneo's south-western tip where shallow water and reefs made night movement so dangerous that Carse again reduced speed and sent Cain forward with the leadline. For the next hour the only sound was Cain's deep voice softly intoning: "Mark five . . . deep four . . . by the mark three . . . by the mark three . . . by the mark. . . . "

Finally Carse called to Lyon. "We could easily hit something. I think we'd better anchor for the night."

"Right," Lyon said.

"Anyway, Paddy says it'll rest the engine. She hasn't stopped for nearly a fortnight."

But when they had anchored, the sudden lack of movement and the quiet worried everyone, but Paddy most of all, who was so attuned to his engine that he could sleep beside it and yet wake at the slightest change in its voice. After he had cleaned his oil strainers he lay on deck, but every time he dozed off he woke almost immediately, listening for the engine beat, before he realized where he was and why the diesel was silent. Before dawn he was below again, and at first light the ship woke when he spun Mickey Mouse to produce air pressure to start the engine.

Within an hour the *Krait* had passed Tanjong Sambar and had turned north up Carimata Strait, between Borneo and the island of Billiton, and almost immediately they ran into sail— two boats hull down to port and starboard—and an hour later two bigger ships about five miles to port—a Canton-type junk with brown sails polished by the early sun, and a Batavia-type, both making in fast towards Borneo. By changing course the *Krait* was able to avoid the junks, though for much of that day the lookouts were calling red and green sightings and the helmsman was manoeuvring to keep clear.

Just before the noon change of watches this day Paddy appeared at the wheelhouse sadly shaking his head.

"What's wrong now?" Carse asked.

"It's the bloody Army," he said, wrinkling his nose. "The next time Paddy McDowell goes to sea it'll be with sailors. It's like this. I notice the old crate's a bit sluggish-like an' I can't find why—like drivin' a car with the brake on a notch or two. I can't make it out.

"But when I go aft ter sit on the throne what do I find? Mister Crilley—Corporal Crilley—is doin' his laundry. Half the ship's bloody washin' is trailin' at the end of a rope about fifty yard astern. 'It's a good way ter get things clean,' 'e says.

'It's a good way,' I says, 'ter lose us a knot or more when the bloody Nips is after us.'"

Paddy shook his head and spat.

"Soldiers!"

Daylight next morning unwrapped the *Krait* in the middle of twenty-two small sailing craft and one big brown junk— Jones counted them—but now there was no need to alter course, for the other boats, as they sighted the Japanese flag, scattered like water-beetles.

Now the sea was turquoise patched with green islands—a swept and dusted sea except for countless pink and deep purple jellyfiish rocking in the *Krait's* wash, and a lone turtle, a splash of dull gold set in opal, riding the surface.

Past many names this day of islands like flyspecks on the chart—Bawal and Chempedak, Onrust and Mengkudu, and by next dawn Pelapis was abeam, and inland on Borneo, but far away, was Mount Pahing, and south and west were the dark blue peaks, magnificent but sulky, of Carimata Island.

Then, near the little island of Masa Tiga, south of Pontianak, the *Krait* swung north-west, and in a little while the sea began to darken and to move and the first cloud-drift showed wind.

They had reached the South China Sea at last, and away across it, where the enemy was gathered, was Singapore.

12

THE ISLANDS of the Rhio Archipelago hang down like a string of beads almost from the end of the Malay Peninsula to Sumatra, and through these "Thousand Islands", as they are called, slicing north-west from the South China Sea, are narrow reef- and island-strewn straits—Rhio, Dempu, Temiang, and others—which lead, directly or indirectly, to Singapore.

Operation Jaywick's plan of approach, which would confine the *Krait* mostly to narrow shallow waters free from big-ship patrols, was to use Temiang Strait, roughly half-way down the archipelago, to cut across to the edge of Durian Strait, which separates the Rhio islands and those off the coast of Sumatra, to drop the raiding party with their canoes at Durian Island, between Kundur and Suji islands and about thirty-five miles south of Singapore, and to then hide among the mud and palms of one of the Sumatran rivers where the canoemen, after the raid, would rejoin her at a point to be fixed.

This broad plan, which had been worked out in Melbourne

and Z.E.S., had seemed sound, but the nearer the *Krait* moved to Singapore the less the officers liked it and the more critical and cautious they became, so that Carse was not surprised when, with Borneo sinking astern, Lyon put his head into the wheelhouse and said, "Get someone to take the wheel, Ted. It's time we all had a natter."

Carse handed over to Cain, and joined the three other officers in No. 3 hold. Young had been sent on deck.

"I think we'll have to alter our plan of approach," Lyon said immediately, from his bunk. "I don't like it—and I know you all don't either. One of its weaknesses is how to hide the *Krait* successfully where there are certain to be people. We need only one person to see her to give us away."

"I've been wondering," Carse said, "if it's a good thing to try to hide her at all." He looked at Davidson. "As Donald has often said—we're a Jap fishing boat."

"The *Krait* is safer where everyone can see her?"

"Exactly."

"Correct," Davidson said, his jaw like a spade, "but two other things worry me—the long stretch of fairly open water between Durian Island and Singapore, and the poor getaway down Durian Strait."

"Even if it isn't patrolled," Page added, "which it probably is."

He sat cross-legged on the deck. He seldom sat any other way and could even "walk" with his legs curled under him, like a Siamese approaching his King.

"Let's decide about the *Krait* first," Carse said, in his slow deliberate way, his head on one side. "This is just a suggestion, but I reckon the *Krait* would be safer where she is now—over near Borneo."

Lyon tapped his open palm with his fist.

"I've been thinking much the same thing. Look at it this way. We haven't seen a thing Japanese since Lombok, so it's a fair assumption these waters aren't patrolled, or if they are, at least not regularly."

"It's also my guess," the navigator said, grinning sardonically, "that after you boys hit Singapore there's going to be a big blue. The Nips'll be out like green ants looking for you. . . . I don't mind admitting I'd be glad to be well away when they're going mad around the nest."

They looked at each other in the hold's half-light.

Davidson spoke. "One point. The ship would be doubly exposed crossing to Borneo and back. If she's seen about too much some inquisitive fellow might start asking damned awkward questions. Except—I'll admit—she would hardly be suspect when coming back to the trouble area."

"Ted and the others have to take their chance," Lyon said

bluntly. "But I agree. The *Krait* should be safer over this side when the balloon goes up. The Japs are hardly likely to look for their attackers near Borneo."

"Don't be too sure," warned Page. "It's the Nip Air Force we'll have to keep our eyes skinned for. They'll think we came in by sub, and they'll put every plane they've got over these shallow waters."

"True, but while the flap's on it's much easier for us to hide than for the *Krait*."

The lookout called and Carse jumped for the ladder. Cain leant out of the wheelhouse. "Red four-five, but miles away."

"O.K. Keep away from her."

He dropped down the ladder and said: "Is it settled? After leaving you the *Krait* goes back to Borneo?"

Lyon nodded.

"Now, what about Donald's query?"

Lyon unfolded a chart on his knees. "I think Donald's right —but first things first." He tapped the stiff paper with a finger. "Up Temiang Strait to Pompong Island—here. That's our immediate objective. It's very small and uninhabited because it has only one little spring which at this time of the year doesn't give more than a quart of water an hour. When we get there we'll decide where to go next, otherwise we'll be making stabs in the dark. Durian Island may be too far for us. We just don't know."

"It's too damned open," the big man insisted. "We need a more covered approach within reasonable paddling distance of Singapore."

"I'm inclined to agree," Lyon said, "but let's finally decide at Pompong."

Carse noticed that as he bent over the chart again Lyon was smiling—eagerly, like a little boy.

Back in the wheelhouse Bob Page lifted the hinged top of the bunk and dragged out the first-aid kit from among Carse's clothes and other gear.

"Back in a jiffy to take over, Ted. Poppa has some skin off his shin."

When he returned he replaced the iodine bottle in the box and held up a flat metal case.

"Seen this?" he asked. He clicked open the case. It contained a row of small flat dull-yellow objects like sections of a small orange.

"Lozenges."

Carse peered at them. "We haven't had a cough in a thousand miles." He picked one out and put it in his palm Now it reminded him of a flat tree bug—a reddish one.

"See how they're shaped," Page pointed. "Curved to go under the tongue. . . . Cyanide."

Their eyes met.

"One bite and it's all over. Ivan brought them—just in case. But we're not taking them with us."

"Leaving them with me," Carse said, dryly. "Nice little playthings to be sleeping on top of. . . . But why the change of plan?"

"We've decided that if anything goes wrong—if capture is certain—we'll shoot the boys and then ourselves."

Carse's mouth twisted. "When was this pretty little how-do-you-do decided?"

"Above Lombok. . . . We can't be captured. We know too much."

"I hope the boys haven't heard of this. It wouldn't be too good for their morale."

"No, they don't know."

Carse handed back the lozenge and watched as Page put it in its case and returned the case to the kit and put the kit under the bunk and pulled down the lid.

They'll do it, too, he thought, cold and empty and suddenly aware of loneliness and time.

"Sorry for the hold-up, Ted," Page said, taking the wheel. "How are the eyes?"

"Oh, not too dusty."

"Wish we had something for them. Salt water's about the best thing I can think of."

"Salt." Carse almost spat the word and Page looked quickly back at him. "Salt," he said again. "I wish to God it would rain. Not a skerrick since Cairns. I feel I'm made of salt."

Page didn't speak but wondered what was the matter as Carse stretched out on his bunk and lay there thinking angrily, impotently, of the waste of war, of Jones and Huston and Falls, the three men who didn't know; thinking of war and its ruthlessness, its necessary ruthlessness, and of its impact on men and what it did to them, to their minds, their souls, and how it would leave them when all this was over.

He couldn't sleep, but slowly the anger drained out of him and soon he was calm. He lay watching the sunlight splashing the wheelhouse window, then propped himself up, cursing the pain in his swollen elbows, and filled in his log and added:

"It seems peculiar that we should be cruising at our leisure through these seas with no sign of challenge, but there is a feeling of deep anxiety all the same. This is definitely not of the Lombok type, but it is there."

He lay back, thinking again of the three men, half-hearing through their names in his brain the soft panting of the exhaust. Then he raised himself again and added these words:

"Each day as the sun goes down I mutter a heartfelt, 'Thank God'."

On 15th September, when the *Krait* was only one hundred and forty miles from Temiang Strait, Carse's eyes looked, as someone said, like raisins set in lipstick. The inflammation had worsened and now they burnt and itched and throbbed as the needles of the glare stabbed at them. This morning in the dawn twilight he had been able to take his star sights—on Betelgeuse, the planet Jupiter and Canopus, one of the Dogs—but he had then found that his eyes were so bad that he could not accurately match the lines on the vernier with the graduations on the arc of his old sextant, and had to call Davidson to do it for him.

And to add to his worries, and his discomfort, his elbows were now badly swollen and had begun to develop fluid sacs because of the repeated bumps in the cramped wheelhouse. The helmsmen sometimes banged themselves if they moved carelessly or the ship lurched in a sea, but Carse, who spent nearly all his time in the wheelhouse, often cracked his elbows when he swung off or on his narrow bunk, and even the repeated jabs of pain did not make him be more careful.

Even Crilley's cheerful good morning, as he handed the inevitable porridge and pancakes through the flap, failed to get more than a grunt from Carse that morning, for too many hours on duty, too little sleep, and the relentless nagging responsibility of a ship against the sea and the unseen but ever-present enemy were beginning to scour his vitality.

"A junk, Donald," Carse said, pointing, as he handed over at noon. "We seem to be on converging courses."

"I don't care if it's Christopher Columbus," the big man growled. He scratched his bottom. "I wish to God it would rain."

He bent over the compass. "A spot of fresh water might help those eyes. . . . Any better?"

"A bit since the cloud cut the glare."

Within an hour the big junk, her decks heaped with cargo under her high brown sails, was only two miles away on the starboard beam, nuzzling into the choppy sea like a heavy hairy animal drinking, and everyone now, except Davidson at the wheel and the mast look-out, watched her from under cover, watched amazed as she drew level, held her position, then moved ahead.

This was too much for the crew. Someone sniggered and then they all began to laugh at the sight of the clumsy junk passing at almost double their speed.

"Paddy . . . Paddy . . . Paddy," they chanted, and when the engineer's head appeared at the top of his ladder they demanded together, "And who called the old bastard an engineer?"

Paddy waited his chance, and when the leg-pulling began to ease he barked, "If the bloody apes on that thing are anythin' like the bloody apes on this they're swingin' by their 'floggin' tails pushin' her along—not jist sittin' on 'em."

But the junk was only a few hundred yards ahead when, without warning, the wind swung to the west and brought heavy cloud-banks trailing a sea mist, and with the change the junk began to wallow and slow down. Soon the *Krait* caught and passed her, but as she vanished astern in the thickening murk, which cut visibility to less than a hundred yards, they experienced their first fright since Lombok when a 10,000-ton Japanese tanker, enormous above them, cut across their bows and was gone almost before the helmsman could spin the wheel.

Thirty seconds later the *Krait* was pitching and rolling in her first storm, a real "Sumatra", since leaving Cairns. Tormented gusts sliced the wave peaks and flung them at the ship, so that as one hit the wheelhouse another was on its way. Then they were out of the violence into almost solid rain, such rain as few of them had seen, and for the next hour, without a falter, it was like massed silver arrows fired into the sea.

As the rain began, shouting men who couldn't hear a sound above the wild drumming scrambled out on deck. They plunged forward, to drop their sarongs, to dance a wild corroboree. On No. 4 hatch, around No. 3, way forward at the mast, brown-stained bodies, white from navels to dangling scrotums, swayed and whirled and drank and screamed with open soundless mouths, and as they whirled, rain-washed buttocks glistened, paper white against the curtain of rain, against the sea. They were marine creatures, resurrected from the dark green places into the light.

Only Davidson, gummed to the wheel, steering blind, couldn't join the dancers on their narrow stage above the flattened sea. He shouted with frustration, loathing the others, but couldn't hear himself and wasn't heard until Carse, naked and streaming, relieved him. Then he, too, dropped his sarong and leapt into the ice-cold rain.

In an hour— a little more—they emerged, after collecting as much rain as they could, through the storm's back-door, and saw the setting sun for a moment between dark banks. Then the clouds embraced and the grey light over the sea came from El Greco as the waves raced away to shatter against the horizon.

But the men were gay as they covered their pebble-smooth skins with the hated dye and put on their wet sarongs. All knew that tomorrow, a few hours, a few miles ahead, death could come with discovery, but as later they drank their steaming tea tomorrow seemed remote as the first star above the masthead.

Only the helmsman knew when, at midnight and in moonlight, the *Krait* crossed the equator.

The little ship edged out of the night into the severe dawn of 16th September. The sea was pewter and among the overcast were lumps of black rain-cloud almost too heavy to stay unaided in the sky.

Carse felt happier as he realized that visibility would be poor and likely to continue so, and that it would be a day of no glare; his eyes, although still inflamed, were better after the cold rain bath. He knew that this was the testing time when he, and the others, would need all their strength and alertness, and he decided that, until the raiders were dropped and the immediate job was completed, he must go without sleep—must stay at the wheel.

At full dawn the *Krait*, after her slanting run across the equator, was ten miles north with low cloud to the south, and above that cloud, like a sentry watching them, was four-thousand-foot Linga Peak, thirty miles away, with a long white brushstroke—a waterfall, a landslide perhaps—down its side.

The Rhio Archipelago—at last.

Three hours later, with long Sebangka Island away to port, and when the *Krait* was closing with the entrance to Temiang Strait, they had their first scare of the approach itself when Jones, the bow lookout and the only man showing except the helmsman, saw a Japanese plane between them and Sebangka.

"Action stations," Carse ordered. "Half-speed."

As the *Krait* slowed to reduce wake visibility the guns, already on deck, were manned and magazines snapped on. But the plane, instead of altering course, continued towards Singapore, its engine note echoing and fading like the end of an argument among the clouds.

"She must have seen us," Lyon called, from behind the wheelhouse, as he put down his Sten. "It's a good sign."

Now, with black-haired Jones up the mast, looking more Japanese than a Japanese, they were in the narrow strait between many reefs and low dark islands embroidered with palm, and some with native huts in brown lines and clusters just back from the sea edge. Now, too, the sails began, and for the next five hours they often had to alter course to keep away from native craft—from the smallest sailing canoes with palm-plaited sails to big two-masters and a junk they couldn't avoid with leering blue, white and green eyes painted on her stubborn bows. But the craft which interested them most, and aroused their covetousness, was a beautiful white Marconi-rigged yacht, European in every detail except for her Malay crew, and probably part of the loot from captured Singapore or the captured Indies.

As Cobber Cain said, watching her through a split in the curtains, "This is just like Sydney Harbour on a Saturday arvo."

But it wasn't, as they were soon to learn.

Visibility was still poor, and they were making a slow approach to their objective of Pompong Island, at the western end of Temiang Strait, when Jones reported the partly-obscured crosstrees of a mast, and then the mast itself, which appeared to be moving round the end of a lcw island.

Carse didn't wait. He called for full speed and steered for the protection of an island cluster to starboard, but the *Krait* had travelled only a few hundred yards when Jones called, "It's a wreck. The mast's sticking out of the sea."

"Half-speed, Paddy," Carse called, relaxing his grip on the wheel, as Lyon said to Davidson:

"One of the escape ships from Singapore. Might even be the *Kuala* or the *Kung Wo*."

They reached heavily wooded Pompong and circled, but although the island had two small beaches they were open and gave no protection.

Carse decided to investigate another small island a couple of miles away, and they had just anchored, and Cain was in the dinghy searching for a break in the reefs when a Japanese seaplane, her yellow floats glistening, roared low across them.

Men under cover grabbed their guns and waited for her to return, for they knew what that would mean. But she continued south and disappeared.

"Getting interesting," Davidson said casually.

And Carse knew, now that every moment was dangerous, that the big man was beginning to enjoy himself.

Cain returned and reported failure, and as he tied the dinghy to the stern and climbed aboard, Lyon said, "Pompong looks the best place for the night, Ted. What do you think?"

"Tonight only. Too many reefs and rips—too many people around here. One pro-Nip could make it tough for us. With an early start we may find something a bit more private nearer Singapore."

"We may have to go to Durian yet."

"I hope not. It's too damned far."

They anchored off Pompong's eastern beach just on dusk, alone now, for the last sail sighted had been two hours before. Davidson, Cain and Jones went ashore and buried, near a twisted tree at one end of the beach, two cans of emergency rations and a four-gallon can of water, and when they returned

Davidson carefully explained where the cache had been made.

"You never know," he warned, "but your lives could depend on knowing where it is. So don't forget it."

He brought back with him more reminders of the escape from Singapore—a rusty British Army waterbottle and two clips of .303 ammunition found in the sand where jungle and beach met.

After dark the *Krait's* mast was lowered to reduce her silhouette, but instead of coming down noiselessly it slipped and crashed to the deck, narrowly missing Cain. And they had just finished their evening meal, and were talking in scared whispers after the noise the mast had made, when two searchlights chased each other across the northern sky.

"Ten to fifteen miles away," Lyon said quietly. "We're only getting their glare."

Carse went to the wheelhouse and studied the chart under a shaded torch. He came back forward.

"Up Dempu Strait somewhere—and certainly on our way."

The muted roar of engines brought everyone on deck two hours before daylight. It came from the south—far south— yet across the water, through the pre-dawn mists, the engines could be heard rising and falling as they sobbed into silence.

"Our friend," Page whispered. "Must be a seaplane base."

"On that bearing they're on Chempa Island," Carse whispered back. "It's about the only place they could be."

The engines revved again, a throaty muttering which lifted to a steady roar that seemed alarmingly close in the chill air. Their note faded, then returned, steady and threatening.

Paddy lifted one of the curtains.

"Four of 'em—an' the one on the left has a dirty carburettor."

His whisper was like a lion with laryngitis. Muffled sniggers came from aft.

"Shut up, Paddy," Jones said, trying not to laugh. "This is serious."

"Serious," Paddy said. "It's been serious for weeks. It's serious me bein' where Paddy McDowell bloody well is now."

Again the engines died, muttered, died. Everyone waited, reaching south with their ears, their tingling skin.

The engines didn't start again, but the light came reluctantly that morning as though it was afraid. The island crept out of the dark and became just a little darker than the dark. A bird slid across the fading stars, calling, calling.

The galley flickered as the tireless Crilley lit the kerosene stove. Men shaved and bent over the side and washed their faces. And in the silence of this sea world a toothbrush sounded like a scrubbing brush on a floor.

Then from the island, and almost as though they had been amplified, came three words, which nobody understood although Lyon, who spoke the language, knew they were Malay. The men froze—waiting.

"No talking," Lyon whispered, and the order whispered aft.

The light grew. It was day. And with the day an old grey-haired Malay in a blue sarong, and two little naked boys, came out of the trees carrying a small canoe which they dropped near the water.

For a moment they stared at the *Krait*. Then they ran back into the trees.

"Paddy," Carse called softly, urgently. "Let's get going."

"Aye, aye, skipper."

He dropped below. Soon the propeller was turning. The *Krait* began to move, out and away from Pompong, heading north and then north-west through Dempu Strait and beyond through the gathering overcast towards the last of the islands shrouding Singapore.

Hour after hour that day they searched for a raiding base until eyes ached with searching and minds and bodies hurt with the mounting tension, for every island that looked suitable proved on closer examination to be either guarded by reefs or inhabited—and inhabited by people who clearly feared the filthy Nippon flag at the *Krait's* stern, for fishing canoes scuttled for beaches and pagars and even children faded into the jungle if the ship showed any sign of stopping.

Unspoken questions, hidden fears, hovered like bats above the *Krait* that day as men together, cemented by a common purpose and a common fate, mastered the frantic little panics which swept across them like wavelets and rolled on.

Carse, who never left the wheel, noticed many things during those crawling hours among this wasteland of antagonistic sea. He was continuously thirsty, a dry-retching sort of thirst no water would relieve. He had no urge to smoke. And fear was inside him, like little stones dropping into a well deep in his guts. He noticed, too, that the other men either talked too much and too aimlessly, or were too cheerful, too gay, and that in between these phases were dead patches like burnt grass when all sound ceased and the silence throughout the ship was almost frightening.

Lyon, his eyes unnaturally bright, spent most of the day sitting on the bunk behind Carse, talking little, but watching, watching. Page had a new nervous alertness about him, but when he smiled, which he did a lot, it was without humour. Of the officers, only Davidson seemed at ease, though once he winked at Carse, a thing he rarely did, and said, "Tedious, isn't it?"

Early they sighted one of the Japanese floatplanes, but far

away, and later a big transport passed over heading for Singapore probably from Java. Carse was still watching this plane, as they cruised along Galang Island, when he heard Lyon move suddenly behind him.

"I'll swear that's an O.Pip over there," he said. "Look—above that building—the open space in the trees."

He reached for the glasses on the shelf above, but Carse whirled and slapped down his hand.

"For Christ's sake—you'll give us away."

And to the crew he called, "Keep under cover, and tell Paddy full speed."

He stared at the clearing, less than a mile away.

"My eyes are lousy, but it looks a bit like a tower."

"It is. It's an O.P. all right. That's where the lights came from last night."

Slowly they passed, and even more slowly it seemed they drew out of sight.

"I wonder if they've reported us?" Carse said. "Now we'll have to stick to this course until dark. They may check."

"I'd love to know what they thought of us."

Carse wiped the sweat from his forehead. "Here's hoping they thought we were a nice Nip boat making for Singapore after catching fish for the Emperor. If they didn't we'll soon know."

Much later he reached for his log, which he kept on the shelf with his navigation books, and propped the dark green ledger on the spokes. Then he picked up the pencil from the window ledge in front of him and on page 17 of the log wrote:

"September 17. 1415: Sighted O.P. Station on Galang Baru. Increased speed on A/c so as not to appear as a loiterer. I don't know how the day is going to end. We have been zigzagging and zigzagging all day long from one deserted looking spot to another only to find that we are approaching a worse one. Out of the frying pan into the fire would be appropriate, but it does the system no good. We have been looking for a place to anchor, but the population is against us. As long as we keep moving, no matter how aimlessly, we do not seem to excite suspicion, but I don't think we can do it for long. We are within about 30 miles of Singapore and still getting closer, waiting and praying for dark. No lovers ever longed for darkness as we do."

On, on they cruised through that endless afternoon under the overcast, their sarongs belted with sweat, the skin around their eyes stretched with the strain of waiting, the fear of showing fear.

The *Krait's* wake traced a pattern between the islands as they went up Dempu Strait and then almost west into Chombol

Strait, south of Bulan Island, where twice they were at action stations—once when they sighted a motor boat, and later when what looked suspiciously like a naval picket boat, with men in white who culd have been sailors, emerged from behind an island and went away from them.

Lyon finally decided that Durian Island, the dropping-point they had planned to use, was too dangerous as a raiding base, a decision which meant that an island had to be found in the next few hours unless they were to spend another desperate exposed day aimlessly searching.

They had seen one island—Pandjang, it was called—miles back which looked promising, but had kept away because of the many native fishing boats in the area. Now they decided to return to it, but not in daylight, and so continued on their course along Chombol Strait, with engine throttled down, as they waited for the sunset to melt and the dark to follow the final hush of this interminable and awful day.

When night rushed in at last, and just before they turned, the evening-scattered clouds beyond the *Krait's* bow began to glow, and gradually the glow increased to a soft glare high above and ahead of them in a great arc across the northern sky.

Carse was so tired by this that he watched the reflection in the clouds for a minute before he realized, almost with a shock, where it came from. Of course, he thought, and then said, "There she is," and Lyon, who had been dozing, opened his eyes and saw the glare and knew.

"The lights of Singapore," he called excitedly. "Donald . . . Bob!"

In those moments, with Singapore in sight, or at least the reflection of its lights, men forgot their weariness, their fears, in the violent excitement of discovery, and even Paddy climbed on deck to growl, "So that's where the little bastards live," before dropping below again to increase speed as Carse swung the ship in a wide turn.

As they headed down Chombol now, to seek and find Pandjang Island in the dark, a searchlight brushed the sky far ahead, and Lyon said, "That settles it. It was an O.P. all right."

But they didn't see it for long, for within minutes their world was blacked out by a Sumatra almost as violent as the one which hit them in the China Sea. Gusts dived at them like wasps, rain battered them, spray tinkled against the wheelhouse where Carse struggled to hold the bucking *Krait* and to navigate out of the island-studded strait where any moment he knew they could hit a reef or be blown ashore. Then, right ahead, an almost dazzling light jumped into the wet blackness, like a lone lamp in a dark lane, as he turned the wheel he instinctively knew that the light was at the end of a fishing pagar he had noticed on the way up the strait, and that the pagar was not far from its entrance.

At reduced speed he guided the little ship, feeling his way through the blackness with the aid of the friendly light, approaching it and passing it, and even giving it a last wave with both hands just before it disappeared and the rain began to ease.

They reached Pandjang Island at 10 p.m. and, approaching cautiously, with Cain on the leadline, were able to anchor only twenty yards from a tiny white sand beach they had noted earlier in the day. But although the rain had stopped the sea was still too rough to risk a landing, and as they waited everyone worked at the forward holds to prepare to drop the raiding party.

The restless deck was heaped with gear, which was being assembled and sorted, when, without warning, a boat passed not a hundred yards off. Because of the wind, still blowing in strong gusts, nobody heard the powerful engine until the boat was opposite them, and already moving away. But an hour later, when the same engine note was this time heard returning, they began to suspect that the boat was a Japanese patrol, and this was confirmed when she passed every hour, though farther out in the stream.

At midnight the sea was still so rough that Carse decided to look for a beach on the other side of the long thin island; but they had only half-rounded the island when the wind died and back they went to the original anchorage, where it was soon possible to launch the dinghy.

At 1 a.m. on 18th September, sixteen days since leaving Exmouth Gulf, Joe Jones rowed ashore with Donald Davidson, who searched the jungle behind the beach and even climbed a small hill, but could see no light or hear sounds which suggested the island was inhabited.

Marsh and Berryman then began the long job of ferrying the gear ashore—the canoes in their canvas bags, the paddles and sails, the heavy limpets and their attachments, the tins of food and water, the arms and ammunition, the medical kits and clothes, and even the bag of gold guilders from under Carse's bunk . . . everything the raiding party needed until the narrow beach was heaped with bags and boxes. Once Berryman was half-way to the beach when the Japanese patrol passed. He stopped rowing and, like the others aboard, froze until the engine faded.

While ferrying was being completed the four officers conferred. No pick-up point had yet been selected. No rendezvous time had been fixed. These decisions had been left to the last, although they had been discussed, because of the difficulties encountered in the long search for an island dropping point.

"Where do you think you should pick us up?" Lyon asked Carse.

"Why not here? We're only about thirty miles from Singapore."

"It's too close, Ted. I'd prefer Pompong—I think we all would."

The others agreed.

"It's much farther," Carse warned. "It means you'll have to paddle at least fifty miles—and you'll already be tired."

"But the *Krait* won't have to run the gauntlet of the O.P. on Galang again. That's a bad risk."

"It'd be just as simple to come here. I'd pass the O.P. at night, coming and going."

"Don't forget that," Davidson said.

The distant searchlight was sliding down the sky.

"And don't forget our friend the patrol," Page added.

"No," Lyon said, firmly. "It's far too risky. Pompong it is—even if we have a longer paddle."

"O.K.," Carse agreed. He was so tired he couldn't argue any more, though now he felt that Lyon was probably right. "When?"

"We've allowed ourselves about twelve days for the raid," Lyon said. "It's the eighteenth today—say midnight on October first-second."

"Right. Midnight October first-second. Now, what about recognition signals?"

"Better not. We'll find you."

Restless against the side the dinghy bumped hard and bumped again.

"Hold her off," Carse called quietly. "She's making too much bloody noise."

Lyon spoke. "If anyone is not back on the deadline the ship will sail immediately for Australia."

"That's too rigid," Carse protested. "I'll keep the R.V. but if those I pick up can't tell me for certain the others are dead, then I'll come back at midnight in forty-eight hours."

"Fair enough." It was Page.

"Agreed," said Lyon, finding Carse's hand in the dark and gripping hard.

At 4 a.m. all gear was ashore, and it was time to go. The crew gathered amidships to farewell the raiding party, the three officers, Lyon, Davidson, and Page, and the three ratings, Falls, Jones, and Huston.

"Well, good-bye, chaps," Lyon said quietly. "We'll see you in about a fortnight."

"Good luck, sir."

"Give 'em hell."

"Cheerio, Happy."

"Buy me a beer, Poppa."

Bob Page shook hands with everyone.

"Look after yourself, Bob," Carse said, and could say no more.

Davidson gripped Carse's hand in both his, turned quickly and got into the dinghy.

Lyon put a hand on the navigator's arm and whispered, "Remember, Ted, if a couple don't come back, don't worry and don't wait after the forty-eight hours. You'll know for certain they're dead."

Then they were gone, and Moss Berryman was back with the dinghy, and it was on board, and the anchor was up, and the propeller turning.

As Carse swung the *Krait's* head towards Dempu and Temiang, towards the distant China Sea, he wondered why his sore eyes were stinging and realized that he was crying.

As they moved away he looked back only once into the dark that was Pandjang Island, and felt that he would never see them again.

13

WHEN DAYLIGHT reached Pandjang Island a family of otters were playing like puppies among the rock pools near the little empty curve of beach new-swept and patterned with the myriad feet of crabs.

But behind Otters' Bay, as the Jaywick raiders named their landing point, the six men were still sorting and hiding their supplies among the trees and tangled undergrowth of this their rear base. As the others worked, Davidson left to search the narrow island, but in an hour he was back, silently parting the jungle wall which surrounded a waterhole they had found below a spring.

"There's a kampong—a small one—less than half a mile on the other side," he explained. "No tracks or footmarks coming this way, but we'll have to be careful. Keep your voices down."

"We're in luck—even water laid on," said Lyon. "But before we sleep we'd better hide the emergency stores."

Falls pointed. "There's a broken cliff along there—looks good to me."

He led the way to where fallen rocks had made natural caves obscured from the sea by undergrowth.

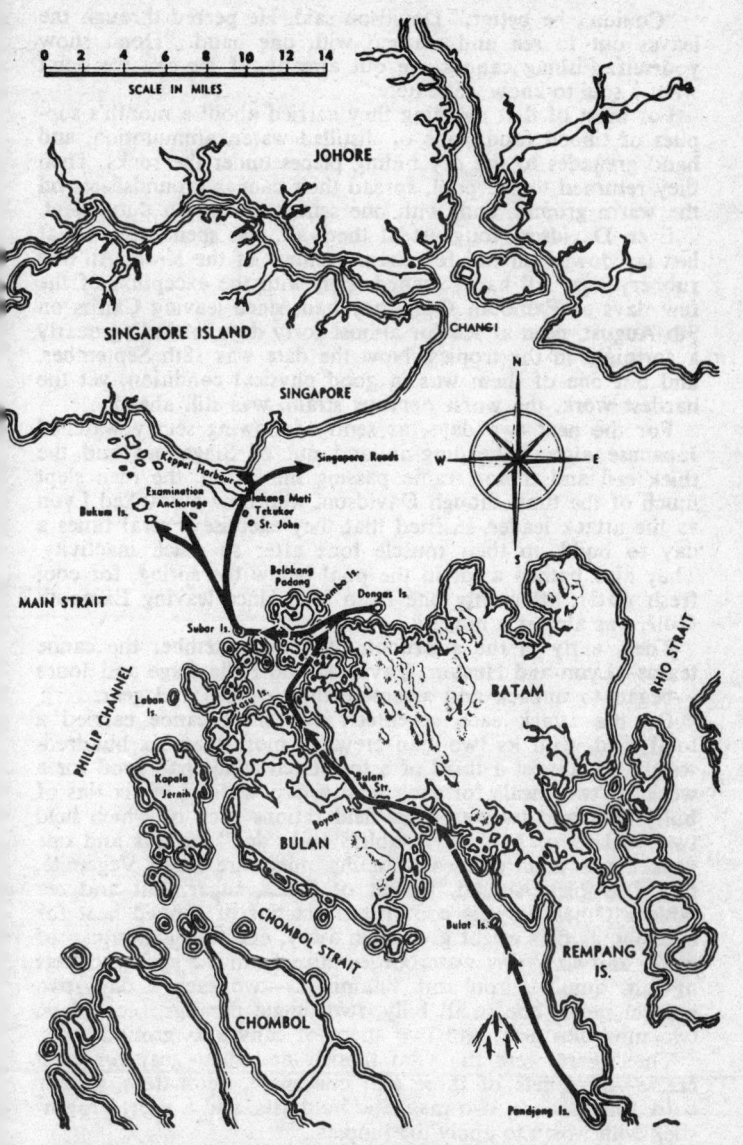

Route of Operation Jaywick's successful three-canoe attack from the rear base of Pandjang Island through Bulan Strait to Singapore.

"Couldn't be better," Davidson said. He peered through the leaves out to sea and warned with one hand. "Don't show yourself. Fishing canoes are out already. If we can we don't want a soul to know we're here."

For most of that morning they carried about a month's supplies of tinned food, cans of distilled water, ammunition, and hand grenades to the dry hiding places under the rocks. Then they returned to the pool, spread their canvas groundsheets on the warm ground, and, with one sentry always on duty, slept.

Even Davidson, toughest of them all, was spent when he at last lay down. All still felt the movement of the *Krait*. All had rubbery legs. All had softened. For, with the exception of the few days at Exmouth Gulf they had, since leaving Cairns on 9th August, been at sea for almost forty days, including nearly a fortnight in the tropics. Now the date was 18th September, and not one of them was in good physical condition, yet the hardest work, the worst nervous strain, was still ahead.

For the next two days, as sentry following sentry watched Japanese aircraft heading in and out of Singapore and the thick sail and motor traffic passing the island, the men slept much of the time, though Davidson, who now outranked Lyon as the attack leader, insisted that they exercise several times a day to build up their muscle tone after so much inactivity. They also bathed a lot in the pool below the spring, for cool fresh water, after only one fresh bath since leaving Exmouth Gulf, was almost a novelty.

Then, early in the afternoon of 20th September the canoe teams—Lyon and Huston, Davidson and Falls, Page and Jones—began to unpack and assemble their canoes and gear.

On the attack each seventeen-foot black canoe carried a total load, with its two-man crew, of more than six hundredweight, or almost a third of a ton. Each canoe had food for a week, at two meals for each man a day—a total of six tins of bully beef and twelve Army field rations each of which held two packets of M and V tablets and "dog" biscuits and one packet with a tin of meat, biscuits, miniature tin of Vegemite, tin of tropical spread, packet of P.K.s, sugar, salt and tea tablets. Other supplies comprised: six tins of canned heat for cooking, as fires might give them away, one four-gallon can of water and six Army waterbottles filled from the spring, tablets of salt, quinine, iron and Vitamin C—two each a day—two enamel mugs, one small billy, two jungle parangs, binoculars, two mosquito nets, and two strips of canvas as groundsheets.

Then there were the vital limpets and their gear for each canoe—three sets of three and one spare, detonators, primer cord, time pencils, two magnetic holdfasts, and a short broomstick with which to apply the limpets.

When canoes and cargo were ready just behind the beach

the raiders stripped and again dyed themselves, especially their faces, hair and hands, and after a late afternoon meal of tinned meat, chocolate and water, they dressed for the long journey.

Each man wore over a khaki shirt, a black two-piece suit of water-proofed japara silk, which narrowed and gripped at wrist and ankles, two pairs of black cotton socks, and black sandshoes with reinforced soles; and each man carried on a black webbing belt, which could be slipped off while paddling, a .38 revolver and 100 rounds, a sheath knife (Davidson also wore a throwing stiletto), and a short loaded rubber hose, and in zipped suit pockets a small compass and a small first-aid kit containing bandages, needles and surgical thread, powdered sulpha, and morphia bottles with needles attached.

When they were dressed and equipped Lyon took the flat tin of cyanide lozenges from one of his zip pockets and showed them to Huston, Falls and Jones—the same lozenges Page had told Carse were not to be taken on the raid and which Carse never knew during the attack itself were not still under his bunk.

"These are cyanide capsules which take effect in five seconds," Lyon explained to the three. "I thought you had a right to know I have them—just in case. I'll distribute one each before the attack."

"Thanks, sir," Falls said.

And that was all.

In the flooding dark they carried the canoes down the beach and had just put them in the water when they heard the now familiar engine of the night patrol boat. They froze, standing in the water, although they knew they could not be seen against the dark island mass, and followed the moving sound, and far out saw the outline of the boat heading south-east.

"About as long as the old *Krait*," Davidson whispered, "and four times faster. We don't want to tangle with her."

They waited until the engine note had filtered away before loading the canoes—explosives and their attachments forward with the water-can, food at the stern, waterbottles, arms and folded black silk sail between the canoemen, and black collapsible mast clamped along the starboard decking.

During the afternoon they had buried all tins and scraps and carefully searched the camp area so that not even a thread from suits or shirts, caught in a bush, could give them away. They did not worry about tracks in the sand or jungle because they knew that by morning the tide and the crabs would have wiped them away.

Ready at last, and in the velvet blackness of that early evening, the six black men got into their black canoes. Even at a few yards they were almost invisible to each other as Davidson and his partner Falls, who were to lead, dipped the black, knife-edged blades of their single paddles and the three canoes moved out of the little bay in tight arrowhead and turned north-west, away from Pandjang and up along the coast of larger Rempang Island.

Averaging about two miles an hour, they paddled only eleven miles and were exhausted by midnight when Davidson pulled in to the small rocky uninhabited island of Bulat, near the entrance to Bulan Strait, which would lead them between the big islands of Batam and Bulan to Singapore. Weary and sore, since they had last sat in a canoe three weeks before, they landed on a sand-spit, unloaded and carried the canoes to a grove at the base of cliffs which sparkled like mica against the late-risen moon, and slept.

But it was here on Bulat that they learnt their first, and nearly their last, lesson, for both Davidson and Jones woke at daylight, and for some reason they could never explain, got up immediately and looked out to sea—and there was a sampan trailing the Japanese flag at her stern heading slowly in towards their hiding place, and there also were two of the canoes only partly hidden, and, worse, some of their supplies actually outside the trees and on the beach.

They belted the others awake and, sprawled in the undergrowth, revolvers cocked, watched fearfully as the sampan anchored just off the beach, in full view of the bags on the sand, and stayed an hour. And not once, before it pulled out, did anyone on board even appear to glance at the beach, though Japanese were on deck several times.

"This ought to be a lesson to us," Davidson exploded as the sampan disappeared.

It was anger at himself more than the others.

"By God, we won't get another chance. In future everything must be hidden before we even think of food or sleep. Our necks depend on it."

He pointed to the end of the two canoes, distinguishable against the white sand, the dark background of the bush.

"Look at them. I could kick myself for being such a fool. I should have made sure they were under cover."

But they were all responsible—and knew it—and the mass feeling of guilt was comforting.

In silence they moved farther into the trees among the stale metallic smell of wood-rot and damp earth where the canoes became part of the protective shade. And there they spent the day sleeping, only the duty sentries watching the many islands, dark patches on a pale green quilt, for patrols using Bulan Strait.

They woke in the afternoon, unshaven, dirty, backs aching,

thigh and arm muscles stiff from the unaccustomed strain of paddling for hours encased like grubs emerging from a cocoon, in the small manholes of the slim canoes.

Jones sat up first, stretched his arms, tried to straighten his back, groaned, sniffed and sniffed again.

"Poppa—you stink."

Falls, who was lying on his back, sniffed too.

"You don't smell too good yourself."

Jones experimented. "I am a bit high."

They all stank, not merely of dried sweat, but of sweat mixed with a foul odour from their damp silk suits—an odour like long-sour milk, but worse. Even when they took off their suits, which they did from then on whenever they could, the smell clung to their bodies, even when they scrubbed themselves with wet sand.

The suits, so close-woven that they did not allow air through and did not dry quickly, were the one failure of their equipment, although they did keep out the mosquitoes, which was important. Everyone agreed that jungle-green slacks and shirts would have been more efficient—and cooler. But it was too late for wishing. The suits were all they had.

There was no water on Bulat, so in the late afternoon, when the sea was clear of native boats and fishing canoes, the men had a quick swim and Davidson even took a photograph of his companions, up to their necks a few yards off the beach, against a distant island and a native kampong.

The black raiders left their hideout on Bulat at dusk and began their dangerous penetration of Bulan Strait, little more than a ditch between the low dark masses of Batam and Bulan islands. In the next ten hours they travelled less than nine miles.

From the start, those animistic demons of the Malays, the spirits of the waters, seemed to have combined to deny them passage of the strait, which was not much more than a mile wide along its main channel. Even in fairly still water, heavily laden canoes are difficult to keep on an even course, but among the rips and whirls between the islands the canoemen soon lost formation and at one time were actually driven backwards. Along one island Lyon and Huston lost control and crashed beam-on to the bow of the canoe paddled by Page and Jones and nearly overturned.

Lyon was physically the weakest of the six. He had lost weight on the voyage, he lacked the intensive canoe training of the others, and even Huston's strength and stamina never completely compensated for his frailty. Compared with the others, Lyon and Huston were an unbalanced team, and a source of worry to Davidson, the operational leader, though only to Page did he voice his concern. Lyon, however, possessed other strengths which kept him going—faith in himself and his idea, fanatical determination to return to avenge the capture of Singapore, the later capture of his family.

All night they paddled along their corridor of darkness before the clouds came down to cover a chalky, short-lived moon. Sometimes they made less than a mile an hour, sometimes two, until, with dawn just ahead, and disgusted with their poor progress, they dragged their canoes in among the mangroves on Bulan Island.

Concealment was thin, as they were to realize often during the day. At first light a dog's bark sounded almost beside them. Then a man shouted and children called to each other. Peering through the leaves the raiders saw that they were within a few hundred yards of a kampong on the little island of Boyan, and that other kampongs were like rabbit droppings along the low shores of the strait.

"I hope that blasted dog minds its own business," Davidson whispered.

"He didn't hear us getting in here," Lyon said, almost cheerfully. "And we made a lot of noise."

"Probably thought it was a croc."

Davidson grinned as he saw the startled looks among the Australians.

"Plenty in these parts. Surprised we haven't seen some."

They laced the small mangrove branches to help hide them from the canoes and sailing boats already using the strait only a few yards away. They laced some of the leaves overhead to give a little shade. Then, after breakfast of tinned meat and biscuits, they stretched out in this desolate place of mud, on the sharp mangrove roots, on the waterworn stones in patches among the mud. And somehow, among the stench of ancient tides through which even their own personal stink penetrated, they slept—waking at calls from the village, a dog-fight, the dry thump thump of women pounding rice, the high cries of boatmen passing so close that the sails of a junk came between them and the sun.

As small crabs scampered over them, with dry clicks and scratchings on the black silk, they slow baked, itching with sandfly bites, in their windless tunnel among the leathery leaves, the mud welling between their legs and under their arms, black mud on black saturated clothes.

In mid-afternoon a whipping rain began. It fell on the leaves like gravel. It turned the mud into thick stout. It abolished all other sound. It hung like thick grey mosquito net between the hideout and the village. They had to shout to each other, yet were safe in the knowledge that their voices would not carry. But they didn't mind the rain. It refreshed them, even cleaned them. They drank from cupped hands under streaming leaves, and were able to conserve their own water-supply. They even shaved.

Wet, but more cheerful now, they left the mangroves early, with the tide, as lights flickered among the huts on the little island, as the voice of a woman singing seemed to cool the steamy evening air.

Before midnight they were out of Bulan Strait, and two hours later, and with the glare of Singapore's lights in the sky north of them, for they were much too low on the water to see the direct lights, they waded ashore, after a reconnaissance by Davidson and Falls, along a mudspit to land on Dongas Island, just off the north-west coast of the big island of Batam.

It was 23rd September—twenty-one days and two thousand miles since leaving Exmouth Gulf, forty-five days since leaving Cairns—and their target, the harbour of Singapore, was only eight miles away.

In the morning the black raiders found they had come ashore at the island's only real landing place, a strip of beach, at the head of a miniature inlet, backed by jungle, and behind that a sand clearing on the edge of a mangrove swamp. The cover was good, and into it they carried the canoes and supplies and established their camp.

Lyon and Davidson had in Australia selected Dongas as Jaywick's forward O.P. and attack base. It was small, mostly jungle-covered, had water and was, on all information available, uninhabited. It was also high enough—this was a deciding point—to give the attackers an uninterrupted view into Singapore Harbour, though still, at about eight miles, a long-range view.

Davidson, after they landed, had searched the immediate camp area, but at first light he disappeared again to return with the news that they were alone on the island and that, so far as he could see, no one had been there recently. This was welcome information since it strongly suggested that even Malay fishermen did not use the island. Davidson then led the others round the swamp to high ground where, among jungle cover, they could see over the tops of trees across to Singapore.

This was the moment they had been waiting for, but for Huston, Falls and Jones their first sight of the big base lacked the impact they had expected. They were excited, but Singapore, behind her gauze of distance across the flickering water, was remote and almost meaningless, just another distant island among weeks of islands, almost an anti-climax after having come so far. After two thousand miles, more than half of them through enemy-controlled water, it lacked personal association or memory beyond a name on a map, a city of surrender, a lost division. It was there, to be attacked because it was there, and only in the thought of attack was this moment significant to these three as they gazed across the strait through the leaves of Dongas.

"Just another island," Huston said.

"And a lot more bloody paddling," Falls added.

But to the others, and particularly Lyon and Davidson, the first sight of Singapore was an emotional catharsis—the past and the present rushing to meet each other across eight miles of sea, nineteen months of waiting. Across there was part of their lives—familiarity, friends, children born, gunfire, defeat, humiliation. Across there was the climax of a wild idea, parturition of defeat and death. There, too, was impossible attainment and pride regained and personal retribution—Lyon for a wife and child, Davidson for brothers, Page for a father.

The reticent Lyon could not stop talking. The talkative Davidson was unusually silent.

"Look, Donald—Fort Canning—the Cathay—the Swimming Club. . . ."

The familiar names spilt among the leaves as Lyon moved the long Army telescope, then brought it back to begin again, searching and finding the past with all its associations, pleasant and grim.

At last he handed the telescope to Davidson.

"Singapura—City of the Lion."

And laughed—a little hysterically.

Davidson traversed, along the low curving waterfront until the Johore coast jumped into vision, then back quickly to the Changi area where twelve thousand prisoners were less than fifteen miles away, then back to study Keppel Harbour, part of the Examination Anchorage, and finally the Roads opposite Singapore city.

"Ships everywhere . . . some big fellows . . . must be a hundred thousand tons just inviting us to call on them."

Davidson lifted the telescope again and the camouflaged oiltanks on Pulau Sambo, less than three miles from Dongas, slid into view.

"Plenty of activity there. We'll have to be damned careful not to show ourselves. Those tanks look only a few hundred yards away."

"Were those the lights we saw last night?" Jones inquired.

"Yes," Lyon said. "The oiltanks were one of Singapore's landmarks before the war. They were silver then."

"Why camouflage them?"

"The Japs play with camouflage like a kid plays with paint."

"Where's Changi?" Falls asked. "I knew a bloke in the Eighth Divvy."

Lyon pointed towards the end of the island, so far away that it was smudged haze.

"Poor bastards."

Back at the camp at last they cleaned the canoes and examined them to make sure they were not damaged, and then they sorted their supplies, equipment and explosives so that they could move quickly if evacuation was forced on them. Then, before posting sentries and sleeping, for all were tired, they stripped their stinking suits and hung them under the trees to dry and air. They loathed those suits, even though they had worn them only a few days, and yet, in one way, they were fortunate to have them, for the suits played an important part in helping them in their adjustment to each other under the close and exacting personal contact of the Jaywick raid.

A truism among canoemen is that your best friend can become your worst enemy if you paddle in the same canoe too long. A canoeman often becomes suspicious of the man in front or the man behind, and after hours or days of weary paddling suspicion develops and dislike begins. One man imagines that his partner is not paddling hard enough or is paddling inefficiently, and soon imagination becomes conviction and trouble starts.

But even under the most difficult conditions friction never developed among the Jaywick raiders because of the type of men they were, their sense of dedication, and the mutual admiration between officer and man, though, with the exception of Page, the relationship between the two was rigid, even on the raid. As Joe Jones once wrote: "The boys always referred to Davidson as Davo. Other than that we had no nicknames for the officers. It was very much an officers-and-ratings show. There was no such thing as calling an officer by his Christian name, as often happens with Army shows of this nature."

True, they were a small, highly skilled group facing a common enemy under the most dangerous conditions, but there is yet another explanation why the raid, apart from the reasons already given, was one of superb human co-operation without personal friction of any kind. The reason was the stinking suits, which became a source of hatred on which all could concentrate their discomfort, irritation, exhaustion and pain on this long and fearful journey through the dark.

The raiders slept that day and most of the next, but as they lay in their shorts or naked on their strips of canvas under the matted trees, two men on four-hour watches were always at the O.P. on the rise. There they watched Japanese shipping moving in and out of the port, watched for any sign of patrols.

They watched the courses steered by small ships and native boats for evidence of minefields—although they knew the port had controlled mine zones—and Japanese aircraft for reconnaissance over Singapore's immediate approaches.

The city had no blackout, not even a brownout. At night they could look past the lights of nearby Sambo right into Singapore, where headlights were clearly visible along Beach Road. But the harbour had no navigation lights, which seemed inconsistent with the glowing city behind, yet Japanese thinking often failed to blend, as soldiers who fought them found, with Western man's.

Not one sentry during those tensely tedious hours saw any searchlights, any evidence of sea or air reconnaissance, any evidence of port security. As Davidson remarked, after they had compared their observations, "The Nips don't seem to be taking any precautions. They probably feel pretty sure of themselves—and with a lot of reason."

That afternoon Ivan Lyon, who was with Huston, hurried back to camp at least an hour before the end of their watch. The others heard him coming, sweeping the vines aside as he ran, and wondered fearfully if it was an alert.

"Thirteen ships—all together in the Roads." He was panting and streaming with sweat. "Looks like a convoy getting ready to sail."

Davidson was on his feet. "What's the tonnage?"

"At a guess an average of five thousand—about sixty-five thousand. But three are tankers."

"That leaves us ten—three each and one to spare."

The others watched the big man's face, watched him thinking, assessing, making up his mind.

"The tide won't help us," he said, sticking out his chin. "But it seems too good to miss."

Lyon nodded. "We might not get them all together again."

Davidson jerked his head at Page. "Do you feel strong enough, Bob? Any more of that sickness?"

"No, only the gripes yesterday. I'm fine now."

"Right. Let's have a crack at them."

They called Huston and plastered the brown stain on their faces and hair and put on their black suits, grumbling at the smell, and at 8 p.m. they carried the canoes through the trees to the water, loaded the rusty limpets, tins of emergency supplies and waterbottles, and headed for Singapore, with the lights on the oil island of Sambo to port.

Now, because eye-level was only a few feet above the sea, they lost the direct lights of Singapore and did not begin to pick them up again until they were much closer to the outer Roads. But even then they could not see the ships because dark hulls and riding lights merged with the dark-light patchwork of the city background.

At midnight they were still more than two miles from the Roads and paddling with all their weight across-tide to keep the erratic canoes facing the target area when, from Fort Canning or the Cathay Building—they never knew which—a searchlight snapped on.

Slumped forward, faces turned away, they froze, knife-edged paddles slicing the water, and for half a minute, their brains and guts like ice lumps in sweating bodies, they waited, floating helpless in the glare, waited for discovery.

The light snapped out and from the three canoes came six hisses as the men, who had been holding their breaths, exhaled. But for another few minutes, as the tide pushed them east, they continued to freeze because of the danger that the light would come on again.

Then they began to paddle, but at 1 a.m. Davidson whistled his thin Burma bird-call signal and they came together.

"Hopeless," he said. "We can't do anything with this current. Make back independently."

Davidson-Falls and Page-Jones were back in camp at Dongas before daylight, but Lyon and Huston were missing.

All day the four waited. They couldn't sleep, couldn't keep still, but prowled aimlessly between lookout and camp. And in the afternoon it rained, a miserable cold rain, after an electric storm had rattled the island.

"I can't believe they've been picked up," Page insisted, the dye dripping out of his hair. "The Nips are much too quiet."

Then at dusk the missing two returned—exhausted, scarlet-eyed, staggering under the weight of their limpets.

"Where have you been? What happened . . . what . . . ?"

Lyon waited for the questions to stop.

"We've been on Dongas," he said, with a frail grin.

"On Dongas . . . here?"

He slumped onto one of the limpets and wiped the rain out of his eyes. "We got lost. We landed only a few hundred yards from here, and didn't know it was Dongas. The island looked different in the dark. We spent the day in the swamp."

Huston looked almost old. "We only found out a little while back. Then I crawled out of the mangroves and picked our original landing place."

"You both look all-in," Davidson said. "Did you get any sleep?"

"A bit," Huston said.

"Good—because we must move tonight."

"Tonight," Huston began.

His eyes appealed to the silent Lyon.

"Sorry," Davidson said, "but with the tide as she is Dongas

117

is no place to attack from. We must find another island further west."

Six silent, grim-faced men ate, hid their supplies in an eroded gully in the jungle, and carried their operational gear and food to the beach.

The night came tearfully, and later it was black and wind-swept with angry splashes of rain when they began to paddle, past the lights of Pulau Sambo, past Belakang Padang, through islands only a little blacker than the night. Then the wind dropped and the clouds thinned and the sea smelt of weed mixed with garlic.

Arms ached, backs ached, as they forced the canoes against the tide-race between the islands. A boil on Davidson's bottom stabbed and throbbed. A blister on Huston's left hand burst and stung as though acid had been poured on it. Only the strongest, Davidson, did not reach the point that night when the body worked only under the lash of the mind.

Near dawn they found arid Subar Island in the mist, seven miles west of Dongas, and landed on shingle at the foot of fallen boulders. But this was no hiding place and they had to stagger and slip with their gear and then their canoes to the top of this tiny rocky island where, among scattered bushes and bracken, the only cover, they crudely camouflaged the canoes with leaves and rocks, then dropped and slept.

That morning, as the light of 26th September uncovered them, even Davidson, who kept first watch, had almost reached the stage where he no longer cared.

14

THE HEAT sprawled heavy and wet on Subar, and among the rocks too hot to touch the leaves of the sparse bushes were curled and rough like dried tea-leaves.

The heat on the windless, shadeless rock, above a sea flashing like aluminium strip, was so malevolent that by mid-morning sleep was impossible. The six stripped, draped their canvas groundsheets between rocks and bushes and, crawling naked beneath their shade, slow-broiled in the sweat of their stinking bodies.

They were hidden from the sea sixty feet below, where junks and ketches, proas and sampans, passed and re-passed in an endless regatta of brown sails; but they knew that a low-flying plane might see them—a chance they had to take—though none of them cared what happened that day; discovery could not be much worse than the heat and the thirst and the weariness like a weight on their bodies and on their spirits.

All that morning, as the heat-clouds climbed on the backs of other cloud way behind them over Rhio, way ahead of them over Singapore Island, the duty sentry lay between two rocks sweeping the sea right and left for signs of Japanese patrols, staring until his eyes ached and vision blurred and the target island only eight miles away retreated further into its blue haze.

North-west across Main Strait was misty Bukum Island and the Examination Anchorage among the scatter of islands, reefs and rocks which cover the south-west coast of Singapore Island. North, the island of Blakang Mati, a dim smudge against the land, covered Keppel Harbour and the docks, and past St John Island was Singapore Roads opposite the obscured city.

But not until mid-afternoon, when the cobweb of haze lifted —though it never cleared completely that day—was it possible to see Singapore Island with any clarity and to study the target areas and plot some of the shipping. For an hour Donald Davidson lay wedged among the rocks trying to make an appreciation of the numbers, size and position of ships in harbour. Lying there, traversing the long telescope, holding it rigid for minutes at a time until his arms ached, he knew that an unlucky flash from the glass, seen by a Japanese O.P. or one of the passing boats, might arouse suspicion and uncover them. But he also knew that at this stage of Jaywick, with attack only a few hours ahead, this risk had to be taken.

At last he snapped the telescope shut, crawled back to the others, and pulled a water-stained chart from his canoe and spread it on the ground.

"There's still so much haze it'll be easier to follow on this. Here we are—Subar. A bunch of ships are in the Roads— there, that area—probably the convoy we saw yesterday, but it's too far away to tell. There looks like a ship—a big one— right at the Tanjong Pagar end of Keppel Harbour—here, behind Blakang Mati. I can just see it around the end of the island. Now, the Examination Anchorage—this open space— has several ships in it, including a tanker I'm sure, and ships are at the wharves on Bukum—this island near the anchorage."

He looked up. "Is that clear?"

The Australians grunted. Lyon, who knew the harbour well, having sailed over it often before the war, lay with eyes closed, listening.

"Right. Now— this is the plan. Falls and I will take Keppel Harbour. There's a boom—I can just see what could be the old boom pylons—but if it's impossible to get inside or if the ships there are no good, then we'll go on to the Roads and piddle on the Nips there. Major Lyon and you, Huston, will attack anything you can get alongside in the Examination Anchorage, and Lieutenant Page and Jones will attack shipping at Pulau Bukum."

"What's the distance to Bukum?" Jones asked.

"About six miles—almost straight across from here."

"I'd paddle twenty to get away from this bastard of a rock," Huston said, and spat.

Davidson ran a dirty fingernail along the clear strait between Subar and Singapore.

"If it's anything like the other night there'll probably be a cross-current here—a nasty one. You'll have to allow for that. Otherwise you might be swept too far along."

Lyon opened his eyes and sat up, wearily running his fingers through his hair.

"It's the twenty-sixth today and our R.V. with the *Krait* is midnight October first-second, so we must attack tonight. . . . We haven't much time up our jumpers. I suggest that Lieutenant Davidson's canoe—the fastest of the three—tries to reach Pompong first to hold the *Krait* for the rest of us. Of course, it may not be necessary—but it's a precaution."

Page spat out the pebble he had been sucking and said, "That's a good idea. We could easily be pushed to get back in time."

Davidson waited. The others nodded. It was not really their decision.

"I was going to suggest something like that. You never know what fun and games any of us might strike getting away from here."

He folded the chart. "Then it's settled. Falls and I won't go back to Dongas. We'll move on tonight and hole up somewhere along the way."

"Good show," Lyon said, lying back and closing his eyes.

As the sun dropped towards the distant islands, towards far-off Sumatra, the withering heat of that day began to drain off Subar, though even at dusk Falls insisted the rocks were still hot enough to grill a steak, if anyone, as he said, was crazy enough to want to grill a steak on Subar. But with the easing of the heat morale lifted and men, practically sleepless since the day before and now facing a night of action and days of paddling after that, started to prepare almost eagerly to leave their island hiding place. With their last tins of canned heat they boiled more billies of tea and ate their last meal of meat, limp chocolate and vitamin pills, and scratched holes for the empty tins among the still hot rocks. They had started packing their gear, just as the sun disappeared, when they heard a plane approaching and dropped where they were, faces to the earth, as a Japanese army transport—the only plane near Subar since daylight—spluttered over with engines throttling back, losing height as she made for one of the fields on Singapore Island.

"I'll bet anyone a quid they never even looked at us," Page said, waving the razor he had begun to dry-shave with just before the plane appeared. "If that Jap pilot was anything like ours all he was thinking of was an iced tankard of saki."

Lyon looked up from the bag he was packing. "Anyone who mentions iced tankards again will go on a charge."

In the quickening dusk they pulled on their black suits, slapped more brown stain on their faces and hair, and prepared to leave the little island. Down through the tumbled rocks, to the shingle on the eastern side, they first carried the heavy limpets and the emergency supplies and water, and then fetched the long canoes and put them into the sea and loaded them and rested.

Now that the attack was about to start, from inside the enemy harbour, within less than ten miles of Japanese headquarters itself, they were almost light-hearted as they waited restlessly for the first stars, not conscious any more that they needed sleep or that their bodies, after a journey of two thousand miles to achieve the "impossible", to fulfil the "wild idea" of one man, could not be driven much further.

"Time to go," Davidson said at last, and in that moment, like a thin chill cry within, was fear, and then it was smothered by a muttered curse as someone slipped on a stone, the dull thump of a canoe bow on rock, a faint splash, the dark movement and never-to-be-forgotten finality of attack beginning.

Davidson and Falls, who had decided to leave earlier because they would have to paddle farther than the others during the night, got into their canoe, settled their legs and nervously checked their gear. Then, as hands fumbled for hands in the dark and faceless voices called good luck, paddles swirled and they were gone.

Twenty minutes later the two other teams pushed off from Subar and headed in across the black water under a moonless sky for the lights of Singapore.

"Down!" the leaders whispered as the searchlight beam splashed into the sea to port.

Way forward in their seats, their faces almost on the rubber decking, the two teams froze as the light played with the water, then edged towards them, yard by yard with awful logic as though it knew they were there.

Jones, in front of Page, sideways watched the creeping glare and saw the sea flowing across his vision like melted silver, and wanted to be sick. Nearer the light came and Lyon, in the other canoe, his body folded into pain, his eyes watering with the strain, pleaded "Not now, not now," over and over again in a monotonous voiceless chant.

The searchlight leapt skyward, up and up, then down, down to fall into the sea to starboard, and around them the water was acres of dazzling white light and in it they floated, black and motionless, like drifting logs.

Jones began to count, a gabble of sounds divorced from time: "Eleven, twelve, thirteen"—like a bell in his brain—"thirty-one, thirty-two" . . . on and on . . . "sixty, sixty-one, sixty-two, sixty-three. . . . "

The light went out.

Paddles snatched at the sea. The canoes slid forward, faster and faster. . . . A hundred, two hundred yards, three hundred. . . .

The light snapped on again, to fall where they had been, to follow the same inexorable pattern—down, forward, up in the air and over as though the men on the light had orders to jump some object, a ship perhaps, in the harbour. But this time the canoemen, drifting stilled in the twilight edge of the glare, knew they could not be seen.

Subar was five miles and two hours away, back across the currents sweeping Main Strait, and now, at 10 p.m., and about a mile from their target areas, the two teams stopped again to prepare for their separate attacks. As the black canoes lay together the teams arranged their limpets in their groups of three and set the fuses for explosion at five o'clock the next morning—a seven-hour delay. Each limpet also had a one-minute delay fuse, and the agreement was to press this fuse, if discovered fixing the limpets, and to paddle at top speed away from the ship before the charge or charges exploded. This fuse, for use only in extreme emergency, was designed to give the attacker at least a chance to get away and to be a warning signal to the others.

When the teams were ready they gripped hands across the water and separated, Lyon and Huston moving on towards the Examination Anchorage, and Page and Jones swinging left and heading for Bukum Island.

The lights along Bukum wharves wallowed and glittered in the water as Page and Jones slowly approached the island and stopped. They were no longer in the dark, for the sea around them now glowed with reflected light like a polished floor.

"Aren't we a bit close?" Jones whispered.

"For God's sake keep your voice down. . . . No, they're looking from light into dark."

Even Page's whisper seemed dangerously loud to Jones, who realized then, and later, that the most difficult thing at night and when under tension is to whisper quietly.

Page signalled with his right hand, and silently the paddles dipped and feathered, dipped and feathered, the water slicing down their shaved edges as they moved parallel to the wharves.

Then they stopped again in the thick salty twilight, conscious of the sweat trickling out of their hair and the heat inside their suits and their sweat-sodden backsides on the hard seats.

Opposite, where the Arabic calligraphy of the numbered wharves was white on black, a 5000-ton freighter was high in the water and obviously empty, and next to her was a small coastal-type ship with a long barge moored under her stern, and farther along a big low-riding tanker with red markings like mah-jongg symbols on her black stack.

As they watched, light spluttered violet-blue and illuminated one end of the barge and the wharf piles high above the barge.

"Welders," Page said, and again Jones noticed how unnaturally loud the whisper sounded in the still air close to the water.

They moved closer, narrowing the gap between them and the wharves, so that they could now hear the cries of working men above the grumble of winches.

"Target, freighter," Bob Page said, after another interval of watching. "Make for the middle—the darkest part."

Page aimed the canoe and they dipped together and headed in, from twilight to half-light into full glow, half-expecting any second to hear shouts of discovery, a rifle shot, the stutter of automatics. Then they were in the freighter's shadow, up against her bulging belly, and for a minute or more they held the canoe with their paddles against the tide while their eyes adjusted to the dark and they could see clearly the black wall of the ship beside them.

Now Jones felt between his knees for the metal holdfast and eased the small magnetized frame onto the side of the ship, being careful not to let the magnets clang as they gripped. Then, as he held the holdfast cord with one hand to keep the bow of the canoe close to the ship, he pushed against the side to force the canoe's stern away from the ship as Page fitted the broomstick into the hole in the top of the first limpet, put the limpet over the side, reached down and, four feet under the water, eased the magnetized limpet onto the freighter.

As Page worked the broomstick out of the attached limpet, Jones released the holdfast, grabbed his paddle lying on the canoe's decking, and controlled the backward drift of the canoe as Page fed out the white cordtex, attached to the limpet, until the next position was reached. There the long-practised routine was repeated, and with the second limpet attached they again drifted along the side, Page feeding out the cordtex until the third position was reached.

At last all three limpets were fixed—the first on the engine-room, the others on the two holds, and all linked by the white cordtex and set so that the combined thirty pounds of plastic explosive would explode at 5 a.m.

As Jones released the holdfast for the third time he nearly dropped it into the sea, his hands were trembling so violently, and his mouth was so dry that his tongue seemed too big for his mouth and upholstered with hard scale. Yet he was astonished to realize how alert he was and how physically alive he felt at this moment, as though every nerve, every muscle, every blood-vessel was functioning with perfection.

Paddles out now, they moved the canoe along the ship and under the flare of her bows and hung onto the rusty anchor chain and rested there. They were in the shadow of the wharf and only ten feet from the barge on which men were working at the other end among an argument of escaping steam and the violet crackling from the welder's torch, and above on the wharf itself Japanese, Chinese and Indians gabbled and shouted as they trundled cargo.

Page and Jones, more confident now after successfully limpeting their first kill, were holding the canoe against the anchor chain and eating a well-earned supper of limp chocolate when some primitive sense of danger warned them simultaneously. Cautiously they lifted their eyes to the wharf glow above them and froze.

Directly above them, and standing almost on the edge, was a Japanese sentry with slung rifle, his face under his peaked cap bisected by shadow. He stood there for several minutes, like a photograph, looking out to sea, then he cleared his throat, searched deep for the phlegm, and spat. The gob slapped the water beside the canoe as he eased the weight of the rifle on his shoulder and turned and strolled along the wharf.

Page touched Jones with his paddle. In went the blades and soundlessly they glided out from the anchor chain, waiting in the shadow of the barge for the sentry to move well down the wharf before paddling across the lighted area and into the welcome dark as sparks from the welder, working at the stern of the small ship, sprayed like a bunger fuse on Guy Fawkes night.

"I'm glad we're out of that," Page whispered.

"Me, too. I didn't feel a bit brave."

Jones opened a packet of chewing gum and handed a pellet back, as they rested, deciding what next to do, drifting. Then, well away from the wharf, which held no other worthwhile targets except the tanker—and tankers are hard to sink with limpets because of their many compartments—they saw the lights of another ship to seaward and let the drift take the canoe towards her. They had spent more than an hour on the first attack. Now two more had to be completed.

The classic approach for a limpet attack is to drift with the tide towards a ship's bows so as to be masked by their height and flare, but as Page and Jones approached their second target in what they guessed was nearly a five-knot race the glare from the lights on Bukum was just sufficient to dull-polish her port side, and they were about to head to starboard when they noticed what looked like some of her crew leaning on the starboard rail. They were not sure that the group was not part of her structure, but the burst of a cigarette confirmed their suspicion a few seconds later and the canoemen continued on and soon were alongside where Page back-watered as Jones tried to clamp the holdfast, failed, and got it on at the second attempt.

Their target was a big modern ship with three sets of goal-post masts, engine aft, and so low in the water with cargo that the attackers felt certain she had moved only that afternoon from the Bukum wharf. But there was too much reflected light on her side and on her port water for safety, and the two Australians worked as quickly as they could in the dangerous glow.

The first limpet went on, with a soft water-muffled clang, in line with her bridge, and the other two limpets were fixed to her aft holds. Then Jones had the holdfast off and they slid aft with the tide and away from her to be caught in a new and slower rip flowing eastward which took them, almost before they realized it, towards another ship like a smudge across the faint outer glow from Bukum.

They soon saw, however, that the rip was swinging them away from her, and began to paddle hard across the current until they could let the canoe sweep under her stern. They came in so quickly that they bumped her rudder and hung on, panting, fearful that the noise had been heard, while the current gargled and the water heaped up along one side of the tilting canoe.

This ship was an ancient, heavily loaded tramp, and so rusty that when they got against her the holdfast magnets would not grip on the sheets of flaking rust. She stank of rotten weed and acid and salt as Jones tore off enough of the corrosion to get the holdfast to grip. But their problems had only just started, for Page had to reach deep into the water to tear at the ship's plates with his nails to clear spaces for the limpets, for even their magnets, which were more powerful than those on the holdfast, would not at first grip on the flaking surface. This was difficult and painful work, and dangerous, too, because the scratching against the ship's side might attract attention. But at last they were away, sliding down the dark with one of the lights of the limpeted tramp receding and disappearing like the tail-lamp of a departing train at the end of a long platform.

The glow from Bukum was a mile away when they stopped and Page bent forward and tapped his partner on the shoulder with his paddle.

"Thanks, Joe," he said.

"Thanks, Bob."

Jones lifted the holdfast overboard and let it go without a splash. He reached for the spare holdfast and dropped it over, too, as Page ditched the spare limpet, for there was no more need for them now. They were just extra weight now the attack was completed.

And then, slumped in their sweat, they were both so violently tired they never wanted to move again—a frightening, sick sort of weariness that seemed to drain their bodies of all energy and wrap their brains in heavy wet cloth.

For minutes, as the canoe drifted on the dark sea, they did not stir. Then almost imperceptibly they recovered and a cool singing elation swept their dragging weariness away.

"We've done it," Page whispered hoarsely. "Joe, we've done it."

Slowly they began to paddle towards Dongas.

It was nearly 2 a.m. on 27th September.

And only when they were half-way back did Jones realize that two huge saltwater boils had developed on his right knee and that they were throbbing.

Lyon and Huston, after separating from Page and Jones a mile from Bukum Island, went on into the Examination Anchorage where they thought they would have no difficulty locating and limpeting targets observed by Davidson that afternoon from Subar.

But they were soon disillusioned, for whereas the lights on Bukum had been both a danger and an advantage to Page's canoe, the blackness of the anchorage and the shoreline hills behind the western end of Keppel Harbour made their approach extremely confusing and difficult.

Ships were in the anchorage. They knew that. But from almost sea-level the attackers could not see them against the coast of Singapore Island, and they could not tell in the dark, with distances almost impossible to judge, whether the lights they did observe were on ships or on the island itself.

Lyon and Huston paddled around, stopping every few minutes to observe and listen, but an hour passed and they had still failed to find a ship. They moved towards one light for nearly ten minutes before they realized that it did not seem to be getting any closer and that it must be on the island.

For nearly two hours they searched, disheartened and worried, before Lyon saw a red light in the direction of Blakang Mati Island, and guessed that it was one of the tankers seen from Subar.

He whispered, "Red four-five. If it's a tanker we'll put all the limpets on her and make sure."

"Right, sir."

They moved towards the red light and soon picked up the muddy silhouette of a tanker against the soft glow of the city behind Blakang Mati. Slowly they circled, noting with excitement how low she was in the water, then edged forward and came in under her stern where, covered even from the starlight, they were in almost total darkness.

Working cautiously along her port side, for they could hear voices, and even distinct words, on deck, they put their first set of three limpets on her engine-room plates. Then they moved astern, slung another set of three around her propeller, and Lyon was about to put on the last of the third set of three on the starboard side of the engine-room when he felt that he was being watched and looked up.

Not ten feet above them a man, his head out of a porthole, was looking down on them, the lighter patch of his face clear against the blackness of the ship's side and the night sky.

Huston, who was gripping the holdfast cord and holding the canoe's stern away from the tanker so that Lyon could apply the last limpet, sensed from Lyon's sudden stillness that something was wrong and was about to whisper when the man above sniffed.

Not daring to move, hardly breathing, they waited for a challenge, for the general alarm that would inevitably follow, for the searchlights which would begin their thin cold probing. But for minutes all they heard was the soft slapping of the sea against the tanker's side, shrill voices high above them on deck, muffled sunken sounds deep inside the ship like far-off wind instruments.

The man above had a cold, for he sniffed wetly several times and cleared his throat, but he still didn't move and Lyon crouched almost in the sea, wondered if he would have time to fix the limpet, which he had in his lap, and to press the one-minute fuse if they were discovered. He was still wondering when the man withdrew his head and a few seconds later the raiders heard a faint click as a cabin light was switched on and a thin pipe of light came from the porthole. Now they waited for the man to return, for a torch to stab at them, for a shout in Japanese, and the muscles of Huston's neck were tight cords with waiting. Then, with new hope, he thought: he must be going to bed. Then he felt Lyon move as with infinite care the leader fitted the broomstick into the limpet, put the limpet overboard, and down into the water and slid it gently, without a sound, onto the tanker's plates.

Huston waited tensely as Lyon eased out the stick, then he released the holdfast and the current swept them along the tanker and away.

"Do you reckon he saw us?" Huston asked, when they were out of range.

"If he did he probably thought we were a fishing canoe."

Huston wiped his face with his sleeve. "I'm glad we've used all the limpets," was all he said.

They turned seaward—for Dongas.

Davidson and Falls, who had left Subar before the other canoes, paddled hard across the tide and were past The Sisters and through between the islands of Tekukor and Blakang Mati by a little after 9 p.m.

They rested for five minutes, as a searchlight measured the sky, before diving deep among the shadows along Blakang Mati—where the barracks of the British fortress island were now lighted by the Japanese—and moving along the channel towards where the boom pylons at the Tanjong Pagar end of Keppel Harbour were visible against the city glare.

They were moving easily, almost enjoying the rhythmic thrust of the long thin bow, when Davidson, whose night vision was uncanny, saw a light and realized it was moving towards them. At first he could not guess its distance or speed, then with alarm he knew they were in danger of being run down.

"Go for your life," he called, as he dug to swing the canoe, and together their paddles gripped the water to force her closer to the island. And then, as the light seemed to gather speed and rush at them, they worked frantically, and the light was on them and beside them as a big steam ferry thumped past not ten feet away and went on into the night trailing ribbons of sparks from her spatular funnel.

"My word," Falls said, "that was close."

They seesawed in the wash, the water splashing over them, and then they were clear and paddling on to the boom.

Now they stopped at one of the rusting buoys and sat forward, tense and watchful, feeling for danger with their eyes, their ears, their skin, testing the air weighted with suspicion.

They could see no boom-defence vessel, no boom patrol of any kind. Crouched, still they let the canoe drift out so that the buoys were no longer close together like big onyx beads but strung in a long line, an etching of separated darkness on darkness. Now they could see that the boom gate was open, that the way was clear and apparently unguarded.

"Looks clear," Davidson whispered.

But Falls heard the words so clearly that he hissed a warning.

"What's wrong?"

"Too loud."

"Balls."

Cautiously they moved back and then along the boom, like two black cats along a wall, yard by yard until they reached the entrance. They waited there, a minute, two, straining the dark. Then they turned the corner and drifted through—a long thin shadow.

They were inside Keppel Harbour, and then they heard singing, high, clear and close in the still night air, with shouts like inverted commas reaching above the voices.

"Our friends beating it up at the Yacht Club," Davidson whispered.

The Yacht Club meant nothing to Falls—except that Japanese, enemies, were noisy, enjoying themselves, and dangerously close, and that he would much prefer to be thousands of miles away, safe at home.

The raiders moved across to the east wharf where there were two small ships not worth limpeting, and then went under the wharf so that they could examine the harbour in safety. But the decking dripped monotonously on their heads and down their necks, and the piles wallowing in the restless water trailed gardens of weeds which stank, and they came out again and went on, searching for targets.

The long main wharf was empty, but by keeping in its shadow they reached the entrance to the Empire Dock and saw ships inside and the masts and funnels of others and heard the nattering of winches, but the whole area was floodlit and active and Davidson decided they were wasting time.

As they turned an ocean-going tug came down harbour, so they waited before following her out, and as they paddled through the boom and headed for the Outer Roads the party at the Yacht Club had reached the shouting stage.

There were ships—plenty of them—in the Roads off the business heart of Singapore. Davidson and Falls could see their blurred shapes as they approached, though they also noticed that reflected light from the glowing city, over which the smoke from Chinatown was drifting like fog, made attack, except on the seaward side, dangerous. As they came closer a sampan went by, but the man paddling with a stern sweep did not see them, even though they were not a dozen yards away, and the lights of a car or truck crept along Collyer Quay past Clifford Pier and the brilliantly lighted Fullerton Building and disappeared as the vehicle swung to cross the bridge over the Singapore River.

A clock ashore chimed the quarter-hour—a chill and lonely

sound to the men in the canoe—as they selected their first victim, a heavily laden freighter, and drifted under her bow and along the side to the engine-room.

Now it was almost slack water, and Falls had no trouble clamping the holdfast; but as he held the canoe steady and pushed against the side, he wondered why Davidson, generally so expert, took so long to fix the first limpet, and cursed at the delay when he knew that one glance from a sailor, having a final cigarette, might discover them. His impatience increased when he saw that, although the ship shielded them from the lights of the city, the Roads were not completely dark, and even in the seaward shadow of the ship reflected light from the sky made the water like oiled copper.

The first limpet took so long to go on that Falls, who knew that speed under these conditions was vital, gave a sigh of relief when the signal came to release the holdfast and move to the second limpet position and then the third. But not until they had attacked their second ship and had reached the third did he know what had caused the long delay.

Ashore the Victoria Hall clock called 1 a.m. as they made a stern approach to their third victim, another engine-aft freighter, but this ship was showing so many strong lights aft that even under the gloom of her counter the reflection from the water polished their faces like the light from a fire at night.

Two limpets were on and Davidson was about to fix the third when Falls glanced over his shoulder and nearly dropped the holdfast cord.

Davidson, his face glistening with sweat, his mouth like pliers as he pushed the broomstick into the top of the limpet, was wearing a monocle.

So that was the reason, Falls thought, as he gaped back at his companion.

And it was, for as Falls had waited, cursing, for Davidson to fix the first limpet on the first ship, Davidson, with a limpet resting on his knees, had fumbled in one of the zip breast pockets of his suit, and had crossed to search the other pocket until he found his monocle. Then he had screwed it into his eye, and had slipped its cord, made from finely plaited fishing line and blackened with boot polish, over his head. And only then was he ready to attack.

Now, as the holdfast came off the last ship and the tide took them along her side and away from her lights, Falls, who knew that Davidson's eyes were perfect—better than his own— and that he did not need glasses and never usually wore a monocle, didn't know whether to laugh or to hit Davidson over the head with his paddle.

First daylight was leaking into the sky that morning of 27th September when Page and Jones grounded on the bent beach of Dongas at 4.45 a.m. After ten hours in the canoe their backs ached, their necks were stiff, their legs felt like plasticine, so that when they got out they collapsed in the shallow water and had to drag themselves onto the sand with their hands.

Lyon and Huston, who had reached the hideout island half an hour before and who, though exhausted, had been able to recover a little from their all-night paddle, hobbled to their aid. They massaged their legs and backs and then, as they pulled up the canoe and unloaded her, pumped questions at the two men on the sand.

"How many did you get?" Lyon demanded.

"Three," Page said, groaning at the pain in his back as he tried to ease cramped muscles.

"Good show. We put all ours on a tanker—couldn't find any others."

"That should burn up some of their precious oil."

As Page began to knead his leg muscles, feeling them tingle as the circulation slowly returned, Lyon asked, "Did you hear an explosion—dull as if it was under water?"

"Yes—not long after we'd started back." It was Jones, who had managed to stand, but who swayed on still numb legs.

"We thought someone had pushed the tit," Huston said, rubbing Jones's legs. "Gave me a touch of 'em."

Page looked up. "You don't think it was Donald?"

"I'm sure it wasn't." Lyon said quickly. "There was no alarm. . . . If he got three we should have seven kills."

"We'll soon know," Jones said, and even his voice was tired. Page could stand now, though unsteadily. Slowly he exercised.

"What's the time?" he asked.

"Time those limpets were going off," Lyon said. "We'd better get up to the grandstand."

They staggered to the camp with the canoe, and, still tottering, and snatching at vines for support, half-scrambled, half-pulled themselves up to the O.P. on the rise.

Although the light was growing, the lights on Sambo were still strong and the sky glow from Singapore like a false dawn. They waited, but only a few minutes, just time enough for the sea below the O.P. to push aside the gloom and emerge —like dark grey linoleum. Then from across the strait came a dull dry explosion like a distant bomb-burst as the combined flash of thirty pounds of plastic explosive smashed the plates of Jaywick's first victim.

"Thar she blows," Page said, sitting up and wincing with the pain in his back.

Huston punched Jones. "You beaut—you bloody beaut."

Lyon shaded his torch and looked at his watch.

"Five fifteen. . . . Not bad."

They waited, staring into the half-light, waited five minutes, six minutes, before the second explosion, much louder than the first, seemed to roll across the water, reach them and roll on behind them across little Dongas and fall into the sea.

And as the sound was lost the lights of both Singapore and nearby Sambo blacked out, and in their place a ship's siren, faint and plaintive, began to wail like a bird in a fog.

"Two," Lyon said.

"And now they're worried," Page added.

In the next twenty minutes they heard five more explosions, two close together. But that was all.

"Seven," Lyon said. "What was your tonnage, Bob?"

"Hard to tell. Between fifteen and twenty thousand."

"With our ten-thousand-ton tanker that gives us, perhaps, thirty thousand, and with another twenty thousand from Donald we should have fifty thousand."

"And that's a lot of ships and cargo the Nips can kiss their arses to," said Huston.

Jones yawned and rubbed his eyes.

"What I'd call a decent night's work."

He yawned again. "I could sleep for a month."

(They didn't know it then, but figures later released gave Jaywick seven ships sunk or badly damaged, including the 10,000-ton tanker *Sinkoku Maru*—a total of between 36,843 and 39,111 tons.)

Now it was daylight and as the young sun spilt into Singapore Harbour Lyon could just see, through his telescope, a ship near Bukum Island with her bows high in the air before black smoke, vomiting from the burning tanker, covered the Bukum Anchorage area and spread like a stain along the waterfront. But before it reached the Outer Roads opposite the city, and blacked out Singapore to the raiders, he could see many ships, including tankers, leaving the target areas and cruising aimlessly, and all could hear the ceaseless crying of their sirens.

The great raid had been successful, but the raiders were too exhausted to appreciate their victory. In the sixty hours since the afternoon of 24th September, when they had made their first attempt to raid the Japanese convoy from Dongas, they had slept little and in that time had paddled between forty and fifty miles in Singapore waters.

Only Lyon, as he shut his telescope, seemed to feel excitement he could not control. Although even behind his brown stain disguise he looked thin and ill, and nearer to collapse than anyone else, he could not stop talking, and his bloodshot eyes glittered unnaturally in his dark face as he shook hands with his companions.

It was Jones who brought Lyon, brought them all, back to reality when he pointed across the strait and said calmly, "And here they come."

Far away and high they could all see the speck over Singapore Island. It was 6.30 a.m. and the first Japanese Army plane was up.

The search had begun.

Twelve planes were in the air all that day. Most of the morning they searched west of Singapore for the "submarines" which had attacked across the Indian Ocean from the British Eastern Fleet's base at Trincomalee in Ceylon and through Malacca Strait between Malaya and Sumatra. Only in the late morning and in the afternoon did the planes switch their search to the east and south, and then they patterned the islands and narrow waterways of the Rhio Archipelago, the China Sea and way south to Sunda Strait, between Sumatra and Java.

But out of the tanker smoke, too, which covered the harbour of Singapore, came naval patrol boats and fast sampans to make a day-long sea search which passed Dongas many times and continued until dark, while small low-flying float planes skimmed the islands covering Singapore.

"Carse was right," Page said, as they watched the first enemy plane. "The green ants will soon be running all over the nest."

By 8 a.m., when the first naval patrol boat had been sighted, or something which looked suspiciously like one, Lyon decided to move from their camp near the beach because of the danger that the systematic Japanese might come ashore on Dongas. And so, while Jones remained on guard at the O.P., the others moved canoes and supplies down into the mangrove swamp, and, as carefully as possible, smoothed away the more obvious signs, like footprints, of their occupation.

In the swamp they lay in the evil ooze and tried to sleep, but now that they were no longer the hunters but the hunted, sleep would not come. Their bodies cried for rest, but their brains, their instincts, would not let them. They dozed and woke, dozed and woke, conscious of the searching engines above them and on the sea around them, knowing that at any hour, any minute, the Japanese might land to search Dongas and that they would have to fight and certainly die.

Hour after hour as they listened to the search, lying in their bath of mud and sweat, trying to sleep and failing, trying to ease the pains of their bodies, they knew with fear that only the leaves which hid them were not enemy.

And all the time, beyond their immediate discomfort and

weariness and fear, was the added knowledge and added fear, whittling at them; that they still had at least fifty perilous miles to paddle through alerted waters and that they might not have the strength to reach the *Krait*—if the *Krait* had not already been captured or blown up—if the *Krait* still existed to rescue them.

This was their worst fear, that having come so far and achieved so much, they still had only a doubtful chance of survival.

All that day, as sentry followed sentry at the lonely watch on the hill, the men on Dongas slept little and thought a lot, listening, even in their half-sleep, to the voices of the engines, jerking upright as a plane came near or a boat passed, sinking back as the voices receded.

Three times motor sampans were near the island, and twice floatplanes, their angry wing-circles flaming like little suns, roared over the island, just above the trees.

Shortly before sunset Page scrambled down from the O.P. to report a grey naval patrol boat approaching and travelling suspiciously slowly. Then he climbed back to the hill to watch through the leaves, his heart pounding, as she passed along the island, not fifty yards from their landing beach, her powerful engines throttled back, an officer in white near the stern examining the island through glasses.

At dusk the black raiders, mud-covered and stiff, came out of the swamp and prepared to move. They were still weary, but they had at least rested, and now, as though nature had decided to help them, they were alert as spiders and their despondency and fears had left them.

As Page remarked, almost brightly, while they shaved: "So far so good. Thank God nothing is ever as bad as you imagine it to be."

They made tea and ate their first meal of the day, and then with supplies waiting hidden at Pandjang Island, their rear base, they sank in the swamp any food and water-cans they did not need so that the canoes would be almost empty for the paddle back first to Pandjang and finally to Pompong Island.

In that black evening of 27th September, twenty-four hours since they began their attack from Subar, they launched the canoes and headed towards Bulan Strait, the way they had come.

Their R.V. with the *Krait* at Pompong Island was midnight on 1st-2nd October.

As Lyon and Huston, Page and Jones were preparing to leave Dongas, Davidson and Falls had already quit their hiding place in the mangroves seven miles away on the north coast of the island of Batam, and were making towards the entrance to Rhio Strait, which separates Batam and Bintang islands, and about seventeen miles from Singapore.

After their attack on the ships in the Roads, Davidson had decided to get as far away as they could from Singapore that night, and to continue their escape through Rhio Strait, which, though more used by shipping, was much wider than Bulan Strait and therefore more difficult for the Japanese to patrol.

Davidson and Falls had also heard the exploding limpets, though they had counted only six explosions, had seen the far-off smoke of the burning tanker, and had been just as aware as the four on Dongas of the Japanese search, as they lay among the mangroves of Batam Island waiting for the covering dark.

When it came the two gaunt unshaven men, who like the others had slept little, began the hardest journey of their lives, for this was the evening of 27th September, and they had to reach Pompong Island by 1st-2nd October to hold the *Krait* for the others, a journey through waters controlled by the now alerted Japanese and a native population intimidated and afraid.

Moving only at night they circled northern Batam and came south through northern Rhio Strait, spending the first day on an island in the strait, and the next, after narrowly missing detection by a patrol, at the old camp on Pandjang Island. There, after their first good sleep for days, they filled their bottles with spring water and took a few packets of dry rations from the hidden supplies under the overhanging rocks. Davidson wrote a note on the back of a strip torn from a chart and left it, weighted with a rock, on top of the food packs.

"We are proceeding to R.V.," was all it said.

That night they slipped past the roving searchlight from the Japanese O.P. on Galang Island, but later were nearly swamped by a Sumatra which forced them to heave-to for two hours, frail bow thrashing the sea, before getting ashore on an island in Dempu Strait where they spent the day in the jungle near a native fishing village.

They finally reached Pompong Island, twenty-three hours before the R.V. with the *Krait*, at 1 a.m. on 1st October, more than three days after leaving their temporary hideout on Batam Island, and after thirty-three hours of paddling.

They had just enough strength to drag the canoe into the trees before falling beside it to sleep for the next fifteen hours.

Helped by the currents after leaving Dongas on 27th September, Lyon and Huston and Page and Jones reached the entrance to Bulan Strait in less than two hours, but half a mile inside the strait they almost crashed head-on into an anchored Japanese patrol boat which showed no lights and, fortunately, had no lookout. Page and Jones, who were leading, did not see her until they were a few yards away and had just time to swerve the canoe and drift past, so close they could have touched her with their paddles. Lyon and Huston, who were farther out in the stream, did not see her at all and did not stop.

They continued down Bulan Strait, but by midnight were so exhausted that they landed on southern Batam Island and, beyond a thin belt of mangroves, hid the canoes and themselves among trees on the slope of a low hill which in the morning proved to be an old Chinese cemetery, dotted with vault-like graves dug into the slope. They could not have found a safer place for, although they could see a village down the strait, nobody came near the cemetery.

They went on that night to reach their rear base at Otters' Bay on Pandjang Island early on 29th September, after fighting to keep afloat in a storm which nearly pushed them ashore on a rocky point outside the southern entrance to Bulan Strait.

At Pandjang, after finding Davidson's note, they bathed in the spring pool, ate, and slept most of the day and night, intending to move on the next night to Pompong Island, but on the afternoon of 30th September another violent storm, which blew for hours, delayed them. Huddled shivering under the streaming trees, they discussed what to do, and Lyon finally decided to miss the first R.V. with the *Krait* and to go on the following night to keep the second appointment. But in the sparkling dawn of 1st October he suddenly changed his mind—although he knew they still had two days in reserve—and made the most dangerous decision of the entire raid—to break their rules and risk a daylight passage between Pandjang and Pompong.

His reason for this decision was that he preferred to try to to make the first R.V. with the *Krait* at midnight on 1st-2nd October rather than expose the ship to yet another passage of Temiang Strait to keep the second and last pick-up forty-eight hours later; and although the others were scared of a daylight journey, and distrusted his desperate decision, they didn't dispute it.

With only fifteen hours to go to keep the first R.V., Page and Jones started for Pompong at 9 a.m., and Lyon and Huston followed an hour later. They used their blue silk sails at first, but had to take them down when the wind changed.

Although they had rested at Pandjang, days of poor food, little sleep, long hours cramped in canoes, and the strain of avoiding the enemy had almost destroyed their reserves of strength. They came close to collapse that day. Their backsides, covered with rashes from the friction of the sweat-soaked suits, stung and itched. Their eyes, attuned to night work and unaccustomed for nearly a fortnight to the water glare, were burnt so badly they could hardly keep them open. The water in the bottles became so hot they had to sip it like hot tea.

All day, against a slapping headwind, they paddled south-east, counting their strokes to give them the strength at the end on each slow dozen to go on and to paddle another dozen and another, concentrating on other things, on homes and families, on iced beer and the simple comfort of a bed, so that sometimes an hour would slide by without pain or the terrifying thought that the *Krait* might go without them. This ever-present fear, now they had evaded the enemy for so long, now they were so close to rescue, kept them going. The thought of detection became almost secondary to the thought of being left behind.

Keeping seaward of scattered Malay fishing canoes they passed the Japanese O.P. on Galang Island, hardly caring if they were discovered, though they were so low in the water that their canoes from a distance closely resembled those of the Malays and evidently aroused no suspicion. They fitted into the emerald seascape of those islands and channels so well that float planes from the Japanese base on Chempa Island were low over them twice during the day but showed no interest. Only once, when they rounded an island and skirted a group of fishing canoes, did dark heads turn and watch them knowing immediately, as they saw the long sleek canoes, that they were alien.

In the late afternoon, after eight hours of ceaseless paddling, Page and Jones pulled in to a beach where Lyon and Huston joined them soon afterwards. There, slumped on the damp sand, without moving, exposed to enemy eyes, they lay for an hour. And then they went on together, driving their bodies, close now to a numb sort of terror of missing the *Krait*, of being left behind.

On, on they paddled, their burnt eyes scarlet, their sunburned lips rimmed with white salt, their movements mechanical, their minds hardly functioning any more. On, on through the endless black night until at 3 a.m. the next morning, 2nd October, and eighteen hours after leaving Pandjang nearly thirty miles behind, they reached what they thought was the pick-up anchorage at Pompong Island.

But they couldn't find the *Krait* and, frantically now, they criss-crossed the anchorage, searching with near-blind eyes for the ship.

At last they could go no farther. They drifted in to a beach, fell into the shallow water and, crawling, staggering, falling, crawling, they dragged the canoes up the sand and dropped.

15

FOR TED CARSE and his crew of seven the fortnight after dropping the raiding party at Pandjang Island on 18th September was a time of ominous waiting, of mounting apprehension mingled with an illicit kind of boredom, for while the black raiders were stalking, attacking and retreating from Singapore, the other men of Jaywick were miles away, in the China Sea and among the islands off the Borneo coast, wondering, as day heaped on day, if they would ever see the others again, wondering, too, how long they themselves could continue to move about undetected.

True, they were not within sight of the enemy, as the raiders were, nor were they enduring any physical hardships except the strict confinement in the little *Krait* with its severe water rationing and declining food supplies. But they knew that at any moment they might be challenged or reported, and every man was aware that if they had to fight their chances of survival and escape were slender and that their extinction would mean the end of the raiding party.

They didn't dare stay in any one place for long, except at night, because of the danger of attracting attention, and so, day after day, the *Krait* moved on, an endless passage without destination, an aimless steaming which took them fifteen hundred miles among the islands off Borneo as they waited for news of the raid and for the time to once more cross the China Sea to pick up their comrades.

On 19th September, after dropping the raiders at Pandjang and heading east to the St Esprit Group, in the China Sea halfway between the Thousand Islands and Borneo, Carse wrote in his dye-stained log:

"Our present job reminds me very much of the anxious father waiting outside the maternity ward for news. The only difference is that his worries and anxiety pass, as a rule, with the arrival of his baby in a few hours or so, while ours is to drag on for a fortnight, and when the time comes we expect a lusty overgrown family of six."

Waiting was a theme repeated again and again by Carse in his log, and by Horrie Young in the diary he kept as he sat beside his radio in No. 3 hold during those days off Borneo—waiting and the lack of news, the lack of any sign, direct or indirect, from the enemy to reassure them or to warn them.

Carse entered this on 24th September: "This waiting about is the worst part of the trip so far. If we had an objective it would not be so bad, or if the weather was fine and we could work on the ship. *Krait's* bottom is getting very dirty—green weed about four inches long. If the raid is a success we are thinking of renaming the ship the *Singapore Terror*. . . .

"Our cook is certainly living up to his nickname of Pancake Andy. We get them at least once a day. When this cruise commenced pancakes were one of my favourites. But if I ever look at one again I'll be sick. Andy Crilley has done an excellent job—but oh, oh, for a loaf of bread and a good sirloin steak."

25th September: "No indication on the radio of any raid on Singapore. . . . This waiting is not easy. . . . News of the raid would be very welcome. . . . Everyone on board is pining for land. It is now 23 days since we set foot ashore."

26th September: "No news yet about Singapore. All the Japs seem to be doing is to try to impress their civilian population with the vast superiority of the Imperial Japanese Air Force and the vast numbers of men who will be needed to take their gains off them. No mention of Lae, Salamaua or Finschhafen. . . .

"Commenced scraping bottom at last. . . . After wearing sarongs for so long we will probably be arrested for indecent exposure when we get back. The loose sarongs I think are the main reason why none of us has contracted skin diseases. . . .

"It seems peculiar that we should be drifting around this part of the China Sea with men working in a dinghy alongside scraping *Krait's* bottom on a beautiful day just as if Mr Tojo had never been heard of."

27th September (afternoon after the raid when the Japanese were searching): "Leading Telegraphist Young picked up what appeared to be a recall signal to a flight of nine planes, each of which replied independently and then closed down. He reports that the lengthy construction of dots and dashes he heard was Japanese Navy code, and from the strength of the signals the planes were close to us. This recall might mean the Japs have caught the raiding party or have abandoned the search. We should certainly know when we make the rendezvous."

28th September: "Our black dye is running low. We have only enough left to paint ourselves twice more."

29th September: "Began to make back across the China Sea to keep the rendezvous. We don't know if we're walking into a trap."

30th September: "By tomorrow night we should know the fate of the raiding party—and our own fate, too."

Their long wait was nearly over.

"All weapons and grenades ready," Carse ordered as the *Krait* neared Temiang Strait in the afternoon of 1st October.

The sea was oil, after a storm which had delayed them, and, as they approached, Linga Peak, away to the south, changed from blue to pink-blue to black, deep-etched against the evening sky. Then its high edges blurred and spread as the light faded. Then the peak was gone.

"Half-speed," Carse called, and heard the order echoed to Paddy below as Cobber Cain, the skin behind his knees almost white through the faded stain, went forward to the lookout position in the bows.

Slowly they approached, out of the darkness of the China Sea, to make their third passage of Temiang.

The navigator's eyes had improved, helped by more sleep during the time of waiting, but the fluid-filled sinuses in his damaged elbows were worse and stabbed with pain every time he bent his arms. The fluid sacs were the size of duck eggs and their skin, which had resisted the last of the stain, was blue-white and polished. His elbows were nagging now as he stood at the wheel, but he hardly noticed the pain as he focused into the dark ahead wondering what would happen that night, thinking in a detached sort of way that he might not be alive in the morning, for only a few hours before Horrie Young had reported still no mention of the raid on Singapore or Tokyo Radio.

Had the raid gone in? Had it been successful? Did the silence mean that Lyon, Davidson and the others had been captured and that the Japs knew? Carse decided there were only two theories and only one certain answer. The raiders were at Pompong, waiting to be taken off, or the dark strait the *Krait* was penetrating was leading to a Japanese ambush. It was one of those two, but midnight 1st-2nd October was the R.V. and that R.V. must be kept.

They went past a kampong fire, and then another, flickers of human life in this world of water and islands under anchored stars, in a hot thick stagnant silence which made men lick their lips nervously and swallow too often and think too much. Throttled back they moved along the strait until, near midnight, Carse called softly, "We're getting close. Man all guns."

They nosed forward, aware only from the whispering of the exhaust that they were moving, and then as they came to the end of Temiang the navigator recognized the darker mass of Pompong Island and turned towards it.

It was 12.30 a.m. on 2nd October—half an hour late—when Cain soundlessly lowered the small anchor on its hemp hawser; but the current was so strong that the anchor wouldn't hold and Carse ordered the heavier one down.

As guns covered the beach—Cain with the Lewis, Crilley

and Berryman with Brens, the others with Stens and Owens—Carse had already decided that if the Japs were waiting for them it would not matter if he called in English.

"Ship ahoy," he hailed once, just loud enough for anyone on the beach to hear.

Then they waited, and in the silence stiff as calico Carse could hear someone near him breathing, or was it his own breathing, he didn't know. Dimly his eyes picked up the pointing weapons, the crouching shapes of the men, the faint glow from the beach sand.

"Look," Cain whispered.

A thin shadow against the beach seemed to be moving. It was moving. The trap could be closing.

"Don't fire unless you're fired on," Carse whispered.

The shadow appeared again. Then the watchers lost it. They strained for sound, but there was no sound.

Another minute passed.

Then every gun barrel swung as, without warning, Davidson slapped the gunwale and called, "It's good to be back."

"You bloody fool," Carse snapped at the dark shape as Davidson clambered aboard. "Why didn't you answer my hail?"

The big man laughed. "I wanted to see how well prepared you were."

"You wanted. . . . You're lucky you weren't drilled—and that would have finished everything."

"Sorry, Ted," Davidson apologized as he held the canoe steady for Falls.

Carse was still angry at Davidson's thoughtlessness as he listened to the noisy welcome which continued for the next ten minutes. He couldn't stop it, and Davidson did nothing to control the men. This is even crazier than Donald's action, he thought.

It's like a football club reunion. It's endangering everything. And where are the others? Why aren't they back?

"Everything went off well," Davidson was explaining. "We counted six explosions—three ours, I think. We saw a big oil fire, probably from the oil wharf at Bukum, but we were a long distance away."

He continued to describe the raid.

When the first clamour of their safe return was over, Davidson and Falls sat on the deck and drank mugs of Crilley's cocoa, but there was still far too much noise and at last Carse said, "If you don't all pipe down you won't be alive to pick up the others." And to Davidson he said, as the crew quietened, "Where *are* the others?"

"We haven't seen them since the night of the raid. But they'll be all right. We came ahead to hold the *Krait* for them. I left a message for them at Pandjang."

"How far were they behind you?"

"A day, perhaps—probably less."

"The major wasn't in very good shape," Falls reminded.

"That probably explains why they haven't reached Pompong," Carse said, his anger gone now as he realized that the noisy welcome had been like the blowing of a safety valve, a release after weeks of tension, and how glad he was to see Davidson and Falls, and how worried he was about the other four.

"I'll wait till dawn—just in case they turn up. It's too dangerous to muck around here."

"And then?" Davidson asked.

"They've still got forty-eight hours to make the second R.V. That should give them plenty of time if they're coming."

"They'll be back," Taffy Morris said, out of the dark, "I know the major."

"It might be a good idea, " Falls suggested, "to put some food ashore. The planted food was gone when we got to Pompong."

"Those bloody Malays," Carse said.

He called to Berryman and Marsh, who had just lifted Davidson's canoe aboard. "Get some tins and bury them in the same place as before. The others might need them."

While the two men went ashore, Davidson and Falls slept, and even the dull pre-dawn roar of the aero engines at the Jap base on Chempa didn't wake them.

But at first light Carse could wait no longer, and as the anchor came up and he turned the *Krait's* head once more towards the China Sea he grinned wearily at the tireless Cain.

"If we go up and down Temiang many more times, Cobber, we'll be laying an ownership claim to it."

Bob Page opened his eyes and saw a small scarlet crab among the greasy mangrove roots a few yards away at the end of the beach and as he watched the crab cleaning its face with its nippers he couldn't remember where he was, though he was aware that his body, all his body, felt battered and bruised.

He shut his sore eyes and opened them again and tried to think. Crabs. . . the beach at Pandjang. . . .

Pandjang? No, that wasn't right. Pompong . . . Pompong . . . the R.V. . . . He sat up quickly, with a feeling that something was wrong, and looked about him. His eyes sorted the leaves along the jungle edge and swung to the mangroves and out to sea. And then he saw her, a mile off and going away, down Temiang. He was on his feet now, bending and shaking the others into sodden consciousness and pointing.

"The *Krait*—she's gone without us."

They watched her going away until an island in the strait covered her, and then they looked into each other's eyes and looked away, and Page, staring about him, said, "No wonder we missed her. We're on the wrong beach."

"By God, you're right!" Jones exclaimed. "We should be on east beach."

"She must have been there all the time."

Lyon, whose face was haggard, aimlessly combed his hair with his fingers.

"It doesn't matter," he said, hardly above a whisper. "We've still got forty-eight hours to the next R.V. . . . *Krait'll* be back."

You hope, Jones thought, but couldn't say it.

Lyon nearly fell, and held his head in his hands. Then he looked up and in an expressionless voice said, "We'd better get the canoes under cover."

They slept most of that day, four stinking black motionless bundles in the black jungle shade, but when they woke in the middle afternoon, still feeling battered, they were hungry for the first time for days, and even Lyon had lost his gaunt look and had recovered some of his strength.

"As soon as it gets dark we'd better move to the other beach," he said. "But we need food. . . . Fishermen use this island—sometimes sleep here. There may be come here now."

Page glanced nervously at the others. "Do you think that's safe? What about the rations Donald planted?"

"He and Falls probably used them. . . . No, we'll have to take the risk. The gold will work wonders."

And then he stared into the undergrowth and said, almost to himself, "We could be here for weeks, if the *Krait* doesn't come, before we get away."

"A cheerful cove you are," Page said. "After the last week the last thing I want to do is paddle to Australia."

"Australia," Lyon said, a rumour of a smile in his tired eyes. "I can think of better ways—pirating a junk and sailing her to Ceylon."

Page knew he meant it. He had done it before. He would do it again.

From his canoe Lyon pulled out his canvas bag of gold, dropped a handful of the Dutch guilders into one of his zip pockets, and went into the trees.

Page shook his head. "I don't like it. I don't like it a bit."

But an hour before dark Lyon was back with a native basket filled with cooked fish between young banana leaves and a mess of cooked vegetables.

"No rice, sago, baked potatoes or caviar," he said, cheerfully. "Thanks to our friends the Japs, trade is at a standstill and the Malays are out of everything, including clothes."

"Can they be trusted?" the realistic Jones asked.

"I think so—at least while our gold lasts. Even if we're here for months we'll still be able to eat. I found a camp of fishing Malays—a dozen of them—from one of the other islands."

"What did they say?" Page asked, and added, dryly, "They could see you weren't exactly a local."

"They knew I was a Tuan, and didn't ask questions. The oldest fellow told me none of them cared who won the war so long as the Buginese sailors start operating again and trade gets back to normal."

They ate, and in the short twilight paddled the four hundred yards to the other beach and hid the canoes and slept.

Next morning, when they were all stronger and hungry, they found traces of a camp, a small trampled area which they decided could have been used by Davidson and Falls. But when they dug for the food cache—the only one they knew about was the one left originally by Davidson—they couldn't find it, nor did they find the food planted by Berryman and Marsh the night before.

While Lyon went for more food from the fishermen, Page, Jones and Huston began to build a hut of plaited palm leaves, since they had all agreed by this that if the *Krait* didn't return to Pompong by next morning, 4th October, then they would have to presume she had been captured and they might have to stay on the island for weeks before they could get away.

3rd October was a day of suspense, for apart from the question mark over the *Krait*, the others didn't believe, as Lyon did, that the fishermen would not report them to the Japanese.

As Page said to Jones, "The Japs'll feed and clothe them if they give us away. They must know that. It's too big a temptation."

Their restlessness increased as the afternoon faded. Page, sitting cross-legged, plaited palm leaves, lifting his head often to listen. Lyon went to the beach many times, or paced up and down, a thin mask of the man he had been that day more than a month before when they sailed from Exmouth Gulf. Huston climbed a tree and sat camouflaged among its leaves gazing down Temiang. Jones fiddled with the canoes and later cleaned the boils on his knee and bandaged them.

Before dark they lit a fire, for they could see smoke from the fishing camp, and boiled water for the last of their tea and ate strips of cold fish and pieces of stringy vegetable which tasted like tainted onion, and small bananas. Then they brought the canoes to the beach edge and sat on the sand in front of their just-hidden bows.

Although they had rested, they might all have been recovering from a long illness. They had lost a lot of weight and their faces were thin and pointed. The dye, faded and streaked, helped accentuate this thinness, and exhaustion of body and spirit showed across eyes that seemed to have stretched, across sunken, crudely shaved cheeks. They were the faces, the eyes, of men who had been driven too long.

They waited, not talking any more for they had nothing to say, not even Page and Jones, the strongest of the four, not even moving in this questing eternity of time, only looking out now across the glow of beach, across where beach became dark water, into the dark.

They waited, their feet on the harsh sand, knowing that their future was now being decided.

They waited.

In their night vision the sea was black and the sky which joined it a different black, and in between a foreign shape, black, too, moved. They didn't see it, not at first, only when it was closer, and then their strained eyes didn't believe it was there until across the shadowed blackness the call leapt to meet them.

"Ship ahoy!"

As the echo bounced against the tree wall behind them they were on their feet, hugging each other, laughing, shaking hands.

"The *Krait*!"

They snatched the canoes, dragged them across the sand into the water, and as they dug with their paddles Lyon called, "*Krait* ahoy," and called again, not caring how far his voice might carry in the still air.

Then they were alongside and arms reached for them and pulled them out of the canoes and lifted them aboard, and everyone was slapping backs and grabbing hands and laughing and asking questions which nobody answered, and again there was too much noise and nobody cared until the first wild welcome was over.

And then, for the first and only time in the history of Jaywick, Lyon called for drinks all round.

Carse brought a bottle of Beenleigh O.P. rum from under his bunk—the first bottle touched since leaving Exmouth Gulf —and Page shared it with fourteen mugs lined up on No. 4 hatch.

Only Paddy refused, and although everyone tried to persuade him, he wouldn't drink.

"It's no good," he said. "If I had one after all this time I'd want twenty, an' then Paddy McDowell wouldn't know if the old crate was goin' ahead or astern an' how in hell would we all get back home?"

They opened tins of emergency rations and spread the meat

and chocolate and the rest on the dark deck and talked with full mouths, like schoolboys at a midnight feast, and Page held up his mug and said, "Thank God that's over", and Davidson, in a clean sarong and wearing his monocle, which he had displayed all day much to the amusement of the crew, lifted his mug and said, "Yes, I think we should all thank God."

When the celebration was over the six raiders went to their bunks and hammocks where they slept for the next twenty-four hours. And as the canoes were lifted aboard and packed in their bags, Carse turned the *Krait* away from Pompong and began his sixth and last passage to Temiang.

At 3 a.m. on 4th October they cleared the strait, and at daylight, on a direct course for Carimata Strait across the China Sea, and then for Lombok, Linga Peak was no longer like an enemy sentry watching them from the high sky, but an old and trusted friend.

16

FAR TO THE SOUTH-EAST over the *Krait's* salted bows, framed in the wheelhouse window, blue Rinjani threaded her needle point through the sea to salute their return.

Lombok, the strait to safety, was almost in sight.

It was 7 a.m. on 11th October—seven days since the *Krait* had cleared Temiang for the last time, fourteen days since the raid on Singapore; and that morning, with Rinjani in sight, with Australia waiting eight hundred miles across the Indian Ocean, nobody had any misgivings about their chances of making their second and final passage of Lombok.

"She was clear last time," Davidson argued between mouthfuls of bacon and pancake, "why should she be patrolled now?"

The other officers, having breakfast on No. 3 hatch, agreed.

"If they patrolled her it was immediately after the raid," Page said, "and that's a fortnight ago."

Lyon tossed his tea dregs overboard. "I don't think we have a thing to worry about."

Since clearing Temiang a curious change had taken place among the men of Jaywick. For the first time, in a month of cruising in Japanese waters, they all felt suddenly, alarmingly safe. A foolish certainty. It broke all their self-imposed rules. It undermined their greatest asset—united vigilance.

That morning—and mornings before—they believed their worries were over. They felt calm, immune, yet the Japanese naval and air bases at Surabaya were only 120 miles to the west, the Japanese military fields on Bali and Lombok were minutes away, the very water swishing along the *Krait's* side was Japanese.

This exclusive sense of inviolability, so irrational, so dangerous, was a violent reaction to all the hardships and dangers they had endured, to the spectacular success of the raid itself. They were relaxed, self-satisfied, positive that danger had been left behind among the Thousand Islands and the China Sea. They were like students who had just sat for an examination after months of preparation. The examination was over and with it all its work and denials and tensions.

All that day they approached, without sail or plane to jolt their complacency, and all day Rinjani pushed higher above cloudless Lombok Island.

It was a day of green and blue illusion.

Although they were closer to Bali than Lombok, they did not see Gunung Agung until late afternoon when, only fifteen miles from the northern entrance to Lombok Strait, they watched her high cone, wedded with a frail ring of cloud, watched later as the sun slid behind her and the sacred mountain lay against a sky of blood and orange and violet.

At dark they were less than ten miles off, and an hour later the *Krait* was nearing the first rips which laced the northern entrance. At 10 p.m., under a high clear moon, she was tossing spray over her shoulder. At 11 p.m. she was through, sliding into the strait among moon-glitter along the fast southern-moving flow from the Java Sea.

Then, at 11.30 p.m., Falls and Jones sighted together.

"Ship. One three five. Approaching fast."

"Hell," Carse said, as his fingers gripped the wheel. "This is it."

The enemy ship was too far away and too far astern to see without leaning out of the wheelhouse. But he could not risk being seen. He called to Jones.

"Joe. Take the wheel—quick."

He got out the starboard side, dived under the canvas flap, jumped to port and squinted through a slit in the tattered blinds.

One glance was enough. Across the clear moonlit strait the enemy ship had white water at her bows.

"Action stations. Jap patrol," he ordered, and as he dashed back to the wheelhouse he could hear feet thumping on the deck and the weapons and ammunition being tumbled out.

"Warship," he said to Jones. "Go aft."

And to Falls at bow lookout he called, "Report to Major Lyon, Jap patrol approaching."

Davidson and Page thumped up No. 3 ladder and, keeping

low, crept aft to their action stations. Lyon followed and dipped into the wheelhouse.

"What do you make of it, Ted?"

"Destroyer, by the look of her. I've altered course to suggest we're making for Bali. It might fool them."

"A bit sudden, wasn't it?"

"Like Granny's vomit."

"If they challenge, we haven't a leg to stand on."

He lifted the bunk seat, dragged out the first-aid kit, and found the tin of cyanide lozenges. He called to Page and handed the tin through the food hatch.

"One for each man."

"Limpets are our only chance if we get near her," Davidson called.

"The few left are battened down in No. 2 hold—with the canoes," Carse reminded him.

"Of course," Davidson growled. "That's torn it."

"If they stop us and we can get alongside we might get a chance to fight and go that way," Lyon said.

"And if not?" Carse asked.

"Then we'll ram her, blow the *Krait* and take her with us. . . . I've already connected the detonator."

Carse knew that soon, very soon, the end would come. He was afraid, but in a becalmed sort of way, and the thought of that final shattering blast of the 150 lb. of explosive in No. 3 hold was no longer terrifying.

He took a quick glance out the port side and saw the warship's bow wave, bridge and mast.

"Must be doing twenty-five knots," he said. "She has the bone in her teeth."

He was surprised how steady he felt.

"I'd better warn Young," Lyon said. "He might have to get a last signal away."

His voice was almost casual.

He crawled along the deck to No. 3 hold and went down, but only to reappear in a few seconds and to stand on the ladder with his head just below the hatch coaming where he could see Carse, but could not be seen from seaward.

"Getting close," Berryman called from aft. "Starting to turn."

"Destroyer," Cain called, more angry than afraid at being caught so close to safety.

"She's too bloody big for the Seventh Division."

It was Pancake Andy's historic contribution.

When the destroyer was not more than a hundred yards to port and still astern, she slowed and turned, parallel to the *Krait*, then moved ahead. Those aft, watching behind the curtains, could see her clearly, but Carse and Lyon were still blind, and from their positions they could not risk even a glance which might give them away.

Slowly the destroyer moved ahead and came abeam. Carse could see her now, her one mast, squat double stacks, the big black characters on her side grey-white in the moonlight. She had no steaming lights, but he noticed a faint glow aft.

He tried to recall her silhouette, but it wouldn't come. Then he remembered, though he wasn't sure.

"*Sigure* class," he guessed, hoping that when the searchlight came on his black-bearded face, wild black hair and stained chest would pass the test of Japanese eyes.

In those moments, as everyone waited for the searchlight shutter to open and its shaft to impale them, waited for the winking light that would be the unanswerable challenge, Carse felt that time had stopped, that the living thing that was himself was suspended between sea and sky, not moving or breathing or functioning any more, but stilled like a full stop between sentences in time. Then, harshly, he felt alive again as the destroyer began to slip astern and he realized that she must have almost stopped her engines and that the *Krait*, helped by the swift current, was moving ahead of her again. Her stacks, bridge, bow slipped astern, and in the narrow wheelhouse he was again blind.

From behind him he heard Davidson whisper hoarsely, "Why doesn't she challenge?"

Now Carse could see her bow again, as she moved ahead for the second time. Her bows passed and then the *Krait's* wheelhouse was level with her bridge, and the moonlight glanced on something metal there, and now he could see her stacks across the glittering water.

For eight minutes she paced the *Krait*, less than a hundred yards away, the sea curling at her bow, the glow near her stern mirroring a hidden fire. Then, just on midnight, she increased speed, turned away and headed across the strait for Lombok Island.

For a minute, two, not a man moved as they watched the destroyer, expecting her any second to circle and return. Frozen in their positions, to their guns, as they had been in those minutes between life and death, they watched her as she dwindled across the moonglow.

Someone coughed. A Bren magazine clicked off. A movement, gentle as a breeze, started aft and travelled along the ship and went overboard.

Page was the first to speak. "Good-bye and God bless you, and if we don't zee you zum more we zank you."

Huston laughed and chopped off the sound, and then all were chattering wildly as Lyon jumped on deck from No. 3 ladder and came to the wheelhouse. He was grinning.

"Funny how thirsty a man gets," he said, and called, "Crilley—tea all round."

Later, when Pancake Andy had produced tea, they were still arguing at the wheelhouse why the destroyer had not challenged.

"I know," Lyon was saying, "they accepted us at face value—a Jap fishing boat flying the Jap flag. But it's too obvious. It doesn't satisfy me."

"It's the only logical explanation," Page argued, and Davidson supported him.

Lyon appealed to Carse. "What does the Navy think? You mentioned you had a theory before someone rudely interrupted you."

"Carse scratched his dirty beard. "The flag and the ship probably tricked them—I'll admit that. But I've got another idea and it could easily be wrong. Look at it this way. It was near midnight. Their watch was about to change. The officer of the watch was not only bored patrolling a ditch like this—he was bloody tired, like me. He was about to hand over his watch, but if he'd challenged he would have lost a lot of sleep."

"In other words," Lyon said, "we could have been saved by one inefficient officer."

Carse yawned. "Let's say one bloody sleepy officer."

Lyon smiled. "My watch, Ted."

At daylight on 12th October the *Krait* had cleared Lombok Strait and was beating into a strong south-easter, and by next morning, when she was about 180 miles south, Lyon decided to break radio silence and call the American Admiral Christie at Potshot, Exmouth Gulf, to warn him that Lombok Strait, which his submarines were using, was now patrolled.

Horrie Young, who already had his receiver tuned to VHM Coonawarra Wireless Station, near Darwin, was not happy breaking silence so close to Japanese airfields, but he encoded Lyon's message and quickly tapped out Coonawarra's callsign three times and added the go-ahead "K".

Young felt sure that a close watch would be kept for the *Krait's* signals, but Coonawarra didn't reply and he cursed them at long range for their inefficiency.

He warned Lyon of the danger of breaking silence again, and didn't try until two days later, when this time he called VIX, Fremantle, and immediately received back the letter K.

Smartly he tapped out in code: "To A.C.N.B. [Australian Commonwealth Naval Board] from *Krait*. Mission completed. For Admiral Christie Lombok now patrolled. E.T.A. 17. A.R."

Back came the letters R.I.

The signal was in Australia.

When Carse heard this he called Paddy McDowell and told him.

"Now it doesn't matter much if that propeller shaft of yours breaks down."

Paddy grinned. "An' if it does we'll get a trip to Fremantle, after all."

Four days later, on 19th October 1943, the *Krait* anchored off the American base of Potshot in Exmouth Gulf.

It was 47 days and nearly 5000 miles since she had headed north for Lombok, for Borneo, for Singapore, and 33 of those days had been spent in Japanese waters to within touching distance of the Japanese fortress of Singapore.

Jaywick was over.

FROM JAYWICK TO RIMAU

ON THAT OCTOBER MORNING, as the *Krait* dropped anchor near U.S.S. *Chanticleer*, a plane was waiting to take Taffy Morris to Perth for medical treatment, Ivan Lyon to Melbourne to report the victory of Jaywick, Bob Page to Canberra to marry Roma Prowse.

Then Ted Carse took the *Krait* on to Darwin where Paddy McDowell, no longer nursemaid to a diesel engine, broke his long drought by drinking a large bottle of O.P. rum—all by himself.

Early in December 1943, the fourteen men of Jaywick gathered at Z Staging Camp in Jordan Terrace, Brisbane, where they celebrated with a nine-gallon keg, and then they scattered, though some were to meet again to make another raid against Singapore.

This was "Rimau"—Operation "Tiger" or, as the Japanese called it, "Tora Kohsaku Tai"—and it was Lieutenant-Colonel Ivan Lyon who led this raid a year after Jaywick, and Donald Davidson, then a lieutenant-commander, who was again his second-in-command.

It was possible to recreate Operation Jaywick because some of those men who celebrated in 1943 are alive, and because of the existence of essential records, including Lieutenant Carse's log of the *Krait* and a brief diary kept by Leading Telegraphist Young.

But Operation Rimau was the raid which vanished, and even long after the war little was known in any detail of how it disappeared and why, and the fate of its members. Because Rimau remained largely a mystery, I never believed that sufficient information could be dredged from the past to make the telling of this raid possible, and so, when I began this book, I regretfully turned what I thought was the final page on Rimau and decided to concentrate solely on Jaywick.

But during my long research on Jaywick, stray fragments of Rimau began to emerge—a name, a phrase, a reference on a chart—and as more fragments accumulated I began for the first time to see its shadowy outlines.

The very totality of Jaywick, the raid which succeeded, was almost a challenge in itself to discover the elusive details of the raid which failed, and more and more as research progressed I had to know more of Rimau. There was inevitability about this, blended with a kind of nostalgic literary foreboding, for the two operations, though separate in method and time, were positive parts of a whole.

Slowly as research advanced, as I learnt more about the lost raid, as it elements became a recognizable pattern of brave and ultimate tragedy, I knew with certainty that the entity that was Jaywick was still not enough—that, lacking a portrait of Rimau, however inadequate, even a miniature, Jaywick and this book would remain forever unfinished.

The story which follows is not complete, can never be complete, because the men who could tell it died creating it. But I have been able to find enough about them, from brief official records and many other sources, and after months of personal search, to describe the lost raid as fully and as accurately as possible—and, unique in itself, to describe it from both sides, Allied and Japanese.

The first part deals with Operation Rimau up to the time it vanished.

The second describes some of my own research problems, frustrations, and discoveries.

And the third, based on those discoveries, is the raid itself—the magnificent failure and what happened to its members—told for the first time.

OPERATION RIMAU

Lieutenant-Colonel Ivan Lyon, M.B.E., D.S.O.
the Gordon Highlanders
Lieutenant-Commander D. M. N. Davidson, D.S.O., R.N.V.R.
Captain R. C. Page, A.I.F.
Lieutenant H. R. Ross, British Army
Lieutenant B. Reymond, R.A.N.R.
Lieutenant A. L. Sargent, A.I.F.
Lieutenant W. G. Carey, A.I.F.
Sub-Lieutenant J. G. M. Riggs, R.N.V.R.
Major R. N. Ingleton, Royal Marines, S.E.A.C. representative
Warrant Officer J. Willersdorf
Warrant Officer A. Warren
Sergeant D. P. Gooley, A.I.F.
Sergeant C. B. Cameron, A.I.F.
Able Seaman W. G. Falls, D.S.M., R.A.N.
Able Seaman F. W. Marsh, R.A.N., mention in dispatches
Able Seaman A. W. Huston, D.S.M., R.A.N.
Corporal A. G. P. Campbell, A.I.F.
Corporal C. M. Stewart, A.I.F.
Corporal C. M. Craft, A.I.F.
Corporal R. B. Fletcher, A.I.F.
Lance Corporal J. T. Hardy, A.I.F.
Lance Corporal H. J. Page, A.I.F.
Private D. R. Warne, A.I.F.

1

Operation Rimau was the child of Jaywick and of Ivan Lyon's compulsion to attack Singapore, for the *Krait* raid was only just over when he was already planning to return.

Originally, Rimau was to be part of a larger operation, a dual attack against Japanese shipping. This combined operation, under the code-name "Hornbill", was to be against Singapore and the Japanese-occupied French Indo-China port of Saigon. The attacks were to be launched simultaneously from the Natuna Islands, in the South China Sea just west of Borneo, after a preliminary reconnaissance of these islands by the secret Force 136 from Admiral Lord Louis Mountbatten's South-east Asia Command in Ceylon. But the reconnaissance, code-named "Kookaburra", was never made, and "Hornbill" was abandoned early in 1944 because resources intended for S.E.A.C. were held for the invasion of Europe.

This left Ivan Lyon with Rimau, which he named after the tiger tattooed on his own chest and planned as a submarine-drop operation based on the use, not of canoes as in Jaywick, but "Sleeping Beauties", electrically powered submersible metal boats which looked a little like Eskimo kayaks.

Lyon's decision to attack Singapore again is questionable. The main argument against such a raid is that to attack in the same place, particularly against the literal-minded Japanese, and to attack where Japanese security had been strengthened after the success of Jaywick, was a grave error of military judgment.

But there are counter-arguments in favour of a return raid —and audacity to attack twice in the same place is one of them. There are other reasons, too: Rimau was entirely different from Jaywick; Singapore was a busy port and many ships meant many targets; Lyon, and Davidson and Page, knew Singapore and its approaches, a big advantage; the Jaywick raid was already "cold" while Rimau was being prepared, so that although Japanese security had been improved, these precautions, if they followed the usual wartime pattern, had probably been relaxed.

So that Lyon may have been right in assuming that the dangers of a second attack were worth accepting, though by using the most skilled men of Jaywick, all in one operation, he risked total wastage of raid-tested specialists in limpet warfare.

It is significant, however, that both Donald Davidson and Bob Page—brave men willing to go on another raid with Lyon against a new target—were suspicious of Rimau, which they joined only because of their deep personal attachment, and at times almost mystic admiration, for their equally courageous

Attack Route of Operation Rimau.

The map on the next pages shows the route taken by the British submarine *Porpoise* from Careening Bay, Garden Island, Western Australia, north through Lombok Strait in the wake of the *Krait* and across the Java and South China seas to Merapas Island, in the Rhio Archipelago, rear attack base of Rimau.

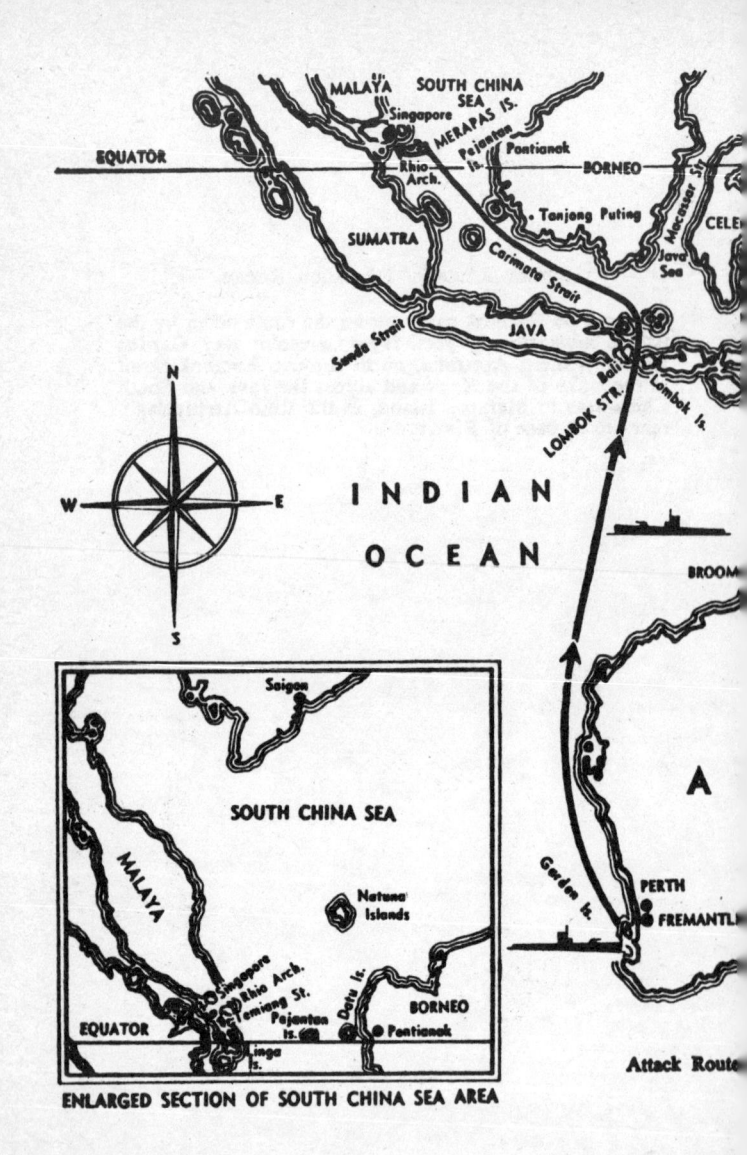

ENLARGED SECTION OF SOUTH CHINA SEA AREA

Attack Route

Wetar Is.   Romang Is.

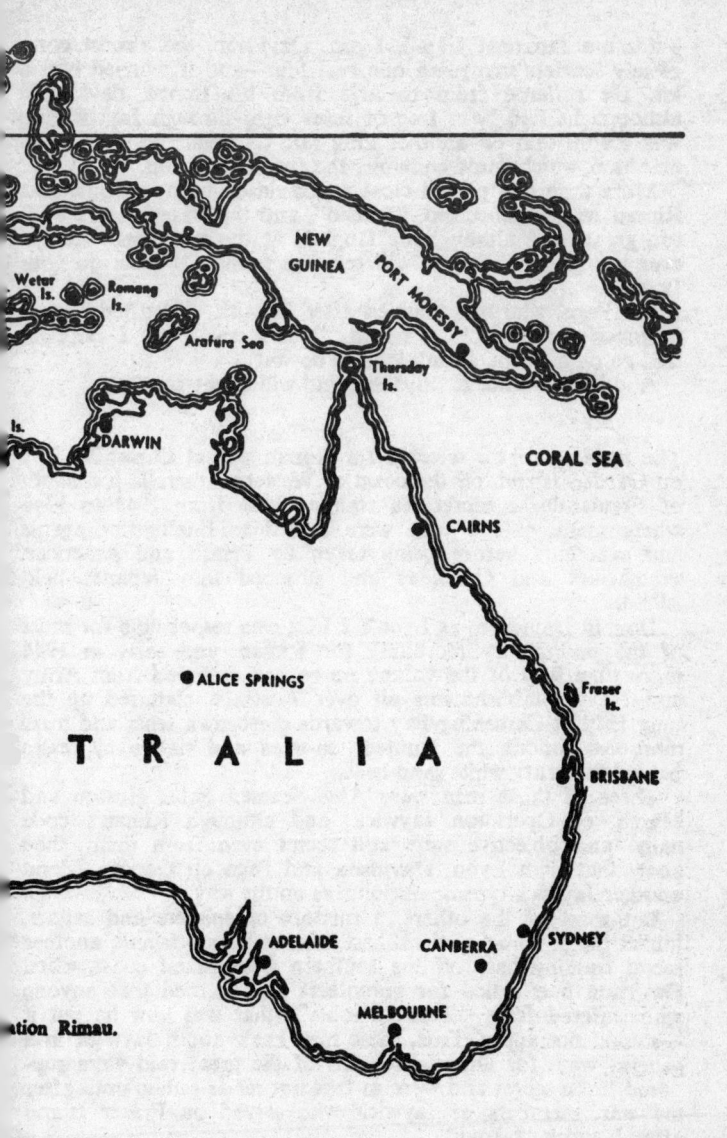

NEW GUINEA   PORT MORESBY

Arafura Sea

Thursday Is.

DARWIN

CORAL SEA

CAIRNS

ALICE SPRINGS

Fraser Is.

TRALIA

BRISBANE

ADELAIDE   CANBERRA   SYDNEY

MELBOURNE

ation Rimau.

but more fanatical friend, Lyon. Davidson, the almost completely fearless man, had one real fear—and it worried him a lot. He suffered from malaria from his Burma days, and although he had been free of fever right through Jaywick, he was scared that on another long raid he might go down with an attack which could endanger the entire operation.

More than one person close to Davidson tried to argue that Rimau was ill-conceived, "loaded", and that the dangers were too great, and although he laughed at the warnings, without ever answering them, he did tell one friend, "I must go with Ivan."

But Page, who had married after Jaywick, distrusted Rimau so much that he told a friend, "Ivan's crazy, but I can't let him go on his own. I can't let him down."

And then he added: "But this raid will be my last."

The training centre selected for Rimau was at Careening Bay on Garden Island, off the coast of Western Australia just south of Fremantle—a secret sea training base from 1943 to 1945 where many gallant men were drilled as Intelligence agents and saboteurs before being taken by British and American submarines and Catalinas and dropped into Japanese-held islands.

Donald Davidson, as Lyon's 2 I.C., was responsible for most of the preliminary recruiting for Rimau, and early in 1944 more than fifty of the volunteers he had gathered from Army and Navy establishments all over Australia clattered up the long jetty at Careening Bay towards the brown tents and mess marquees among the stunted tea-trees and native cypresses behind the gritty white sand beach.

Three of those men were Able Seamen Falls, Huston and Marsh, of Operation Jaywick, and although Rimau's code name and objective were still secret even from them, they knew that with Lyon, Davidson and Page on Garden Island another Jaywick-type operation was on the way.

But most of the others, a mixture of soldiers and sailors, joined blind. Some of them had been at Fraser Island, another secret training base off the southern Queensland coast, when Davidson had called for volunteers and warned that anyone who suffered from "claustrophobia"—that was how he put it —should not apply. True, these men knew about Jaywick in a general way, for although details of the great raid were supposed to be secret and were in fact not made public until after the war, members of Jaywick who served on Fraser Island after Jaywick "talked".

But other men had joined from scattered camps and bases on the Australian mainland, had never heard of Operation

Jaywick, and knew only that they had volunteered for special service that was secret and could be dangerous.

Every man, however, knew the day he reached Garden Island that he could be rejected at any time—knew, too, that during training he could for any reason withdraw without discredit to himself or his unit. Many of these men were in fact rejected, for physical or other reasons, before the personnel of Rimau were finally chosen; but not one man withdrew from choice.

There are reasons why it is remarkable that there were no withdrawals.

Sea training at Careening Bay concentrated on Davis submarine escape apparatus, Sleeping Beauties, and limpet attack with the S.B.s. These held one man, were twelve feet long, and the operator who sat in one—not inside one—facing a half steering wheel and a small control panel, wore what was known as a shallow-water suit, not unlike a frogman's, fitted with oxygen mask and container.

To approach a target the submerged operator "porpoised"— brought his boat near the surface so that his eyes were just above sea level, observed where he was going, then dived, later porpoising nearer his target to make other quick checks on direction and distance. When close to his target ship he brought his eyes above surface again, moved alongside, attached limpets which he carried on the deck of his craft, submerged and escaped.

At least, that was the theory, but the volunteers found the Beauties—one was known as the "Virgin Sturgeon"—erratic, difficult to master, and dangerous. When put into dives they could not be controlled and continued down until they hit bottom. Or they rose so violently out of control that they almost leapt from the sea.

True, these idiosyncracies were part of the routine hazards of learning to master these craft, but men who were there say that few operators ever learnt to handle them properly, and even then the behaviour of the boats was often so chaotic that to have used them in an actual attack would have invited disaster.

Rimau volunteers regarded the training S.B.s as inefficient and dangerous, but when more modern operational craft, for the raid itself, arrived at Garden Island, these were even more unimpressive and so full of new "bugs" that they were almost unmanageable.

The decision to take the S.B.s is hard to understand, particularly as canoes had proved so effective on the Jaywick raid, though Lyon may have been influenced by his memory of the slowness of canoes and of those exhausting hours, which he often referred to, during and after the 1943 attack.

But the performance of the S.B.s was not the only disquieting feature of the preparations for Rimau. Garden Island's isolation was important to the secrecy of the operation and its equipment during the months of training, yet one of the exercises with the operational Sleeping Beauties was in Cockburn Sound against H.M.A.S. *Adelaide* and in full view of hundreds of sailors lining her decks. That this broke security on the secret S.B.s was soon evident, for they were openly discussed in bars on the Western Australian mainland—at Fremantle and Rockingham. Because of this loose talk, which was picked up and reported back, postponement of Rimau was actually considered—and then rejected.

This was probably the right decision, because Rimau's potential target area was so vast, and there were so many harbours and anchorages in that area, that even if word of the S.B.s had reached the Japanese, it could not have helped them much, though it could have led to a tightening of security in all their ports.

The Japanese, however, had no pre-knowledge and knew nothing about the Sleeping Beauties.

After months of preparation the final selection was made of the men who had survived the training period, and the complement of Rimau was established at twenty-two.

In addition to Lieutenant-Colonel Lyon, Lieutenant-Commander Davidson, and Captain Robert Page, and the other three members of Jaywick, Able Seamen Falls, Huston and Marsh, there were five officers, ten non-commissioned officers and one private.

The five included three Englishmen, Major R. N. Ingleton, Lieutenant H. R. Ross (British Army), and Sub-Lieutenant J. G. M. Riggs, R.N.V.R., and two Australians, Lieutenant B. Reymond, R.A.N.R., and Lieutenant A. F. Sargent, A.I.F.

Major Ingleton, a huge, genial man, was a Royal Marine Commando who represented South-east Asia Command on the operation, and Sub-Lieutenant Riggs, also from S.E.A.C., had come to Garden Island to help with training, but was so keen to go on the raid that he persuaded Lyon to include him in the Rimau party.

The eleven non-commissioned men were all members of the A.I.F. They included two warrant officers, J. Willersdorf and A. Warren (both Victorians); two sergeants, D. P. Gooley and C. B. Cameron (also Victorians); four corporals, A. G. P. Campbell (Queensland), C. M. Stewart and C. M. Craft (Western Australia), and R. B. Fletcher (New South Wales); and two lance-corporals, J. F. Hardy (New South Wales) and H. J. Page (Queensland). The private was D. R. Warne, A.I.F.

The two conducting officers, whose job was to supervise the

dropping of the party and then return to Australia, were Major W. W. Chapman, British Army, and Lieutenant W. G. Carey, A.I.F., of New South Wales.

But of all the new personnel with Rimau, only Walter Carey had any personal link through Rimau to Jaywick's beginnings, for he was a younger brother of Sam Carey, who led Scorpion "raid" against Townsville—the raid in which Bob Page had taken part before joining Jaywick. Walter Carey, who had worked in New Guinea before the war, had been with the Australian 8th Division in Malaya, and had left Singapore in September 1941 for Commando training at Maymyo, Burma, and after Pearl Harbour had gone into China as a member of that little-known Australian Commando Force—Mission 204— which spent a year with the Chinese Army.

Just before Rimau was launched, Lieutenant Carey, hoping to give his anxious mother some idea where he was, wrote her saying that by the time she received his letter in Sydney he expected to be feeling just like the goldfish in the bowl on the table in her own breakfast room at Abbotsford. With this subtle breach of security in front of her she immediately guessed that her son was in a submarine—and she was right— for Operation Rimau had already started from Careening Bay, Garden Island, in the British mine-laying submarine *Porpoise* (Lieutenant-Commander Marchant), which carried, in addition to the twenty-two raiders and the two conducting officers, fifteen black Sleeping Beauties, stowed in her mine-space, eleven canoes, and fifteen tons of supplies apart from arms, ammunition, grenades, limpets and radios.

The date of departure was 11th September 1944.

2

THE *Porpoise* entered the Java Sea through Lombok Strait almost a year after the first passage by the *Krait*. She went through at night, running on the surface at fifteen knots, then submerged at dawn way north of Bali and Lombok. She cut through Carimata Strait, between Borneo and Billiton, in daylight but submerged, and that night crossed the China Sea.

On the afternoon of 23rd September, twelve days after leaving Western Australia, she reached Merapas Island, the most easterly island of the Rhio Archipelago about seventy miles south-east of Singapore, which Ivan Lyon had selected as the rear base for Operation Rimau. Lieutenant-Commander Marchant, who knew he was within simple range of Singapore-based aircraft, and only sixty miles from the Japanese seaplane base on Chempa Island, and who had kept the *Porpoise* submerged all day in the dangerously shallow water of the China Sea, cautiously approached Merapas in the late afternoon and in water less than a hundred feet deep made a periscope reconnaissance of the small island.

Neither he nor Donald Davidson, who was once again the operational leader, could see anything suspicious—no sign of natives, beach tracks, canoes, smoke—and at dusk he surfaced four hundred yards from a beach and Davidson and Corporal Stewart went ashore in a canoe.

Three hours later they returned. Their news was good. The island was uninhabited, though old footmarks under their torches showed that the Malays visited a small coconut grove. Over most of the island, which was only one mile long and half a mile at its widest, jungle cover was thick, and they had found one good spring. Merapas seemed so favourable that, on Davidson's advice, Lyon decided to make the island Operation Rimau's "Base A".

By the time this selection was made, Marchant had decided it was too late to land the supplies and for the *Porpoise* to be away from the island by daylight, so he took his submarine well away from land into deeper water and submerged.

After sunset on 24th September he returned to Merapas and once again circled the island, but this time his searching periscope showed him three Malays beside a canoe on a beach— but at the other end of the island from a beach Davidson had selected as the operation's landing place. Lyon and Davidson agreed that the Malays were probably stray visitors from another island and that the decision to make Merapas Rimau's Base A should stand, but the presence of the Malays forced them to alter their plans. The original idea was to hide the supplies ashore and leave them unguarded, but now the leaders realized that the Malays might find them, and, knowing Malays, they knew what would happen to those supplies. There was also a greater risk, not that the natives might report their discovery to the Japanese, but that they would talk about it— and kampong talk travels fast and far.

The only spare man in the submarine was Lieutenant Walter Carey, the No. 2 conducting officer, and Carey, a Commando who knew how to look after himself, agreed to stay alone on Merapas—not an enviable job—to watch the supplies until the operational party returned from their attack on Singapore. Carey knew that he might have to kill anyone who found the supplies or who saw him, but his instructions were that killing should be last-resort action because the disappearance of visiting Malays would draw attention to the island and lead to a search. His job was to keep out of sight.

With this decided, the *Porpoise* was brought to within a

hundred yards of the selected beach and supplies in their sealed tins—enough for twenty-two men for three months—plus a radio receiver, two hundred Dutch gold guilders, and a Bren, Owen, ammunition and grenades for Carey, were ferried ashore in the canoe.

Early on 25th September, the *Porpoise* left Merapas and headed for the island of Pejantan, about 140 miles away in the China Sea between the Rhio Archipelago and Borneo, reaching the island on 26th September—first anniversary of the Jaywick raid. According to Intelligence reports, this island, which was just north of the equator, was uninhabited, and that is why it was selected. A careful periscope reconnaissance seemed to confirm this, and as there was no sign of life either on the many long white beaches or inland, the submarine commander and Lyon and Davidson decided that Pejantan would make a good base for the next vital act in the planned strategy of Rimau.

This act was wartime piracy.

The central point of Rimau was the capture of a native craft large enough to carry the attacking party, with their fifteen Sleeping Beauties, canoes, explosives and operational stores, to Singapore itself. Donald Davidson, who during the *Krait* raid often insisted that a native boat would be easy for any raiding party to capture and use, is believed to have suggested the idea for Operation Rimau—and it certainly has his dramatic, and at times melodramatic, inspiration about it—though it was also part of Lyon's thinking.

For Rimau it was fallible, since any large captured craft would be missed, particularly if the weather had been fine, and inquiries about her might reach the Japanese and lead to a search, and particularly an air search. But, again, the risk was not great because, long before the disappearance of the craft could be questioned, the raiders expected to be out of the area and away.

And so from Pejantan the *Porpoise* went looking for a craft to pirate, and on 28th September she found just what she was looking for. At 4 p.m. that day, near the small isolated island of Datu, about thirty miles off Pontianak on Borneo, her periscope picked up the hundred-ton Canton-type junk *Mustika* making out from the coast on the traditional junk route from Borneo to Rhio.

Running at periscope depth in a flat sea the *Porpoise* altered course, closed and surfaced. At sight of her streaming black conning-tower the junk came up into the wind and stopped, and as the submarine moved alongside seven armed Rimau men, led by Davidson and Lyon, jumped aboard while others covered them from the submarine. The Malay captain and his crew of eight were so astonished that they did not attempt to fight, but the captain protested bitterly when Lyon, as the *Porpoise* slipped astern and submerged, ordered him in Malay to steer a course due west for Pejantan about eighty miles away.

But a junk is useless unless you can sail her, so under the automatics of two of the party the sullen Malays worked the craft and taught the Rimau men how to operate her clumsy sails and how to manoeuvre her.

Then, at dusk, the *Porpoise* surfaced and took the *Mustika* in tow for the night, and at daylight, 29th September, submerged again. In a steady breeze the big junk made six knots towards Pejantan Island, which she reached that afternoon to anchor off a beach on the northern coast.

The *Porpoise* came alongside as dark settled on the China Sea, and all that night the Rimau party and the crew of the submarine worked to transfer the operational stores, explosives and equipment to the junk, which had discharged at Pontianak and was almost empty.

The fifteen Sleeping Beauties had to be manhandled out of the submarine's mine-space and, slung with ropes, lifted aboard the junk and lowered into her holds and lashed down.

But although everyone worked at pressure the transfer had not been completed by dawn on 30th September, and the submarine had to submerge and move into deeper water for the day before returning in the evening.

Early on 1st October—a year after the Jaywick raiders had to keep their first rendezvous with the *Krait* at Pompong Island—the twenty-two men of Rimau went aboard the *Mustika*, and the now terrified Malay captain and his eight men were taken into the submarine in charge of Major Chapman, the conducting officer, to be shipped to Australia. They could not be put ashore anywhere for fear of endangering the entire operation. At 3 a.m. on 1st October the submarine and the junk parted for the last time.

The raiders, under Ivan Lyon, put up the *Mustika's* sails and moved west from Pejantan Island to attack Singapore. as the *Porpoise*, after more than a week in the thin waters of the China Sea, sailed for Australia.

And if anyone deserved a decoration in those dark October hours of 1944, it was Lieutenant-Commander Marchant and his men of that British submarine for the risks they had taken in those shallow transparent waters between Borneo and Rhio.

On 11th October the *Porpoise* reached Fremantle, where Major Chapman handed over the captain of the *Mustika* and his eight junkmen to the authorities. I presume that the nine bewildered Malays were well looked after in Australia, warmly thanked, compensated for the loss of the *Mustika*, loss of employment, long absence from their families, and returned safely to their homes after the war. I only presume all this because I have not been able to discover what happened to them from the time they were landed in Australia.

On 15th October, four days after reaching Fremantle, Major Chapman, with a corporal named Croton as his assistant, left again in another British submarine to keep the rendezvous with Operation Rimau. This submarine was not a minelayer like the *Porpoise*, but was an offensive patrol, and she, too, entered the Java and China seas through Lombok Strait. According to the Australian Army Record, her R.V. plan with Rimau, arranged with Ivan Lyon, was to evacuate the raiders from Merapas Island on 8th November, or fifty-eight days after Operation Rimau's original launching date from Garden Island on 11th September.

But . . . "should the pick-up not take place on that date, the party was to wait a further 30 days, after which they were at liberty to make their own arrangements for escape."

The Official Australian report then goes on to explain what happened:

Besides pick-up of Rimau party, the submarine was detailed for an offensive patrol and was not due to leave this patrol to carry out the pick-up sortie until November 7.

When that day arrived there was still on board 15 torpedoes and sufficient fuel and stores for another fortnight's patrolling.

As his main object was offensive action against the Japanese, the submarine commander was loth to abandon his patrol at that stage in order to pick up Rimau.

In addition, the orders for the party were that they might expect to be picked up any time within a month after the initial date, November 8.

Consequently, the commander decided to delay leaving patrol until such time as fuel and stores and expenditure of torpedoes demanded.

Major Chapman was consulted and he concurred with these arrangements.

Finally it was decided to make the rendezvous on November 21-22.

This decision not to keep the vital R.V. at Merapas Island on 8th November was most curious, because authorities generally agree that the first R.V. in war is the R.V. which must be kept, unless extreme emergency prevents it; any later R.V. is regarded as of secondary importance to the first.

Probably there were other special circumstances, apart from the submarine commander's decision to continue his offensive patrol, which forced him to miss the R.V. with Operation

Rimau on 8th November. But to miss a key R.V., knowing that twenty-three men on a highly dangerous raid could be depending on it, was an extraordinary thing to do. The arrangement with Ivan Lyon must have been more elastic than it sounds.

The submarine continued her offensive patrol until, on 21st November, she made a periscope reconnaissance of Merapas and, after spending that day submerged at sea, returned at night and, at 1 a.m. on 22nd November, dropped Major Chapman and Corporal Croton in a canoe five hundred yards off the island.

The Army record then explains what happened:

The submarine then put to sea with the intention of returning the following night.

At 9.30 p.m. on November 22 she arrived a few hundred yards off the north-west corner of Merapas. Shortly afterwards a canoe was seen coming off. Its occupants were Major Chapman and Corporal Croton and they had some difficulty in getting aboard.

Major Chapman reported that there was no sign of the party on the island. It was agreed that nothing was to be gained by remaining any longer in the vicinity and trying again at a later date, so they proceeded clear and sailed for Fremantle.

On the island Major Chapman had discovered signs which showed the whole party had been there, and had apparently left in a hurry. The evidence indicated that they had left at least 14 days previously. No message had been left, and there was no sign of any fight or struggle.

Once again there are two points in this report which cry for comment. The first is that although the original R.V. had not been kept, the final R.V. was "within a month after the initial date, November 8", or 8th December—and for some undiscoverable reason this R.V. was not kept either.

The second point is that the Rimau party had apparently left at least fourteen days before, or on 8th November or before—and 8th November was the first R.V. which had not been kept.

Late that night of 22nd November the submarine turned away from Merapas and headed for Australia.

Operation Rimau and its twenty-three men had vanished—though not quite without trace as you will see.

THE CIPHER ROOM at Central Bureau stank of worn linoleum, glue, damp paper, grease, food, old cigarette smoke, as, night and day, the electric cipher machines under tired lights argued without stop.

The cipher room was a double garage behind Nyrambla, a late-Victorian stone house at 21 Henry Street, Ascot, Brisbane, and here on the midnight to 8 a.m. shift late in 1944 sixteen sergeant A.W.A.S. were working at their machines. All night the signals had poured into the pigeonholes at the "In" desk—thousands of meaningless combinations of five-letter groups which, when deciphered, became yards of numbers with anglicized Japanese words sprinkled among them, yards of disconnected English words. . . .

Numbers and more numbers . . . troop movements, weather information, air movements, priorities . . . numbers, numbers. . . .

As the signals arrived the girls collected them, went to the code desk against one wall to check the cipher, bent forward to set their machines, began typing, and from either side of the machines the endless ticker tapes—code to the left, clear to the right—spilt on to the floor like froth.

Then the operators gathered the glue-backed tape, took it to another table, slid it over water rollers, snipped it, pasted it on message forms. . . .

The room seemed to shrink with the heat. The girls unbuttoned their khaki shirts at the neck and dragged down their ties. The air was still, stale, a pale sour blue fog.

Near dawn the dry clacking of the cipher machines began to falter as the traffic eased. The operators, red-eyed, stiff, stood and stretched and sighed. They were too tired to speak. Wearily one girl gathered all paper and discarded tape with cipher material on it and went outside to the incinerator near the old well. It was her turn. Every scrap had to be burnt to ash, the ash reduced to powder. Those were the orders.

What a way to spend a war, she thought, as she dropped the paper and tape into the incinerator and bent to strike a match. Her name was Helen Frizell. Her eyes were large, the palest blue, her hair dark brown. She was a staff sergeant.

With a stick she prodded the paper and stood away from the fire, breathing fresh air for the first time in six hours, catching the elusive sweetness of climbing roses on the fence behind the garage, listening to the racehorses clopping in Henry Street, heading for their morning exercises.

She went back at last and another signal, a cable, was in the "Most Urgent" pigeonhole. It had no indication of origin. She studied the words—five-letter grouping. She knew the code, and set her machine and began to type and the tapes trickled from the machine. She stopped and read the words—quickly now. She bent forward and hammered the keys.

It was a Japanese report; monitored, she decided, and brief —little more than a mention of an attack on Singapore and the "capture" of a British officer, Colonel Lyon.

But she was not tired any more, for among the thousands of cold impersonal signals this message had meaning. It was real. It dealt, not with symbols, but with a human being.

What was the attack against Singapore? Who was this man, now in desperate trouble? How had the Japs caught him? What would they do to him?

She went to the pasting-down table and ran the tape over the little rollers turning in stale water mixed with cigarette ash.

And when the new shift came on she was still wondering about that lone officer, and for days his name came back and back, haunting, sad.

Operation Rimau, which she had never heard of, had vanished, and after that night of the single enemy message, until the end of the war, was silence.

4

I WOULD have preferred to remain in the background, merely the voice of the narrator of this story of brave men, but that was not possible.

It wasn't possible because my inquiries into Operation Rimau and why it failed became a personal search—a frustrating but in time rewarding search for twenty-three men who vanished behind the curtain of war, men whose fate probably would never have been established in any detail, and their courage never properly recorded, except for the chance discovery of three unknown graves on which the weeds had only just begun to grow.

By the time I began to seek the missing men of Rimau, in an attempt to complete the story of Jaywick, years had dribbled away, memories had been bleached by time, records—if records existed—were grey with the dust of unknown unguessed places.

Knowing nothing about Rimau, my only problem was where to start.

A few yellowing newspaper reports on Rimau, published soon after the war, were my first clues, mere question-marks like wind-bent trees along a coast. But the fragments gathered during my early work on Jaywick told me that these reports were confused, speculative and inaccurate, for often the writers, not aware that Jaywick and Rimau were separate operations, had telescoped the two raids in such a way that they became a corporate tangle which only the initiate could hope to unravel. But as both operations were secret, and as secrecy about much of their planning and execution was continued long after the war, this muddled reporting was understandable, and certainly no reflection on the writers, as I was to find again and again as I tried to uncover the truth and re-enact the lost raid.

Perhaps you remember, during a treasure-hunt in childhood, that tingling excitement akin to fear when a parent or an aunt called, "Getting warmer . . . warmer . . . cool . . . warmer . . . getting hot . . . ", as you search for the prize. If you do remember you will understand the recapturing of that lost excitement when one night, with articles and reports and other fragments which mentioned Rimau spread in front of me, I noticed for the first time that most of them drew their information, or some of it, from a common source, for descriptions were similar, phrases were repeated, words and times synchronized.

But when I had traced that common source I was both satisfied and disappointed with my discovery. The new information was severely limited and, in places, tantalizingly vague. Vital questions were unanswered. Facts were cloudy. But at least the basic information this common source contained was authoritative. There was no doubt about that.

If nothing else, it was a beginning, and a beginning which led to one man.

His name was Wild.

I never knew Cyril Hew Dalrymple Wild, but through others, and especially his charming wife Celia, I feel I knew this tall, good-looking man with expressive blue eyes extremely well.

He was one of those rare personalities you regret not meeting, for, apart from his bearing, his good looks, his beguiling voice, he combined those characteristics which are among the best in any tradition—sensitivity and kindliness, wit and courage.

He was the son of a bishop—the Bishop of Newcastle in England—and three of his brothers entered the Church. One, the last time I heard of him, was Dean of Durham. Another was a chaplain and housemaster at Eton College.

Cyril Wild, born in 1908, was educated at Charterhouse and Brasenose College, Oxford, where he read "Greats", and his wide knowledge of English literature and poetry, allied to a lively intelligence, deep interest in his fellow human beings, and an exceptional memory, made him a stimulating companion.

While working in Japan before World War II with the Asiatic Petroleum Company, his love of language, of words, led him to study Japanese, including Japanese poetry, and although he never completely mastered the language—who does?—his working knowledge of it, and of Japanese history and customs, was extremely sound.

He happened to be in England when war began and immediately joined the Army, and in May 1941, because he could speak Japanese, he was sent to Singapore, where he served with III Indian Corps on the staff of Lieutenant-General Sir Lewis Heath. At the surrender of Singapore he acted as interpreter between the British and Japanese commands, and suffered the indignity of being ordered to carry the surrender flag.

Cyril Wild was a prisoner first at Changi and then in Siam. He was one of the original group of prisoners sent to Siam in April 1943, as members of "F" Force. A few months later half of them were dead from starvation, disease and brutality.

Because he could speak Japanese he acted as liaison officer between the prisoners employed on the notorious Burma-Siam Railway and the Japanese officers in charge of that construction. He not only spoke the language but understood the curious thought-processes and violent emotionalism of his captors, and was able in many ways never known by the men themselves to help his suffering fellows.

"He seemed to be able to tame the Japs," one man has written, "and spent much of his time battling with them on behalf of the prisoners. From personal knowledge I know that he saved several men from having their hands chopped off."

James Mudie, of the British Broadcasting Corporation, who knew Wild in Changi and at Songkrei Camp in Siam, describes Wild as a man of great integrity. "He was extremely sensitive, had a great sense of humour, a commanding, challenging presence, and, to put it simply, breeding. Even the Japanese officers respected him, particularly for those last two characteristics, as well as for his ability to talk their own language. He understood the Japanese officer class and could handle them—and they knew it."

Mudie, who operated a secret radio at Songkrei Camp, was himself saved by Cyril Wild. The Japanese were terrified of getting cholera, and to conceal his radio work Mudie first lived with the camp burial party and later, when the cholera epidemic ceased, he transferred to the camp hospital.

"I got a bit casual. During the day I usually hid the radio in a latrine, but one morning when the set, a battery, a coil of wire and a pair of pliers were in my hut, I heard a bugle call which was the arranged emergency warning that the Japs had started a search. Fortunately, a friend smuggled the radio out, but the Nips found the other things.

"I knew I was for it, so I quickly got word to Cyril Wild. He didn't attempt to explain. He simply told the Jap officers that the battery, wire and pliers were part of the hospital equipment and were used to set up lights for emergency night operations. They believed him, and the hospital was even allowed to keep this 'equipment'."

As Wild visited many of the camps along that terrible railway he trained himself to collect evidence against the Japanese and to store it in his uncanny memory for the time when the Japs would be defeated. After surviving the railway, he was back in Changi Camp in Singapore when the Bomb fell on Hiroshima and the Pacific war skidded to a stop. In a short article, "Expedition to Singkep", published in *Blackwood's Magazine* in October 1946, he wrote a description of the crazy period that followed before the occupation troops arrived.

The officer who relieved us was Lieut.-Colonel Bob Stewart of the Canadian Army, formerly of the Vancouver Police. He had parachuted some weeks before into Johore from India to join the Chinese guerrillas. One day he arrived in Changi Camp in a Chevrolet roadster commandeered from a Japanese general in Johore Bahru.

Even the Japanese were startled at the contrast between his magnificent physique and our somewhat attenuated frames. With Stewart I spent a happy week touring the island, with a Union Jack flying on the roadster. We visited the Civilian Internment Camp at Sime Road, and all the camps of the Indian prisoners of war. Later, Major Cooper, an aerodrome engineer, arrived from the Cocos Islands in a Mosquito. With him, as his interpreter, I visited all the aerodromes on the island, to measure them up and see that the Japs had taken the propellers off their planes. While General Itagaki still kept up his boasting that he would fight for Malaya and Singapore, we saw his men piling their arms and shuffling northwards across the Causeway in their thousands.

So far the local population had dared do no more than give surreptitious V-for-victory and thumbs-up signs as our car with the Union Jack sped past. But today, as we returned from Tengah Aerodrome, we could scarcely drive through the cheering crowds in Singapore. And the cheering was loudest wherever disconsolate Japanese sentries were still standing beside the road. The explanation came as we reached Keppel Harbour and I saw the first flight of the 5th Indian Division, in their unfamiliar jungle-green, advancing with fixed bayonets past the godowns. We drove down to the dockside and met the general as he disembarked. Almost his first words were, 'Take that Union Jack off your car', which was fair enough; for we were no longer the C-in-C, but amusing after three and a half years under the Poached Egg flag!

The next day Colonel Wild joined War Crimes, and his first job, with Lieutenant-Colonel L. F. G. Pritchard, was to investigate the fate of an American B29 crew believed to have gone down in the Malaya area. This was a job which began, as some War Crimes investigations did, with a "tip-off" from a Malay *sais* who had been driver for Lieutenant-Colonel Koshiro Mikizawa, the unpleasant commander of the Civil Section in notorious Outram Road, the jail which few prisoners, European or Asiatic, left alive.

Mikizawa, who had "lost" twelve hundred Asiatic prisoners from starvation in the last fourteen months of the war, had in July, three weeks before the surrender, been driven by this *sais* to an execution near Bukit Timah, off Reformatory Road.

The Japanese commandant was bland and helpful when Wild questioned him. He had attended an execution in July of some Chinese prisoners. He remembered it clearly. He would be glad to point out the graves.

At Bukit Timah he led the War Crimes men to a trampled area scarred with many graves, some still expectantly open, others so rain-washed that the once-heaped earth had subsided below ground-level. He scuttled among the bushes and rank weeds like an unpleasant crab, peering through his thick spectacles with thin ear-pieces, until at last he found what he was looking for—three mounds so new that the weeds were only just beginning to grow. These, he said, were the graves of the Chinese he had seen executed.

Then why, asked Colonel Wild, were the graves marked with crosses—Christian crosses?

Mikizawa showed his gold-filled teeth. He did not know. But these were the graves where the Chinese had been buried. He was positive. He continued to nod and smile.

Because the authorities at that stage would not allow the War Crimes investigators to exhume, the graves with the plain wood crosses above them had to stay closed. But Wild was so convinced Mikizawa was lying, and that even if the graves did contain Chinese there was still something suspicious about the execution of these men, that he decided to watch for more evidence which might link the Japanese commandant and Outram Road Jail with these graves or with the unexplained disappearance of any prisoners.

Wild felt that the ritual-minded Japanese, with more traditional regard for the dead than for the living, would never place Christian crosses above the graves of Chinese, and the more he thought about these crosses the more convinced he was that they were a first clue to some still unexplained event from the occupation years.

A week later a young Malay chieftain from Singkep Island, which is just south of Linga Island in the Rhio Archipelago, gave new and intriguing information to the War Crimes Department in Singapore.

He was the Amir Silalahi, who had been deposed by the Japanese and who had only just escaped from Singkep in a motor tongkan and reached Singapore.

Before I describe the information the Amir brought, there is an earlier story to tell which not only explains why the young sultan and his report were important to War Crimes, but reached way back into the origins of Operation Jaywick itself and way forward through the *Krait* raid into Operation Rimau. The story is Colonel Wild's, but even he was unaware of the pattern of interlocking events, places and personalities, and of the uncanny inevitability of that pattern, when he wrote the following few hundred words dealing with escape from Singapore:

On 13th February 1942 [two days before Singapore surrendered], as the sun set behind the smoke rising from Singapore, s.s. *Kuala* sailed from Laburnum Steps for Batavia. Her passengers were mainly nursing-sisters, with a party of P.W.D. [Public Works Department] men, some R.A.F. technicians, and a few civilians. They had suffered some casualties from bombing while waiting to embark, and were bombed again without effect before they sailed. At dawn on 14th February the *Kuala* anchored off Pompong Island in the Rhio Archipelago, 300 yards from s.s. *Tien Kuang*, which had left Singapore in company with her. A mile away lay the s.s. *Kung Wo*, with a decided list from bombing received the night before. Boats were lowered to fetch foliage from the shore for camouflage, and two were still away when a flight of Japanese bombers came over at 11.30 to finish off the *Kung Wo*. They sank her in a few minutes. The *Kuala's* turn came next: the first stick set her afire, and two more followed. Women and wounded were sent away in the remaining boats, and the rest of the ship's company, including some of the women, took to the water, supporting themselves on mattresses and spars. Unfortunately the current carried them down towards the *Tien Kuang*, to which the bombers were now turning their attention. Four sticks were dropped, which did little apparent damage to the ship, but killed and wounded a number of people in the water. The last flight of bombers dropped their load on shore, causing further casualties among those who had already landed. The survivors of the three ships divided into two parties of about 400 and 250 and made their way to the north and south of the island, which was about a mile across, covered with dense jungle and uninhabited. Their intention was to avoid the unhealthy neighbourhood of the ships, should the bombers return; for although the *Kuala* was now ablaze, the *Tien Kuang* still offered a tempting target. The ship's whaler was used at night to maintain contact between the two camps and to carry water from a small spring at the north of the island to the people in the south. After dark a party of volunteers boarded the *Tien Kuang* and obtained a quantity of stores and medical supplies. An attempt was made to raise steam, but the sea had risen too high in her engine-room. She was therefore scuttled by opening a sea-cock, before she could attract more bombers.

On the afternoon of 16th February a small sampan arrived manned by three Malays, who said that on all the small neighbouring islands there were more survivors of ships sunk by bombing. They were asked to obtain food and assistance, and set off again, promising to do their best. At 1 a.m. the following morning they returned with small supplies of coconuts and rice. The owner of the sampan, Ali by name, urged that an attempt should be made to reach the island of Senajang, where help could be obtained. Mr I. G. Salmond, who spoke both Dutch and Malay, was chosen for this task, and set off in the sampan, taking with him eight wounded R.A.F. men and one Sepoy. They left Pompong with the Malays about 1.30 a.m. One of the wounded died a few hours later, but the craft was so small that it was impossible to dispose of the body without capsizing. It was therefore kept on board until they could bury it on Senajang, where they arrived about 3 p.m. on 17th February.

Here Salmond hastened to meet the Amir, Silalahi, a Malay chieftain with authority over a hundred islands in the Archipelago. His title in Dutch is "Hoofd der Onderafdeeling Blakang Daik".

On hearing the story of Pompong, the Amir at once pledged all the help of himself and his people to the hundreds of British thus stranded in his territory. He himself set off for the island of Redjai to collect motor *tongkans*, and undertook to send the news by the first of these to the nearest Dutch Controlleur, at Dabot, on Singkep Island. During the next two weeks the Amir worked unceasingly day and night, scouring the islands of the Archipelago with a fleet of *tongkans* and sampans to collect survivors, and stinting his own people of food and shelter in his determination to succour these sufferers of an alien race. He did this out of his great humanity, without thought of favour or reward, knowing full well the danger of reprisals from the Japanese, whose arrival was expected daily.

By the end of February nearly one thousand British men, women, and children had been ferried over to the mouth of the Indragiri River fifty or sixty miles away [in Sumatra], most of them in native craft, but some in small ships of the Royal Navy, such as H.M.S. *Hung Jau*. From the Indragiri River they crossed Sumatra to Padang where most of them were evacuated by the

Royal Navy. Many hundreds in England and Australia today owe their liberty and lives to the Amir Sililahi.

Mr Salmond remained in charge of Senajang and Singkep Islands until the last of the survivors had passed through. On leaving Singkep he took the Amir by the hand and said: "I promise that when the day comes I shall return from Singapore with the British Navy to drive out the Japanese." "No, Tuan," replied the Amir quietly, "I shall come to Singapore to meet you, and we shall return together with the British Navy to liberate my people."

Mr Salmond reached Padang on 10th March, some days after the last British ship had left. There he met a man of the same temper as himself in Lieut.-Colonel F. J. Dillon, M.C., who had been ordered to leave Singapore for India on 13th February. Dillon, too, had risked his own chance of escape by staying for a month in central Sumatra until he had organised transport to the west coast for the many hundreds who had escaped from Singapore. Mr Salmond joined him as interpreter, and with a party of eight officers they left Sumatra in a small sailing junk on 16th March and set their course for Ceylon. When dawn broke on 4th April they were well on their way with a favouring wind, and thought that their worst danger, from the daily reconnaissance from land-based aircraft, were behind them. Instead, out of the mist emerged three Japanese naval tankers, and forty-eight hours later they were all back in Singapore, as prisoners.

August, 1945, found Dillon in Changi Camp, near Singapore, after our sojourn together on the Burma-Siam Railway with "F" Force. (I can only hope that the gratitude of the surviving British and Australian members of that party, which lost 3,100 out of 7000 up by the Three Pagodas Pass in seven months, goes some way to console him for the unlucky chance which overtook him in mid-ocean.)

There is the pattern into which are woven so many things:

Ivan Lyon and his part in organizing the escape route, which Wild describes, for those Singapore refugees across to Sumatra and to safety.

Old Bill Reynolds who helped ferry so many of those refugees from the Rhio islands to the Indragiri River in Sumatra in his little fishing boat the *Kofuku Maru*—better known as the *Krait*.

The *Krait* herself, which inspired Lyon to plan and execute Operation Jaywick and to follow this raid with Operation Rimau.

Pompong Island, at the end of Temiang Strait, which the black raiders of Jaywick used as their rendezvous.

The mast which the Jaywick men saw near Pompong Island—the mast of one of those bombed ships in which escaping people from Singapore died, and from which escaping people survived to remember with gratitude the name of Silalahi.

Add to all this one more name and the pattern, which would seem exaggerated in fiction, is almost complete, for it was Salmond, just released from Sime Road Internment Camp, who was the first man the Amir Silalahi searched for and found when he reached Singapore from his island home of Singkep after the Japanese surrender, and it was Salmond, too, who brought this magnificent young Malay chieftain to War Crimes.

The Amir had two most important pieces of information. The first was that the Japanese, from their Rhio headquarters at Singkep Island, were still terrorizing the islands of the archipelago although the war had ended, and among their garrison were twenty-seven members of the Kempeitai, the Japanese Gestapo, twelve of them involved in the Double Tenth case— the arrest on 10th October 1943 of more than forty British internees in Singapore and the death from torture of fifteen of these people.

The second was that ten British and Australian members of a raiding party had been captured in December 1944, and had been kept prisoners on Singkep until taken to Singapore.

Colonel Wild, listening to the Amir's story, thought immediately of Mikizawa's Chinese graves near Bukit Timah, and although he could see no link between those graves and the unknown men the Amir described, he still felt that a connection might exist to explain those Christian crosses.

Who were the nameless ten? Could they and the crosses belong together? Was the Singkep the link?

But many weeks were to pass before Wild could get to Singkep Island to test not his reasoning but his instinct. As he explains:

> The task of reoccupying Malaya was such that it was not until October that we could take action. Meantime, the Amir stayed on patiently in Singapore. We took him to the Great World Amusement Park and to the Cathay to see "Tunisian Victory". He was an appreciative and forebearing guest, but at the end of each evening he would ask us, "When will the British Navy be coming to liberate my people?"
>
> At last, one morning in October, four M.L.s set forth from Collyer Quay. On board, beside our excellent Naval hosts, were half a platoon of paratroopers under a subaltern; Major Sheppard of the Malayan Civil Service, who had planned the expedition and had himself twice experienced Kempeitai methods of interrogation in captivity; another ex-internee, Mr Leonard Knight of the Police, engaged like Sheppard on the Double Tenth investigation; a Dutch official; myself and Mr Salmond and the

Amir Silalahi, together keeping their engagement of three and a half years before. Next morning the Amir was gazing proudly from the deck at the palm-fringed beaches of Singkep Island and the jungle-clad peaks beyond. On the pier waited the Japanese garrison commander, who had been warned by wireless of our coming. We split into four parties: Sheppard went into the little town of Dabot with Salmond and the Amir to assist the new Dutch Controlleur to take over. Knight set off to organise and arm the police. Another officer with a Malay interpreter inquired into the Amir's story of the missing British and Australian party, while I went up the hill behind the town to the Kempeitai headquarters. On calling the roll I found that one badly wanted man was missing, Miyazaki, a Jap-Malay halfcaste, who had interpreted for the Kempeitai in the Double Tenth, particularly during the torture of the Bishop of Singapore. On the principle of setting a thief to catch a thief, I selected the four toughest-looking Kempei and sent them off in two flying squads to find him. Long before my time-limit of one hour was up, two of the Kempei had brought him back well roped between them, having found him in a small sailing boat, struggling to catch a breeze that would take him to one of the neighbouring islands.

We left for Singapore again that night with twenty-five Japanese squatting in the bows of our four M.L.s. Also among our captives, at the Controlleur's request, was the Malay quisling who had usurped the Amir's place. The Amir himself stood waving farewell to us from the end of Singkep's pier until he and then his island were lost to view in the gathering darkness.

Among our trophies was the administration book of the local police station and a scrap of paper bearing the names of a British officer, a warrant officer, and an able seaman, each pencilled in block letters in a different hand. The admission book, kept in Malay, showed that on 18th and 19th December 1944 six "white men" had been admitted, and all had been transferred to Singapore on 23rd December. A later entry showed that three more "white men" had been admitted on 28th-29th December and had left for Singapore on 8th January 1945. The charge against each was the same, "enemy of the State". Attempts had been made to write the names of some of them, but, apart from those on the scrap of paper, only one was clear—"R. M. Ingleton, Major, Royal Marines, British." Two others were marked "Australian", and one "Australian (British)."

These were the only clues when we took up the hunt for the nine "white men" in Singapore. There was no trace of such people having ever been in a prisoner-of-war camp, and the Japanese were in a conspiracy to tell us nothing. No single survivor, as it turned out, remained beyond that found on Singkep. Yet within a month we knew their story in full, and how and where each one of them (not only those nine, but fourteen of their comrades) had met their end. . . .

5

COLONEL CYRIL WILD had direct access to Japanese Army and prison records and to all those Japanese connected in any way with Operation Rimau. He therefore knew the full story of the raid, particularly from the Singapore and Japanese end, and of the fate of its twenty-three members.

He knew that the Rimau men, instead of having to endure the usual Japanese ill-treatment and starvation, were not only well treated, but "treated with respect, verging on awe", and that a "well-disposed Japanese interpreter" had shown them great kindness and even supplied them with amenities.

He knew they were tried by a Japanese military court and executed, that they were buried in those graves at Bukit Timah marked with Christian crosses, and that Lieutenant-Colonel Mikizawa had probably only been half-lying, and may even have been telling the truth as he knew it, for the Chinese he saw executed were found in unmarked graves near the graves with the crosses.

Unfortunately, Cyril Wild only briefly summarized all the information he had obtained when he wrote his all too short "Expedition to Singkep". He left so much untold about Rimau, so many points ignored or only partly answered, mentioned so few names, and filled in so little of the general background, that it was obvious to me that I would have to know much more before I could hope to re-create the full events of the raid which failed and vanished.

To contact Wild and to ask him to help fill the many gaps in his brief account was clearly the next move, and it was with a researcher's excitement, and expectation that I might soon know the complete story, that I started to trace him.

But Colonel Cyril Wild was dead—long dead. He had been killed, I found, in 1946 in a plane crash at Hong Kong while returning to England from Tokyo, where he had been an important witness at the War Crimes trials.

Now I had to begin again, since I was back where I had started, though later Mrs Celia Wild, of Winchester, England, went out of her way to help me with invaluable information she had gained in Singapore after the war when she joined her husband, with some of the documents her husband had assembled during his investigation—though they did not give me the full answers I needed—and with her personal permission to use her husband's "Expedition to Singkep", which *Blackwood's Magazine* also kindly allowed me to quote.

But use of this article, and the new information, was still not enough, though it produced new clues and opened the way along new paths of research.

I had to find more—more about the Rimau prisoners, their capture and the life they had led in Singapore, more about their interrogation and trial and the trial records Wild mentioned in his article, more about their end. I wanted to know everything —the attainable and the impossible—and all the time I was broodingly conscious that I was searching for twenty-three dead men—men who had disappeared years before, who had been seen in those months before their deaths only by a few unknown enemy Japanese.

And so I began a new search which lasted months and took me to many countries. It was a search by letter, a cumbersome and unsatisfying method which made me aware, as never before, of the limitations in communication which the written word imposes without the direct humanizing contact of personality. I wrote letters, dozens of them, and every time I posted one it was like launching a toy boat—as the Polynesians did—on a river at night and wondering if the tide would ever bring it back.

But all my letters did not go out to sea. Replies came— stamped in Melbourne, Port Moresby, Singapore, Kuala Lumpur, Calcutta, London, Edinburgh and many other places.

Some of the people I wrote to ignored my requests. One man, who could have contributed to my search, I'm sure, sent me a telegram of welcome under the impression that I had been a prisoner of war with him and had just arrived in Sydney from overseas. When I wrote explaining his mistake and asking for his help, I never heard from him again.

Some could not help. Others supplied addresses as possible sources of material. Others still gave me new details of value. But apart from all these personal contacts, my search for the translations of Japanese documents dealing with the military court which tried the Rimau prisoners was almost a full-time spare-time job in itself.

As E. C. S. Jennings, a helpful old colleague in Singapore, wrote: "The stuff you want from Japanese sources is well-nigh impossible. I can assure you that 11 years after, this is not available in Singapore. I have tried to get the materials and have always failed. Someone either carted it away to London or Washington or Tokyo or it was destroyed."

So the translations were not in Singapore. They were not in Australia, or, if they were, I could not find them. Inquiries suggested that if they existed at all they were almost certainly in London. But where? The Air Ministry's Air Historical Bureau was the hottest tip—and it was wrong.

I became a long-distance mendicant peddling the same question all over London—from the Air Ministry to the Ministry of Defence to the War Office, from the Judge Advocate-General of the Forces to the Historical Section of the Cabinet Office, to the Director of Research, Acting Librarian and Keeper of the Papers at the Foreign Office, to the. . . .

On this exasperating journey officials everywhere were extremely courteous and helpful, but. . . . "We do not hold the proceedings required". . . . "I am afraid we do not have copies of the translations". . . . "We have never held these papers". . . . "We regret we cannot help you, but suggest you write to the. . . ."

On and on went the search, achieving nothing, getting nowhere, my inquiries like bats flitting from one vast department to another and on to the next.

Then one day a letter, embossed with the Royal Arms, arrived. It was from the Foreign Office.

"The position is that after the British Forces recaptured Singapore," Mr C. H. Fone wrote me, "the records of the trial were found and examined.

"As, however, there was no proof of any illegality in the proceedings the documents were not preserved in any way and there is now no trace of them.

"Presumably, the sources quoted by Cyril Wild in his article formed part of the documentation of the trial to which he would have had access when accompanying the War Crimes officers at the end of the War. . . ."

After months of search this letter looked conclusive. Sadly I read it again. Even more sadly I filed it. I was defeated, but I still wasn't satisfied.

I argued—I had reached the talking-to-myself stage—that surely historical or research or records section of British Government departments were not designed to misfile, misplace, mislay or lose documents of this kind, and the suggestion that the papers might have been destroyed was unthinkable—almost a form of public-service sacrilege.

I am still convinced the translations exist—somewhere.

But with the Foreign Office letter in my file, and its melancholy message in my memory, I was ready at last to abandon not only the search but my attempt to re-create Rimau. True, from all sources I now knew a lot about the lost raid and the fate of its members, but I still lacked sufficient background against which to reconstruct, as fully as possible, the story of what happened.

Then one evening, while making a final assessment of all the information I had gathered, I halted three times at a name.

That name, Furuta, was mentioned among Wild's documents. It was mentioned in a letter I had received from Mrs Wild. It was in a letter from Professor Sam Carey about his brother.

But the name was not a discovery, a bright little nugget in a panning dish. It was in documents and letters, and I knew that Furuta was the Japanese interpreter at the original interrogation of the Rimau men and at their trial.

Much earlier, I had even considered trying to trace this man, but had rejected the idea as foolish waste of time. I remember even smiling a little at my own wayward thought that it might be remotely possible to find one Japanese—and one Japanese without even knowing his full name—among a hundred million Japanese.

Now I looked with renewed interest at that man's name— and wondered. But how could I hope to trace him among the total population of Japan? Where would I start? Would he have been an officer or non-commissioned officer or even a private soldier? What was his unit and would he have an identification number? Was there an ex-servicemen's organization in Japan? Did Japanese Army records still exist or had they all been destroyed at the end of the war? Was the man still alive? And, if so, would it help me if I did trace him?

The questions tumbled over each other and I couldn't answer one of them. But I decided that if anyone could find Furuta, even among a hundred million Japanese, it would be a man of my own craft, a newspaperman. And the only journalist I had known in Japan had left months before.

I telephoned an old friend, Don Tait, chief of The Associated Press Bureau in Sydney, and explained my dilemma. We both thought the search was hopeless, but he gave me the name of A.P.'s Bureau Chief in Tokyo, John Randolph, and also wrote him a note asking him to help me.

I wrote to John Randolph, apologizing for my impossible request but hoping that, as the loaves and the fishes had once multiplied, it might be possible to find me one man named Furuta, who had once been an Army interpreter in Singapore, among the millions of Japan.

I was so certain what the reply would be that I watched the post box with no more than normal interest, and when a letter with a Japanese stamp arrived I opened it with about the same amount of interest I reserve for bills.

The letter was from Donald K. Baldwin, News Editor of A.P., explaining that he had taken over my request as Randolph was away.

Donald Baldwin wrote:

"One of those rare coincidences for which there is no explanation has, I believe, enabled The Associated Press to find your Mr Furuta.

"When your letter arrived we telephoned the Japan Veterans' Association and the Defence Ministry without success, and I wrote a brief note saying there was little hope that we could find Furuta without a more solid clue.

"A member of our staff, Mrs Yoko Murai, saw the note on my desk and recalled that her former English teacher, a man named Furuta, had worked in Singapore. She contacted the family and it appears that the man you are seeking is Hiroyuki Furuta, No. 51 Chimo-Daita, Setagaya-ku, Tokyo. His telephone number is Tokyo 42-6254."

One name plucked from those bead-like islands dangling from the neck of Asia—because I wrote a letter at a certain time and sent it by a certain mail so that a woman I did not know existed should see a letter and recognize a name. Strange synchronism of stage and time—even to a man's telephone number.

But caution whispered that a name was not enough. Now I had to find if this stranger Furuta could, and would, unwrap Rimau as the Japanese saw it.

Hiroyuki Furuta's reply to my letter was back by return mail, and here are its relevant points, just as I received them, typed in English:

"I am in receipt of your letter, and have noted its contents with much interest and pleasure.

"It has long been my desire to get in touch with the families of the members of the Rimau operation, especially with the wife of Captain Page.

"The reason why I have not written to a newspaper office in Sydney or have not taken any aggressive step in this matter was because I was not sure how I might be accepted by them.

"Captain Page and I developed a keen friendship and he told me many things which I do want to pass to his families.

"I shall be happy to answer any questions that you will write to me. I also have a friend, Major Kamiya, who acted as Prosecutor in the Court Martial on the case of Rimau Operation. He will help me on anything that I cannot answer myself.

"The February issue of one the most well known Japanese magazines called 'Bungei Shunju' offered a prize for a story which started with 'I', in other words, a story of any personal experience. I wrote a story, 'Heroes of Rimau Operation Rest Here', and it got the first prize. If I can get some free time, I might translate this and send it to you, that is, if you think it is of some interest. . . .

"In October, 1950, I was Japan's delegate of Red Cross at the International Conference held in Monte Carlo. . . . "

That letter, the first of many which later were to flow up and down the longitude between Sydney and Tokyo, looked like a new beginning.

Hiroyuki Furuta was born in 1906, studied English at the Tokyo Foreign Language College, and, son of a well-to-do father, was able to continue his studies and spend five years in Europe, Africa, America and southern Asia between 1927 and 1932. In the next decade he operated an import-export business in Yokohama, and in 1944 was called up as a civilian interpreter to the Japanese Army and sent to Singapore.

He interpreted at the War Crimes trials in Singapore after the Pacific war and later at the International Military Tribunal for the Far East in Tokyo in 1946-8. He was Director of Public Relations for the Japanese Red Cross Society from 1948 to 1953, and was Japan's delegate to the International Red Cross Conference in Monte Carlo in 1950. During this period he was also Japanese manager of Unasia Corporation, an American trading company with headquarters in San Francisco.

Since 1957 he has been a theatrical entrepreneur, managing director of Universal Promotions, which imports and exports theatre companies and theatre acts.

Furuta, who is one of the leading Mah-jongg players of Japan, is married with two grown-up daughters, Masayuki and Yoko, both university graduates, and one son, Tomoyuki, now a student at Waseda University.

At the start of our long correspondence, which stretched into thousands of words of questions and answers, of explanations and descriptions, I naturally wondered how much reliance I could place in Hiroyuki Furuta's information.

This was a reasonable doubt, a mental and emotional reservation towards a former enemy which no amount of objectivity could sweep aside. It was also caution dictated by realism that the very thing I had set out to achieve, the accurate re-creation of Operation Rimau would be worthless unless I was completely satisfied that what he told me was correct.

Naturally, as our correspondence progressed, I asked myself many questions. Was his information accurate? Was it deliberately twisted to give the right or the wrong impression? Did his apparent humanitarianism flow from genuine feelings he had for the Rimau prisoners, or from defeat, and only from defeat? Was he attempting to dilute general knowledge of Japanese brutality in Singapore and every other place the Japanese mastered? Was he trying, in his own way, through conscience developed only since surrender, to whitewash Japan for her atrocities by showing that her soldiers, or some of them, did not always behave with studied sadism towards defenceless people?

These were natural doubts to anyone who remembers those tense days in Australia in 1942 when Japanese invasion was regarded as certain, to anyone who knows that 27 per cent of

British and American prisoners of the Japanese died because of the systematic and savage brutality of their captors, to anyone who knows, as Lord Russell of Liverpool has also pointed out in his *The Knights of Bushido,* that each mile of the Burma-Siam Railway was paid for with the lives of 64 prisoners of war and 240 coolie slaves.

I was therefore so sceptical that I was not prepared to accept one sentence without testing it critically, and I was ready to reject all Furuta's information if at any time I was not satisfied of the authenticity of any part of it.

I took the greatest trouble with my letters and carefully studied his answers and, so far as I was able, the alien thought-processes behind those answers phrased in English not always entirely accurate in its grammar or construction. I asked for explanations, and explanations of explanations. I questioned statements, names, words, times. I returned often and in devious ways to points I did not clearly understand, to ambiguities.

And I early noticed that on facts I knew, and knew were vital to the truth of this story, he never attempted to evade or embroider, for I was able to test his replies, and that if he could not answer a question he said so and gave his reasons.

Over the months he also translated and sent me his own prize-winning story, "Heroes of Rimau Operation Rest Here", an article in praise of enemies which had told the Japanese public something of what he knew of the lost raid and the extraordinary reaction of the Japanese in Singapore to the captured raiders.

To me his story was particularly interesting because several months after I received it the British Foreign Office also sent me a translation of it which their Research Section had kindly found for me. I put the stories side by side. The Foreign Office version was in precise English. Furuta's was much freer and less grammatically correct. But except for two or three points, and one particularly which Furuta was able to explain satisfactorily, these two translations were basically identical.

Throughout this international interview—for that is what it was—between myself and Furuta, my experience as a journalist helped me assess Furuta's account of events long past and attempt to balance it with Cyril Wild's and other information in my files, taking into account, of course, that human memory at best, as any police court evidence of an accident will prove, is a frail thing.

Cyril Wild's report on Rimau was little more than a skeleton of those total events in Singapore, but it was authentic because it was based on examination of all relevant documents dealing with Rimau, and careful interrogation of all those individuals linked in any way with the Rimau men.

And one of those Japanese whom Wild questioned at length at the end of the war, before releasing him from jail, was Furuta.

It is important to remember that when Colonel Wild finally closed his investigation no charges were made by War Crimes against any of the Japanese for their conduct in the interrogation, trial and execution of the Rimau men.

And this action by Wild was confirmed from three sources in my possession—the letter from the Foreign Office already quoted, Furuta, and a letter written from the Australian Minister for the Army, Mr (now Sir) Joshua Francis, to the mother of Lieutenant Walter Carey.

Hiroyuki Furuta's account of Operation Rimau was inevitably much longer and more detailed than Wild's summary and the information contained in the documents he left. Furuta was in Singapore, on the spot, and his contact with the prisoners began from the day they reached Singapore. His firsthand story is therefore direct from the inside. It describes in detail how he and other Japanese reacted to the prisoners. Furuta's account contains information which Wild never knew, or knew only in general terms.

As my only consideration was accuracy, and accuracy divorced as far as possible from the emotion latent in this story as you will read it, I had, finally and objectively, to sum up and pass judgment on Hiroyuki Furuta's fidelity. And my only way of doing this was to put Wild's account and Furuta's side by side and compare them in relation to all other information I possessed.

On all fundamental points—those which mattered to the validity of the story, those which might be suspect in any way —the two accounts agreed.

I believe Hiroyuki Furuta is honest, his account reliable, and that his humanitarian feelings for the prisoners, and particularly for Captain Page, were genuine.

Now I can do no more than present this story of the gallant men of Operation Rimau as I collected it from both sides— the British and the Japanese—as I analysed and judged it over many months, and as I accepted it; believing that the story itself, in all its victory of the human spirit, is the ultimate test that it is true.

6

WHEN THE CAPTURED JUNK *Mustika*, with the twenty-two men of Operation Rimau aboard, sailed from Pejantan Island, in the middle of the South China Sea, on 1st October 1944, Ivan

Lyon intended to head straight for Singapore. But he changed his mind and first called at Merapas Island, Rimau's base A, where Lieutenant Carey had been left alone on 25th September to guard the operation's supplies.

At Merapas, the most easterly island of the Rhio Archipelago, Lyon landed some of his men as an added protection for his rear base now that attack against Singapore was about to start, though the actual number of men left at Merapas is doubtful. Although the Japanese believed he landed ten, I think this is wrong, because he needed fifteen men to operate his Sleeping Beauties and several more men at least to stay aboard and guard the *Mustika* during the attack on Singapore's shipping and docks. I am more inclined to accept another report that he left four men at Merapas under Lieutenant Carey and that eighteen men were on board the 100-ton junk when she finally sailed for Singapore.

As Major Ingleton, the Royal Marine Commando, was not a real member of Rimau, but, as the representative of South-east Asia Command with the operation, was really an observer, Lyon's intention was to leave him at Merapas during the raid. But after the *Mustika* left Pejantan, Ingleton pleaded to be allowed to go on the raid and Lyon agreed on one condition—that the six-foot-two Englishman would not be allowed on deck in daylight because, even with his skin and hair stained, and wearing a sarong, his size would be much too conspicuous on the deck of an apparently harmless trading junk.

When the *Mustika* sailed from Merapas all members of Rimau stained their bodies and faces, as in the *Krait* raid, and wore green berets and jungle greens, without badges of rank, when off duty and sarongs when on deck working the vessel. The *Mustika* flew the Poached Egg and the Japanese Military Government flag, which was similar to the Rising Sun except for straight lines which indicated the sun's rays and six characters which read, "Shonan Military Administration Headquarters". The Military Government flag was flown on ships not being used by the Japanese Army or Navy.

The *Mustika* moved almost due south from Merapas—to avoid the heavy sea traffic using Rhio Strait—and turned up Temiang Strait, which Operation Jaywick had used so often and so successfully a year before. Then she continued on north-west until she passed through Suji Strait, and turned towards her target—Singapore.

In the passage through the Thousand Islands which began at Temiang, the *Mustika* passed in daylight within five hundred yards of a Japanese naval anchorage, and Major Ingleton made detailed drawings of warships there. During the passage, too, when a Navy plane dived towards them, Bob Page waved the

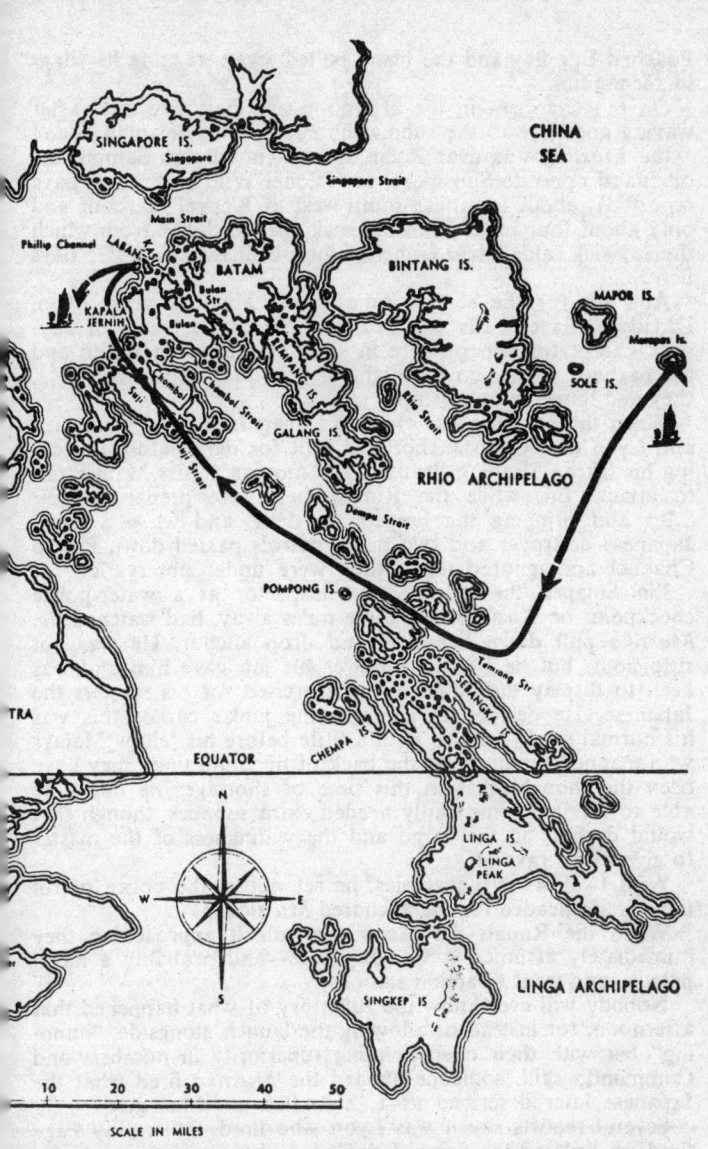

Route of the Junk *Mustika*, pirated near Borneo by Operation Rimau, from Merapas Island, in the Rhio Archipelago, through Temiang and Suji straits to near Singapore.

Poached Egg flag and the plane pulled away wagging its wings in recognition.

On 6th October—in the afternoon and only five days after waving good-bye to the submarine *Porpoise* at Pejantan Island —the *Mustika* was near Pulau Laban (not Pulau Sambo, the oil island opposite Singapore, as Colonel Wild and others have reported), about ten miles south-west of Keppel Harbour and only about four miles from the rock islet of Subar from which the Jaywick raiders had launched their brilliant attack 375 days before.

And so, for the second time within about a year, Lyon, Davidson, Page, Falls and Huston—the canoe teams of Jaywick except for Jones—were in sight of Singapore Island and the harbour where, on the night of 26th-27th September 1943, they had limpeted seven ships.

When the *Mustika* was close to Laban Island the wind died and Lyon decided to anchor and wait for dark before launching his fifteen Sleeping Beauties and moving across Main Strait to attack. But while the Rimau men were preparing their S.B.s and bringing the limpets on deck, and while a small Japanese destroyer and two naval patrols passed down Phillip Channel and ignored them, they were under observation.

Bin Shiapel, the local Malay inspector at a water-police checkpoint on Kasu Island, three miles away, had watched the *Mustika* pull down her sails and drop anchor. He was not suspicious, but he liked the power his job gave him and was keen to display the authority he exercised for his masters the Japanese. He decided to examine the junk's cargo—this was his normal work—and to strut a little before his fellow Malays who manned the junk. At the back of his mind there may have been the thought that in this time of shortages he might be able to pick up some badly needed extra supplies, though that would depend on the cargo and the willingness of the master to give him a rake-off.

With two Malay constables, he set out in the police patrol launch and headed for the anchored *Mustika*.

When the Rimau party saw the launch approaching they immediately assumed it was Japanese—and probably a naval patrol—and went to action stations.

Nobody will ever know the full story of what happened that afternoon, for instead of allowing the launch alongside, "jumping" her with their overwhelming superiority in numbers and Commando skill, someone aboard the *Mustika* fired what the Japanese later described as a "soundless machine gun".

Several reports say it was Lyon who fired. Others say Page fired, or ordered the firing. I don't believe any of this, and for good reasons. Both men were too experienced not to know that the use of weapons so close to Singapore would be catastrophic. And Page, who was junior to Lyon and to the operational leader Davidson, would never have given a fire order.

Whoever it was, some member of Rimau panicked and wrecked the operation.

Although the Australian Army report on Rimau says that all the "natives" in the patrol boat were killed, an unofficial report I have mentions that one man survived. This is correct, for one Malay constable did reach Laban Island to give the alarm—though this raises questions which are almost impossible to answer. With the patrol launch riddled and sunk—the firing must have been heavy—and his two compatriots killed, how did this Malay swim away unnoticed or, if he was seen, why wasn't he shot? The firing had already shattered Rimau's security, and a few more shots would not have mattered. To let this man escape was a major blunder by Rimau, because he was able to report at least two important things—the attack itself, and from a junk flying the Japanese and Japanese Military Government flags.

Ivan Lyon decided that, with the operation's secrecy gone and its future hazardous, they would have to destroy the slow *Mustika* and the secret Sleeping Beauties and retreat as quickly as possible. He estimated that they would not have "more than three hours" before the Japanese heard of the destruction of the Malay police patrol and came in pursuit.

Lyon's "three-hour" estimate may have been based on the knowledge that the Malay constable had escaped and got ashore, which suggests that for some reason they were not able to kill the man in the water or to chase him, though this is difficult to believe as the firing on the Malay patrol boat was at point-blank range.

When the Rimau party began their retreat from Singapore the sun was already down. They raised the heavy russet sails and, in the evening breeze which had swept aside the afternoon calm, the *Mustika* moved slowly south down Phillip Channel. In the quickening dusk the men, turned into the hunted by that fatal gunfire, unpacked the canoes and assembled them on the junk's decks and brought up from the holds the emergency stores, water-cans and bottles, medical supplies and arms and ammunition.

Well after dark, when off the island of Kapala Jernih, west of Bulan Island, and about sixteen miles from Singapore, they blew up the *Mustika,* her holds packed with Sleeping Beauties, with the limpets, and in four separate canoe parties, led by Lyon, Davidson, Page and Lieutenant Ross, started their long, independent and desperate paddle back to Base A on far-off Merapas Island.

That evening of retreat was 6th October, and their first rendezvous with the pick-up submarine on 8th November—the R.V. which was never kept—was thirty-three days ahead.

7

IN THE OFFICERS' DINING HALL at 7th Area Headquarters, Singapore, on Monday, 9th October 1944, Colonel Nagaaki Yoshida, Chief of Intelligence, swallowed a mouthful of rice and bean as he read the message just handed to him in the middle of his lunch.

He frowned, stuffed the paper into his pocket, beckoned to his deputy, Lieutenant-Colonel Cho Kuwabara, and together they rose, bowed quickly to General Kenji Dohihara, and hurried out.

In the long hall—the north wing at Raffles College—officers put their chopsticks down and stared at each other in amazement. To leave before the Commander-in-Chief was extraordinary, permitted only in the most exceptional circumstances. And to leave so suddenly, with such abrupt bows, was against all military etiquette. Unless, of course....

Waves of chatter swept the hall. Something important must have happened. But what?

Over in the corner Hiroyuki Furuta, civilian interpreter attached to Army Intelligence, listened to the excited talk. He knew that only the most important news would drag his chiefs from their lunch, which they always enjoyed, and that this could mean he might be needed urgently.

Though classified as a captain and suffered to be a member of the mess, he was still a civilian, and for a civilian to have the effrontery to move before a commanding general, and especially a general like Kenji Dohihara, of China fame, was to invite the most unpleasant attention—or worse.

Furuta, who didn't dare move, knew only too well that civilians in the Japanese Army were regarded with so much contempt that even junior officers hardly tolerated them and sneeringly called them "next to pigeon".

Sitting there, chewing the last of his lunch, Furuta remembered the story officers told over their saki when they classified rank in the Japanese Army. Generals first, of course, then field officers, company officers, non-commissioned officers, privates, houses, military horses, dogs, carrier pigeons—and then civilians.

He smiled to himself. A "next to pigeon" didn't even think

of moving until the Commander-in-Chief had not only risen, but had withdrawn.

General Dohihara finished his lunch at last and left the hall with his aides, and Furuta, after giving him several minutes' start, grabbed his peaked cap and hurried across the square between the College Buildings to his office in G-2 Section.

The news was extraordinary—and so was Colonel Yoshida's temper. The Intelligence Chief was still cursing Singapore Headquarters when he arrived.

"They've been squatting on the information for days," he snarled, "just squatting on it."

Hiroyuki Furuta learnt that on 6th October, the Friday before, a water-police patrol boat had been sunk by gunfire not a dozen miles from Singapore—sunk by a Canton-type junk flying Japanese flags. Two Malay policemen, one an inspector, had been killed, and another constable had swum ashore. About two hours later a muffled explosion had been heard among the islands further south.

But that wasn't all. The next day, Saturday, an American B24 had circled Bintang Island for nearly two hours, at high altitude, and had appeared to signal to the ground with a lamp, though this report was garbled and didn't appear very reliable.

Worse still, not one word of all this had been reported by Singapore Garrison Headquarters over in Raffles Park to 7th Area Army until a little more than an hour before—just before lunch.

As Furuta says: "It was a great shock to 7th Area Army H.Q. to learn that the enemy had successfully infiltrated so deeply into its defences."

But shock is about all it was—as you will see.

The first reaction to the news at Army Intelligence, where Colonel Yoshida was still furious at the inefficiency of Garrison Headquarters, was that the attack had been made by "remaining spies" left by the British in Malaya—and by spies was meant guerrillas.

But later: "Some of the more intelligent members believed that the action was not the type that would have been taken by a group left by the withdrawing British Army. These members thought that the method resorted to was too daring, even though clumsy, if British guerrillas had been hiding all this time. The theory of left-behind guerrillas gave way to an opinion that it must have been a direct infiltration from the outside world."

Despite this reaction, an extraordinary picture of inefficiency emerges, for apart from a few individuals, like Colonel Yoshida, who were worried about the attack, nobody else at headquarters, after the first impact of the news, seems to have taken the reports of the mysterious junk too seriously. Some of the senior staff even believed that the reports were wildly exaggerated—even though two Malay policemen had been killed and their boat sunk—and laughed at Colonel Yoshida's warnings.

The only action taken by 7th Area Army was to order a company, under Captain Tomita, to search the islands south of Singapore, and even this decision seems to have been made with reluctance; the force sent out was little more than a gesture.

Life in Shonan—the Japanese name for Singapore, which meant "Bright South"—was comfortable and pleasant, even though the Japs grumbled at the tropical heat. Food and women were plentiful. The fighting was far away. Burma, where the war was going badly, was one place you hoped you would never be sent.

Lack of urgency, complacency, the complacency of bored safe human beings no matter of what race. That was the position in Singapore. But this was nothing new. It was an old, old international story of war headquarters far from battles. Except for a few individuals, the staff at 7th Area Army continued to regard the reports of the mystery junk with indifference.

To cover the Thousand Islands with a company—and not a very efficient company—was an impossible task, but Captain Tomita did his best.

After searching for ten days he and some of his men landed from their cramped patrol boat at Mapor Island on 21st October. As Mapor was only about five miles from Merapas, Operation Rimau's Base A, this suggests that he could have been acting on information obtained from the local Malays, though there is evidence that he was not suspicious and that the landing was merely part of his routine search.

Although Captain Tomita was keen, his men, who had been dragged away from the comforts and delights of garrison duty at Singapore, were not happy. They grumbled among themselves and complained that the search was a typically futile "headquarters job" based on vague and probably wrong information. They were casual and uninterested and concerned only with how soon they could return to Singapore.

When they landed Captain Tomita ordered: "The first section will come with me."

Wearily the men shouldered their rifles and followed him along the beach and into the palms.

"We will first search that small hill," the captain said, pointing to a jungle-covered rise behind the beach.

But they had moved only a few hundred yards away from

the sea, and were crossing a clearing, when first one shot, then a Bren gun burst, came from the hill.

Captain Tomita clutched his chest, spun and fell on his face dead. The soldiers sprinted for the undergrowth and dropped on their bellies as the bullets ripped the leaves above them. Uncertainly, they began to return the fire, but visibility was poor and the enemy fire heavy. A man screamed as he was hit as Second Lieutenant Yamaguchi hurried up from the beach with the rest of the men and brought two light machine-guns into action.

Yamaguchi, who had little battle experience, reported later that the enemy used "soundless firearms". "They made a sound not louder than the spatterings of raindrops on palm leaves," he said.

This may have been imagination, though it is the second reference which suggests that the Rimau men may have had weapons fitted with silencers.

He reported that his troops were not familiar with this new weapon and could not determine the direction the bullets were coming from or the size of the enemy force, but he decided the enemy was not in strength or they would have attacked, and his guess was correct.

At dusk firing from both sides ceased, and Yamaguchi decided to wait until morning to attack.

He recovered the body of Captain Tomita and took it back to the patrol boat and ordered the man in charge to cruise around Mapor Island all night to prevent the enemy escaping. Then he returned to near the base of the hill, placed his men and waited.

At first light the Japanese, covered by the two machine-guns, crept up the jungle slope and, screaming, charged. But the enemy had gone. On the hilltop, among trampled jungle, Yamaguchi found some broken packs of emergency rations, a revolver, a broken radio, a notebook, several single sheets of paper with sketches on them, and two Japanese flags.

An extremely puzzled Yamaguchi searched all day, but could find no other trace of the enemy. He decided to report back to Singapore as quickly as possible.

For the first time, with Captain Tomita's death in action, the staff at 7th Area Army snapped out of their tired cynicism and took the junk attack seriously.

Major Koshida, an experienced officer, with a fully equipped battalion of battle-trained troops, and many patrol boats, was ordered to search the whole of the Thousand Islands and not to return until he had killed or captured the enemy force. Before the end of October he had concentrated part of his force in the Mapor area and had scattered search groups throughout the archipelago.

At the same time interpreter Hiroyuki Furuta was sent to Singapore Garrison Headquarters to examine the material found by Yamaguchi on Mapor. He first examined the flags. They were perfect in proportion and colour, but the Military Government flag had one mistake: one of the six characters lacked a dot to make it completely accurate, and Furuta knew it could not have been made in Japan.

With a Japanese Navy Intelligence officer, he then examined several pencil sketches of warships. The drawing was crude, but silhouette and number and type of guns were so accurate that the Navy man recognized ships which used the Rhio Archipelago naval anchorage. He decided the drawings had been made by a "well-trained specialist, not an amateur".

(These were the sketches Major Ingleton had made from the *Mustika*.)

The notebook, a diary, told Furuta little, though it contained the word "Rimau", which he presumed was the name of the party, and repeated references, such as "SB transportation" and "SB disposed", intrigued him. He couldn't guess, however, what these entries meant.

He reported his findings to G-2 Section, and a few days later, after progress reports had been received from Major Koshida, he attended a "Grade A intelligence meeting", presided over by General Kenji Dohihara, the Commander-in-Chief, at which Lieutenant-Colonel Cho Kuwabara, deputy Chief of Intelligence, gave this appreciation:

"The enemy who sneaked into our territory this time proved to be entirely different from the enemies we have known. Their brave action in having dodged our strict watchline to approach near our headquarters is quite unique.

"But there is something else I feel is of great importance. These enemies, when chased into a tight corner by our men, will fight to the last.

"European soldiers are usually good fighters, but when they know they can fight no longer it is their practice to raise both hands and surrender. They never seem to prefer death to being taken prisoner.

"These enemies, however, don't surrender, and there must be something behind this grave determination. We must find out what it is.

"Major Koshida, whose men have just killed four of the enemy, is now sparing no efforts in the pursuit of the others. It will only be I hope a matter of days before he brings in to us these brave and mysterious enemies."

But it was more than a matter of days before the Japanese at Singapore were to see these enemies who now intrigued them so much, and whose behaviour was to have such a significant bearing on their treatment later.

Now it is time to return to that night of 6th October, when the Rimau men blew up the *Mustika,* and the four canoe parties, under Lyon, Davidson, Page and Ross, began their retreat to Merapas.

That evening they had perhaps a hundred miles of night paddling and days of hunted hiding ahead of them, though they did not know that bungling by Singapore Garrison Headquarters would give them a start of three days, and that it was two more days, or 11th October, before Captain Tomita left Singapore with his company to search the Thousand Islands.

Unfortunately, the movements of the four canoe parties, from the time they destroyed the *Mustika,* are confused and conflicting—an almost hopeless tangle of fact, rumour and supposition. The complete story of the Rimau retreat will never be known, although certain facts stand out.

The official Australian Army report, while admitting that the movements of the Rimau men are "somewhat hypothetical", says:

"By coincidence, all four parties met on Sole (Asore) Island where they had a clash with the Japanese. During the engagement Lt.-Col. Lyon and Lt. Ross were killed.

"The remainder pushed on to Merapas. Lt.-Cdr. Davidson was killed en route, but the remainder reached Merapas and stayed until 4 November (8 November was the earliest date arranged for pick-up) when they were attacked by the Japanese.

"Certain Japanese were killed in this action, but the party suffered no casualties. The party then split into small parties and moved south."

The Japanese killed in the Sole Island action were Lieutenant Buraoka and at least seven others.

Colonel Cyril Wild's version is this:

"The Japanese encountered Lyon's own party on Sole Island. In the night action which followed, Lyon and one other officer were killed, after killing the Japanese commander and killing and wounding several more. The remainder reached Merapas Island safely, and joined forces with the other three parties who had likewise suffered some casualties.

"The Japanese discovered them on November 4, two days before the submarine was due to arrive. In the action which followed the Japanese were at first repulsed with heavy losses, but our people were later compelled to leave Merapas and continue their withdrawal to the south."

Conflict in these reports on a number of points is obvious.

The official report says that all four parties were on Sole, which is a small island near Mapor and only a few miles from Merapas, yet Wild says that Lyon's own party was on Sole, but the other officer killed with Lyon was Lieutenant Ross, who was in command of another canoe party, so that at least two parties were on Sole.

Wild didn't know the correct date of the rendezvous with the submarine. He gives it as 6th November, whereas it was 8th November.

An independent report claims that when the Rimau men reached Merapas they found that their base had already been raided by the Japanese, and that they were forced to scatter and fight individually or in small groups on Merapas and surrounding islands.

This report indirectly supports the Japanese contention that the Rimau base around this time was no longer on Merapas, but on Mapor, and there is strong evidence that the Japanese version may be correct.

On 21st October Captain Page was certainly on Mapor, about five miles north-west of Merapas, for it was his party which killed Captain Tomita.

With Page were Major Ingleton and Corporal Stewart and several others whose names are unknown. This group had watched the Japanese land and from the behaviour of the soldiers had decided that, although clearly a search party, they were not suspicious and were probably inexperienced troops. Page ordered his men to pull back to their hill camp in the hope that the Japs would miss them, but as Captain Tomita and his section approached the hill one of the Rimau party fired, either accidentally or through nervousness, and their position was disclosed.

After dark Page decided that as the Japanese now knew they were on the island, and would comb it yard by yard, the only chance to evade further action or capture was to evacuate. Later he noticed that the Japanese patrol boat, which they had watched leave, was circling the island every two hours twenty-five minutes, and in one of those periods, soon after they heard the boat's engine, they abandoned their camp and crept down the hill to the beach.

Furuta says that Page and his party swam away from Mapor. He says they took off their trousers, knotted the leg-ends, filled the legs with coconuts, and used the trousers as floats.

If this is correct they must have either abandoned or damaged their canoes, or the canoes were hidden somewhere near the beach the Japanese occupied and could not be recovered without detection.

It is doubtful if the Rimau men could have swum to Merapas, which was five miles away, though such a swim would not have been impossible for desperate men who knew they would be killed or captured if they did not evacuate Mapor.

The only certainty is that they reached another island.

Although both the official and Wild's reports agree that the major action against the Japanese was on Merapas Island on 3rd or 4th November, and that after the clash the Rimau men escaped south, the Japanese version is that Captain Page and others were still in the area on 8th November—the rendezvous date—for on that day "Page saw Japanese boats gathered in force around Mapor Island". Page and those with him may have actually been on Merapas that day—waiting for rescue by the submarine which never kept the R.V.

From all this conflict of fact and theory, this tragic muddle, one thing stands out. That is the extraordinary length of time allowed between the departure of the *Mustika* from Pejantan Island on 1st October and the main R.V. at Merapas Island on 8th November.

Even when this hit and run raid had to be abandoned within sight of Singapore on 6th October—the attack night—the Rimau men still had thirty-three days before their R.V. with the submarine at Merapas—not days but weeks too long to expect any raiding party to stay in enemy waters and escape detection.

This strongly suggests that Lyon had another plan of escape—probably the sinking of the *Mustika* and the Sleeping Beauties after the attack and the capture of another native boat outward-bound from Singapore.

If such a plan existed—and it is the sort of thing Lyon and Davidson would think of—it obviously was not used during the hurried retreat after the sinking of the Malay police patrol.

Perhaps the reason was Lyon's belief that they had only three hours before the Japanese would start chasing them, that as the Japanese knew they had used a junk all native ships anywhere near Singapore would be searched, and that, as Jaywick experience had proved, they had a better chance with canoes of escaping detection by moving at night and hiding by day.

Evidence suggests that they all got back on Merapas within a few days, perhaps a week, of the failure of the raid on 6th October, and that the parties then scattered among the surrounding islands to wait for the R.V. on 8th November.

They certainly would not have stayed on Merapas because of the danger of drawing attention to their pick-up base, but would have returned there if possible only in time to keep the R.V. with the submarine.

It is almost certain that this is what they did, since actions with the Japanese—on Sole and Mapor islands, and finally on Merapas—were all within a few miles of each other.

Among all this fact and conjecture there is only one certainty: in his two months' search among the Thousand Islands Major Koshida and his battalion killed ten men and captured ten—out of the total Rimau force of twenty-three.

Donald Davidson and, I believe, Able Seaman A. W. ("Happy") Huston, were killed between Sole and Mapor at night when they ran into a patrol boat as it came out from behind a small island. Both men, pinpointed by searchlight, opened up with their Owen guns and fought to the last as the Japs riddled them with machine-gun fire, but in the dark the Japs could not find their bodies in the water and soon abandoned the search.

How, when and where the others were killed among the Rhio Islands is impossible to answer, and even their identities can't be fully established because of the most extraordinary episode of all in the entire history of Operation Rimau.

Three men broke through the Japanese net around the Thousand Islands. One of these men was Lieutenant A. L. "Blondie" Sargent. The others are unknown. They escaped in one canoe, for the canoes Rimau carried were three-man canoes, though for attack work, as in the Jaywick raid, only two men operated them and the third position was used for explosives and stores.

For more than two months these three men paddled from island to island, moving only between dusk and dawn, down the long Indonesian chain. How they evaded capture, how they got food after their supplies were exhausted, how and where they hid, how they survived the endless exhausting nights crouched in their canoe, will never be known.

But a map shows that the voyage they made was one of the most fantastic in the history of war, in the history of the sea.

For nearly two thousand miles they paddled eastward from the Rhio Islands down along Sumatra, Java, Bali, Lombok, Sumbawa, Flores, Alor, Wetar, to Romang Island, north-east of Timor and almost at the extreme eastern end of the Indies, and only about four hundred miles from Darwin, for which they were making.

And at Romang Island the nameless two, after a journey of incredible endurance and courage, met their end. The Army record says that one of the men was killed by a Chinese on Romang Island, and that the other was killed by a shark. Cyril Wild says that "natives" killed one and the other was taken by a shark. The Japanese say both were taken by sharks.

But what of Lieutenant Sargent?

The three men were certainly together at the end, for their canoe either stranded or was damaged on fishing stakes in the sea and they were forced to swim.

"Blondie" Sargent, the only one of the three men then left

alive, was captured after he crawled ashore on Romang. He was desperately thin and almost completely hairless—a condition which had developed after an acute attack of malaria which nearly killed him hundreds of miles back during this fantastic canoe voyage.

These are the reasons, or some of them, why it is impossible to say which men, apart from Lyon, Davidson, Ross and Huston, died among the Thousand Islands.

All that is known is that the other men of Rimau who died in the Japanese manhunt were Sub-Lieutenant J. G. M. Riggs, Lieutenant B. Reymond, Warrant Officer J. Willersdorf, Sergeant C. B. Cameron, Corporal A. G. P. Campbell, Corporal C. M. Craft, Lance-Corporal H. J. Page and Private D. R. Warne. Of the ten men who were captured among the Thousand Islands—Lieutenant Sargent, caught at Romang Island, made the eleventh prisoner—the details of the capture of only one is known. And that man was Captain Robert Page.

Neither time nor place is known, but he was so exhausted and starving that the people of a fishing village took pity on him and fed him. He was asleep in a hut when Major Koshida's men surrounded the village and his kindly host just had time to warn him when two soldiers entered the hut.

Page pretended to be asleep and the soldiers glanced at him and were about to walk out when one took a closer look at the bundle in the corner and pounced. Page did not have the strength to resist.

Those who were captured were held at Dabot on the Amir Silalahi's island of Singkep before being taken to Singapore in two groups, one on 23rd December 1944 and the other on 8th January 1945. These men were Major R. N. Ingleton, Captain R. C. Page, Lieutenant W. G. Carey, Warrant Officer A. Warren, Sergeant D. P. Gooley, Corporal C. M. Stewart, Corporal R. B. Fletcher, Lance Corporal J. T. Hardy, Able Seaman Falls and Able Seaman F. W. Marsh.

8

THE LIGHTS OF CHRISTMAS EVE 1944 were flicking on in Singapore when Lieutenant-Colonel Cho Kuwabara called Furuta to his office at G-2.

"Go to Suijo Kempeitai immediately," he ordered. "Major Koshida's prisoners have just arrived and I want you to help question them. There are six."

Furuta already knew that some of the mysterious enemies had been captured, and as he left headquarters and drove through the crowded streets, among the smoke of cooking fires, the shrill uproar of radio music from shops and eating places, past even a few small Christmas trees with coloured lights on them in windows, he wondered what these strangers would be like who had taken nearly two months to capture.

Suijo or Water Kempeitai—"Military police over the sea area", as the Japanese translated it—was in a building near Keppel Harbour, and there Furuta went direct to the office of the commandant, Captain Norio Hinomoto, who had been ordered by Garrison Headquarters to take charge of the prisoners and to direct the investigation into their attempted attack.

Captain Noguchi, representing Garrison, was already there, and so was Warrant Officer Imanaka, of Suijo Kempeitai, whom Furuta knew at that time mainly as a champion at judo.

"I think we should all work to a plan," the commandant said, offering English cigarettes. "But first we must decide how to handle them."

He mopped his throat with a damp handkerchief. Sweat patches showed under his arms.

"Unfortunately, they have taken a long time to catch, and their information has probably lost some of its value."

Captain Noguchi nodded. "That's true, but it's still important to find out all we can about them. I believe they are mostly Australians. Is that true?"

"Yes. There's only one Englishman I think among the six."

Noguchi grunted. "I suggest we use the orthodox methods."

"With some people they work quickly. With others. . . . " Captain Hinomoto sucked his teeth. "Major Koshida reports that these are very brave men who don't fear death. That is unusual. I wonder if they will talk."

"We can always try," Noguchi said. "There are various methods."

The commandant turned to Furuta. "What's your opinion for men like these? You've been in English countries and know the English way of thinking better than we do."

"I don't think orthodox methods will achieve any real results. With many—yes. But not with these men. Instead of treating them as criminals and using violence, we may learn more from them if we are friendly."

"That's what I feel. I haven't talked to Major Koshida personally, but all his reports say that these are not ordinary prisoners, but special prisoners.

The others looked at Noguchi.

"Perhaps you're right," he said. "These men, as you say, are certainly different from what I've heard."

"This is my impression," Captain Hinomoto said. "Only men who fear nothing would dare attack Shonan in a junk. There seems no doubt these men have the stomachs of heroes."

They then discussed how the examination should proceed and decided that, with interpreters Furuta, Naito, and another to be detailed, they should question the prisoners in separate groups, and later singly, and at the end of each session they would compare notes and decide how the inquiry was progressing and what new lines of questioning to use.

Perhaps I should explain here that I deliberately asked Furuta what was the "orthodox method" referred to by Captain Noguchi which the Japanese used on prisoners, both military and civil. I expected him to deny that torture was used, or at least try to evade the question. Instead, he explained fully.

"The orthodox method was to hit, beat, or slap until a prisoner gave the truth," he wrote. "On many occasions prisoners who refused information were not given food. At the end of the third foodless day they generally started talking.

"According to the interpretation of the Japanese Army, Occidental people are obstinate because they think they have to be obstinate to a certain point. When they are satisfied with themselves that they have been sufficiently obstinate, they start talking. Therefore, cutting food is the short way of giving them the satisfaction that they have resisted as much as they could. This is brutal."

After the four men had planned the conduct of the investigation, Captain Hinomoto told his orderly to bring tea and then said, "I think the prisoners should have a hot bath. They have not washed I'm sure since their capture." He sniffed like a dog and everyone laughed. "They stink—how they stink! I know because I have already smelt them. You haven't."

"And a shave," Warrant Officer Imanaka suggested. "They probably have vermin."

"No." Captain Noguchi was firm. "They should not be allowed razors. That would be foolish." He glanced at the commandant. "That barber you have here. He could shave them."

The commandant nodded. "A good idea."

They sucked their green tea, and then Captain Hinomoto stood.

"Now we should all see them. One is huge—like a great bear. He is their senior officer, a major. Another is young and handsome in the English film way. I'll tell them we don't intend to question them tonight." He looked at his watch. "It's late."

He led them to the first-aid room where one of the prisoners who had been brought to Singapore from Singkep on a stretcher, which the other prisoners had carried, lay on the floor covered with a blanket. His thin pale bearded face glistened with sweat. He didn't open his eyes or move as the Japanese stared down at him. His breathing was ragged. He moaned.

"This is one," Hinomoto said, "but he has malaria badly and is in a coma. The doctor has seen him but can do nothing. He says he can't save him. He will die."

The sick man was Able Seaman "Boof" Marsh, one of the members of Operation Jaywick, who was mentioned in dispatches for his part in the *Krait* raid and who had volunteered again for Rimau.

He died at Water Kempeitai on Christmas Day without regaining consciousness.

The commandant then took them to another room, bare of furniture, on the ground floor, where guards with fixed bayonets watched the prisoners.

"Their jungle greens were filthy and shabby," Hiroyuki Furuta recorded, "and they had nothing except what they wore. They were all exhausted by their long ordeal. Their faces were dirty, yet pale above their heavy growths of beard, and their hair was long and wild. But it was their eyes I noticed most. They glittered feverishly in their bearded faces from exhaustion, the strain of their long flight, and from the nervous tension of capture and imprisonment."

Prisoners and captors stared at each other in silence.

"Gentlemen," Captain Hinomoto said, and Furuta translated, "you have been unfortunate to have been captured by us and are our prisoners. In our capacity as soldiers we have been ordered to investigate your activities, and for a soldier an order is an order.

"But as this is your Christmas Eve we do not want to question you on your holy day. We are not Christians, but we pay respect to those who believe in that religion. I would also like to say that tomorrow's interrogation will be brief. Tonight you will be given a hot bath and will be shaved. We wish you good rest."

To the men, soldiers and civilians, who suffered under the Japanese, who still remember, vividly and bitterly, the countless indignities, slaps, kicks, bashings, torture and starvation they received from many of their captors, and to the kinspeople of those who did not survive months and years of Japanese brutality, those last few hundred words must seem quite unreal, a deliberate fabrication by a former enemy.

I was originally extremely sceptical of this information, because so much evidence exists, from every theatre in which the Japanese operated, to prove that they did not generally treat their prisoners with anywhere near such politeness or human consideration.

It would therefore have been easy to regard this information as false and to reject it and all the rest—except for one thing. After testing it as objectively as I possibly could against all other evidence, both official and unofficial, I decided to accept it. And to appreciate why I believe the Japanese version is true, and why the Rimau men were treated so well and why this treatment continued, you have, as unemotionally as you can, to know and understand certain fundamental facts about the Japanese mental attitude to Operation Rimau and to the Rimau prisoners.

Colonel Cyril Wild says emphatically: "It is clear that from the first they were regarded with respect, verging on awe, by the Japanese, and in consequence were exceptionally well treated."

And again, in one of Wild's War Crimes documents in my possession, he repeats: "Treatment was quite exceptionally good by Jap standards. Prisoners were allowed special privileges and were NOT tortured." The capitals are his—not mine.

The most significant words in these two statements are, without a doubt, "respect, verging on awe."

But why were they treated so well? Why were they regarded with respect, verging on awe?

It is important to recall, when trying to answer these questions, that even before the Rimau men were captured the Japanese regarded them as very brave men. The Japanese considered that only exceptional men would have attempted such a suicidal attack against Singapore, and this opinion was reinforced when they heard that the mysterious invaders, when cornered by Major Koshida's troops, died fighting without a thought of surrender, or were captured only when so exhausted and starving that they could fight no longer.

All were captured. Not one surrendered. That is most vital to this story.

The Rimau survivors, even before they were brought to Singapore, possessed the highest warrior status in the eyes of the almost feudal Japanese officer class. And from the start, and because of this attitude, this veneration for personal courage, they were not regarded or treated as ordinary prisoners but as very special soldiers unlucky to have been caught and to whom respect, deference and, as Colonel Wild says, "almost awe", were due by right as warriors.

In time, and as reports of their bravery and their bearing in captivity spread, the Japanese officers spoke of them as heroes comparable to famous characters in their own fighting services and in Japanese history. They called them the proud words "Yu-shi", which means heroes or courageous warriors.

This is extremely significant, and is indeed the key to the Japanese attitude, for among the heroes whom the Rimau men were placed beside, with full equality, were the revered sailors of the three Japanese midget submarines which raided Sydney Harbour on 31st May 1942. That story is worth recalling.

These 80-feet-long, two-man "midgets"—a composite of two of them can be seen at the Australian War Memorial in Canberra—were launched from five I-class submarines, part of the Japanese 8th Submarine Squadron, under Captain Sasaki, at 4.30 p.m. on 31st May seven miles east of Sydney Heads, after a reconnaissance of Sydney Harbour by Navy pilot Susumo Ito, whose float plane was launched from Submarine I 21 35 miles off Sydney on 29th May.

When they penetrated Sydney Harbour after dark one became entangled in the boom defence nets and blew itself up, and the two others got inside the boom. One of these fired two 18-foot torpedoes at the American heavy cruiser *Chicago*. One torpedo missed the cruiser's bows by twelve feet and buried itself without exploding in a pile of rope under a wharf at Garden Island Naval Base. The other torpedo went under the warship and the Dutch submarine *K 9* and exploded against a concrete dock wall. The explosion sank the old ferry *Kuttabul*, a naval depot ship, and killed twenty-two ratings.

The raiders were sunk by depth-charges that night. None of the men who manned them survived.

Four bodies were recovered from the submarines on 9th June 1942, and the day after these sailors were cremated, the Sydney *Daily Telegraph* published this report:

> A grey-haired woman was the only member of the public in Eastern Suburbs Crematorium yesterday when the bodies of four Japanese sailors were cremated.
>
> The bodies were from two of the submarines sunk in Sydney Harbor.
>
> The woman, in a wine-coloured dress, sobbed softly until the last casket slid away behind a purple velvet screen.
>
> She said afterwards: "I have a son in the Merchant Navy who sails near Japanese-held territory. I would like to think that if anything happened to him he would be treated as Australia treated these Japanese."
>
> Outside, 20 other women and children stood near a Royal Australian Navy firing party and funeral party.
>
> Except for a volley by the firing party and the sounding of the Last Post by a bugler, the ceremony was conducted in silence. There was no service and no prayers were read.
>
> Seven newspapermen were in the chapel when the Superintendent of Naval Services (Rear-Admiral Muirhead-Gould), the Swiss Consul (Mr H. Hedinger), representing the German Government, and a naval officer entered.
>
> Rear-Admiral Muirhead-Gould and Mr Hedinger stood alongside the caskets, each of which was covered by a Japanese flag, until they were slid away.

Caskets containing the ashes of the four Japanese will be given to Mr Hedinger for transmission to Japan.

Four months later, in early October 1942, Tokyo Radio announced that the ashes of the four Japanese sailors had reached Japan.

Thousands of people lined the streets of Tokyo to bow before the ashes of these national heroes, and a Japanese poet, Kihachi Ozaki, wrote a memorial ode praising their valour and daring in breaching "our enemies' greatest city."

When the bodies were recovered from the "midget" submarines the Australian Government consulted local authorities on Japan and the Japanese, including Major George Caiger, formerly lecturer for ten years at the Peers' College in Tokyo, on what to do with them. These experts advised that the bodies should be cremated and sent back to Japan as this would be the correct thing to do, because of Japanese religious beliefs and veneration for ancestors, and also because it would be good propaganda.

The return of the ashes deeply impressed the Japanese. The action was so widely publicized that their servicemen in all theatres of war, from the Pacific to Burma, knew about it.

Here then is one of the reasons why in Singapore the attitude of the Japanese to the Rimau men, whom they regarded as heroes equal to the heroes of their own Naval Special Attack Corps, was strongly influenced by the correct action of the Australian Government in treating the dead sailors of the "midget" raid on Sydney as brave and honourable enemies.

When interpreter Furuta saw the five prisoners on Christmas morning—he never saw the sixth, Able Seaman Marsh, after the first time—he hardly recognized them as the filthy bearded scarecrows of the evening before. They were clean and shaven, their hair had been cropped short, and they had been issued with new khaki shorts and short-sleeve shirts, but no shoes.

He noticed, too, that although their bodies were thin and their cheeks sunken, after weeks of being hunted from island to island, they no longer looked so exhausted that they appeared close to collapse. This morning they seemed almost relaxed, except for the way their still tired eyes watched every move.

The prisoners were now in two adjoining rooms on the first floor. The rooms had large glassless windows which had been barred when Water Kempeitai made the building its headquarters, but no furniture of any kind. The men slept on blankets—each man had two, and more were available—on the bare wood floor. The blankets, Furuta noted, were neatly folded, Army-style, and he wondered what sort of men these were who kept such discipline and morale even in captivity.

On that Christmas morning, when captivity must have been most bitter, the examination of the prisoners was brief and formal, as Captain Hinomoto had promised. The prisoners were divided into three groups in their two rooms. Captain Noguchi questioned Major Ingleton, Captain Hinomoto, with Furuta interpreting, questioned Captain Page and Able Seaman Falls. And Warrant Officer Imanaka questioned Lieutenant Carey and Warrant Officer Warren. They were asked their names, ranks, ages, birthplaces, occupations, the names of their parents, and were questioned about the leadership of their party. These details were taken down and that was the end of the examination for that day.

Captain Hinomoto then told them that they would be allowed hot baths every second day, and those who smoked would be issued with cigarettes, but only during exercise periods, which would start the next afternoon. They would not be allowed to smoke in their cells. He also explained that their food would be Japanese, but on two days a week they would be issued with raw food and allowed to cook it. He promised that food would be plentiful.

Then the Japanese, including the interpreters, conferred in the commandant's office. Their first decision was that, although Major Ingleton was the senior officer, he had apparently been loaned to the operation by the "British Marine Corps" more as an "adviser" than as an active member. As he had deferred to Page on several questions they concluded that Page was, operationally, the most important man among the prisoners, and treated him as such.

The prisoners confirmed what the Japanese already knew from the captured diary that the party called themselves "Rimau", and from that morning they were collectively known to the interrogators, and to other Japanese officers at 7th Area Army and Garrison Headquarters who later met them or knew about them, as "Tora Koksaku Tai", which meant, "Tiger Operation Party or Unit".

One revealing fact is that, although the examining officers and interpreters at Water Kempeitai knew of Lieutenant-Colonel Lyon and Lieutenant-Commander Davidson, they did not seem to know the total complement of Rimau and even believed that some had escaped and returned to Australia—proof that the prisoners, who were never to know the fate of all other members of the party, continued to protect their dead comrades by not mentioning their names.

Someone among the prisoners told the Japanese that Lyon was a Bowes-Lyon and related to the British Royal Family, and they were tremendously impressed that a British "aristocrat" should lead such a dangerous raid. Thus the myth of Lyon's "Royal" connections even reached the Japanese, and probably helped raise the already high standing of the prisoners in the eyes of the Japanese officer caste.

Four other Rimau men were transferred from Singkep Island to Singapore on 8th January 1945, and a few days later Lieutenant Sargent was flown from Koepang in Timor, where he had been taken after his capture at Romang Island.

So that by early January 1945 the ten prisoners—it will be remembered that Able Seaman Marsh had died on Christmas Day—were all together at Water Kempeitai, where they were kept until early February for what was known as their "military interrogation".

Of this examination, which continued every few days for about six weeks, I know only a little, but even before it began certain vital facts, which were important to the fate of the prisoners, were already established by the Japanese, and the prisoners, faced with this evidence—visual evidence which could not be refuted—admitted it.

They had approached Singapore in a captured junk and had sunk a police patrol boat and killed two men; their junk had flown Japanese flags and those flags had not been lowered and the British flag raised when they opened fire on the boat; they had disguised themselves as natives and had also worn jungle greens but without insignia of any kind to denote rank, unit or service.

It was evidence the prisoners did not attempt to deny.

But one part of the examination, described by Furuta, though uncorroborated in any way, is intriguing because it illustrates Japanese methods and shows how trained officers in war can build up a comprehensive picture from the smallest scraps of information.

Under examination the Rimau men never mentioned the secret Sleeping Beauties, but told the Japanese their attack was to have been made in rubber boats carrying explosive limpets which they intended to stick to the side of ships in harbour. They said they had destroyed the junk *Mustika* for two reasons —because they knew the Japanese would search for her and she was therefore only a danger to them if they continued to use her, and because they did not want the limpets to fall into Japanese hands.

Furuta reported this to the deputy chief of G-2 Section, Lieutenant-Colonel Cho Kuwabara, who wasn't convinced.

"Destruction of the junk is obvious," he said, "but if they wanted to destroy the limpets they could have thrown them overboard. I think they're hiding something."

Later, after the three groups of prisoners were questioned separately and then individually about the identity of the two-man crews of the rubber boats, the names of the crew combinations given by each group, and by individuals, varied.

Captain Hinomoto noticed this immediately and decided it was suspicious, and ordered his assistants and interpreters to ask more questions about the rubber boats and the boat crews.

Soon after this Warrant Officer Imanaka told Hinomoto that he was sure there was something special about these boats. He couldn't tell why. It was just a feeling he had. And Hinomoto mentioned this at one of their conferences.

Then, and only then, did Furuta suddenly remember the entries "S.B. transportation" and "S.B. disposed" in the captured diary he had examined, the one found on Mapor Island after Captain Tomita had been killed by Page's party. It was the word "transportation" which interested him most, and he wondered if any link could exist between this entry and the rubber boats they were all so concerned about.

He decided to try to bluff Captain Page, and at the next examination casually asked, "What did you do with the S.B.?"

"What do you know about S.B.?" Page parried.

"I know it was a special boat," Furuta said. "Major Ingleton told me."

"In that case there's no need to keep quiet about it any longer," Page said. "It was a one-man submersible boat."

Furuta rushed off to Hinomoto, who used the same bluff to trick Major Ingleton into confirming what Page had said and describing how it porpoised towards its target.

Although I could not test this story, through Wild's information or other sources, it sounds authentic and, if true, illustrates how in war information of value can be obtained and built up from apparently unimportant beginnings.

Furuta says Japanese Navy men in Singapore were extremely interested in this, to them, new British invention, and tried to build an S.B.—he never knew the letters also meant Sleeping Beauty—but it was never completed before the war ended.

The life of the prisoners at Water Kempeitai, and the attitude of their captors, is known and authenticated.

No special restrictions were placed on them. In their prison rooms they were free at all times to talk, move about, read, sleep. For the first fortnight they were shaved, but after that could shave themselves. They were allowed hot baths and regularly given changes of clothing. Their food was Japanese, and plentiful, generally consisting of boiled rice, cooked vegetables, and dried baked fish, though two days a week they were issued with flour, "hash" meat, as the Japanese called it, and cooking oil. This food they cooked over a wood fire which they were allowed to build outside behind the Kempeitai building. They generally made meat fritters—their favourite. They ate with chopsticks and even held competitions to test their skill. Every day they were marched out to a lawn at the back of the headquarters and allowed to exercise or just sit in the sun for an hour, and some days as long as two. Here they were issued with cigarettes through Captain Hinomoto, and Furuta added his own ration from the Japanese canteen.

Colonel Wild has recorded that, "a well-disposed Japanese interpreter supplied them regularly with books, chocolates, and cigarettes". That interpreter was of course Furuta, and the prisoners owed much to this man who not only supplied them with amenities but spent half his own Army pay of 150 Straits dollars a month- -as independent reports confirm—to make prison life easier for them.

"They wanted to read more than anything," he wrote me. "I had a good collection of fiction and I gave these books to them. I had always liked P. G. Wodehouse and owned many books by this author. I had lived in England and his English humour appealed to me. All the prisoners were heavy readers, but Major Ingleton, a quiet man who did not talk much, read most of all. He liked Wodehouse. I also had a lot of books by Phillips Oppenheim which they all read."

Here, recorded by Furuta at that time, is a conversation between himself and Major Ingleton:

" 'These Wodehouse books are all alike,' Major Ingleton complained. 'Have you anything different?'

" 'Here's a book about the New York underworld,' I said. 'It's by a writer named Damon Runyon.'

" 'Thanks,' he said.

"The next day the English Major waved the book at me.

" 'This is rotten. It's a stupid book. Haven't you anything better than this?'

" 'Only Shakespeare,' I said.

" 'Only Shakespeare,' he said, sadly shaking his head. 'That's the best book of all. Why didn't you say so before?'

" 'Because I was forced to read it so much at school I developed a dislike for Shakespeare. But if you would like it I'll bring it the next time I come.'

"Major Ingleton smiled. 'Right. You bring it next time and in the meantime I'll keep this as a deposit.'

"And he took the Damon Runyon book from me."

After this incident Furuta again recorded:

"One of the other men—I cannot remember his name but I think it was Corporal Hardy—also liked reading Shakespeare, and he and Major Ingleton shared the volume, sometimes taking turns to read aloud to the others. This man told me he had been a professional actor in England before the war. I think he was Hardy, but I am not sure.

"But I must explain that the Japanese Army had a severe restriction on the type of books to be given to prisoners. I was not supposed to give any books which would incite fighting spirit, but I ignored these restrictions. I remember laughing to myself when I heard Major Ingleton declaiming King Henry the Fifth's speech before Agincourt.

"My superiors knew what I was doing, but so great was their admiration for the heroes that they never objected to me ignoring the regulations. I was a good friend to the prisoners. I believed so, and they believed so, too.

"All those who were in contact with the prisoners paid deep respect to their bravery, and nobody ever abused them in any way. The reason for this was natural. They did something which was worthy of great admiration."

Furuta discovered one day that Bob Page loved chocolate, and that "the mere thought of it made his mouth water".

"With the severe food restrictions in Japan I had not seen chocolate for years," he says, "but I was determined to find some for such a fine young man as Captain Page. I made some inquiries and was told that our Air Force had rock chocolate as part of their emergency supplies if they came down in the water or far from their bases. One day the Air Force asked me to help them in a court-martial. It was not part of my Army duties, but I agreed and asked for rock chocolate as compensation for my services. I got it, and next day I brought the chocolate to Water Kempeitai and Captain Page and I enjoyed this booty over Japanese green tea."

But Furuta was not the only one who helped the prisoners.

"Sometimes we were allowed additional rations, such as Amanatto (sugared red beans) or Yokan (sweet bean jelly) and occasionally Daifuki-Mochi (rice cake stuffed with bean paste) which were sold in the canteen. Rations were limited to one pouch of Daifuku for each person Tuesday was a sure day for it, and sometimes we were fortunate on Fridays.

"Members of the Interpreter Section gave all their allotted rations or cakes to the enemy soldiers, for all the members of this section, all civilians, had a feeling of deep goodwill towards them. Headquarters knew all this, but nobody objected, for these were special soldiers. We also had a ration ticket for much better cakes, but my ration for these was soon exhausted and I started buying tickets from other men. Half my pay was happily spent buying things for my enemy-friends."

One of the strangest scenes of the war must have been a day at Water Kempeitai when, at the end of an examination session, officers, interpreters and prisoners began an argument about the merits of judo. The argument started when Lieutenant Carey said that judo was too conventional and stylized and much inferior as a physical art to boxing.

When this was translated the Japanese roared with laughter, and in no time captors and prisoners were all shouting at once and trying to demonstrate why their own sport was superior.

Finally, Imanaka, the judo expert with a "degree of Black Belt", challenged the prisoners to a judo contest.

Commandant Hinomoto agreed immediately and, although it was not time for the daily exercise and sunbake, he marched the prisoners out to the lawn where everybody stripped to the waist.

The guards watched, startled at first, then grinning, as one after another the prisoners tried to throw the challenger. Although they failed, Imanaka, sweat trickling down his chest, complimented the prisoners on their attempts.

"You are all very strong," he said, through Furuta, "much stronger than I thought you were, and you have all some little training in judo I can tell. It might be very difficult for one with the skill of the lowest grade in judo to defeat you. I am astonished you are all so good after such a short study during your war training of what is a difficult Japanese art."

In his diary Hiroyuki Furuta wrote descriptions of some of the prisoners—I wish he had described them all—and these he sent me.

Major Ingleton: "Calm, quiet, imperturbable, a mountain of a man sitting on the floor with his back against a wall with a book propped on his knees."

Lieutenant Carey: "Always cheerful, always telling amusing stories of his experiences. He often insisted humorously that, as his promotion was due on 1st March 1945, everyone should call him Captain in advance. 'You must come and visit me in Sydney,' he told me today. 'You won't have any trouble finding me. Just pick any Carey in the telephone book and he will tell you where to find me. Every Carey in Sydney is a relative.'"

Corporal Stewart: "A fine specimen of a strong good ruggedly honest man who would be at his best under an open sky in a big farm field."

Able Seaman Falls: "A solid young man with a calm mentality. The others call him Pop or Poppa, which means Father."

Lieutenant Sargent: "A man of strong character. Courageous."

But it was Captain Page who appealed most to Furuta as his words show, and this strange friendship, between captor and prisoner, between enemies, seems to have been mutual.

"He was good looking with a slender face and a beautiful old-type moustache. He was manly, brisk in manner and succinct in expression. He was always moderate in his attitude—never too proud, never obsequious.

"I liked Captain Page and he liked me, and our friendship developed amidst the strange circumstances of being enemies. He was really a wonderful man, and in him I saw what a real hero looked like."

Furuta not only deeply admired the younger man, but developed an affection for him that was in some ways close to a father-son relationship. I believe this was genuine affection, for again and again in our correspondence Furuta returns to Page and refers to him with fondness, with admiration, with pride, with a deep brooding kind of sadness.

9

BY EARLY FEBRUARY 1945 the "military" examination of the Rimau men by the Water Kempeitai commandant, Captain Hinomoto, and his assistants had been completed, and the investigation entered a new phase.

But when both 7th Area Army and Singapore Garrison received Hinomoto's report, there were two strongly conflicting opinions among the staff connected with the investigation.

One section of officers argued that the "dauntless courage" shown by the Rimau men should be acknowledged by immediately giving them prisoner-of-war status—which they did not yet possess—and sending them to a p.o.w. camp, though some believed it would be foolish to put them into Changi or any other camp because they would give other prisoners up-to-date information about the war, including Japanese defeats on all fronts, and that this would lift p.o.w. morale, which was already high, to danger level.

The other section, backed by legal men, argued that the prisoners should be investigated to discover finally and legally whether they had broken the rules of warfare—an ironic suggestion, especially to Allied prisoners, who don't need to be reminded that the Japanese themselves broke all the rules.

The "sentimentalists", as the officers of the first group were actually called, lost their argument, and although this was inevitable, as records show, it is intriguing to know that the prestige of the prisoners was so high that some Japanese officers openly advocated that they be granted prisoner-of-war status.

Further examination was decided upon, and Major Haruo Kamiya, senior officer of the Judicial Affairs Section of 7th Area Army, was ordered to take charge of what was called the "criminal investigation".

Immediately, the Rimau prisoners were transferred from Water Kempeitai to Outram Road, the jail so notorious that not many prisoners who entered it ever came out alive.

But before I describe the new investigation, two short explanations, from an Australian and from an Englishman who were in Outram Road at that time, give an accurate and revealing picture of the new "home" of the Rimau men.

"There was a group of people brought into the jail," wrote Mr J. W. C. Wyett, of Hobart, "and it could have been about the time you mention. I had no contact with them, but I do know that some or all of them were executed.

"The jail itself was a massive old structure of stone and was surrounded by a high stone wall, the top of which was encrusted with broken glass. The wall was about 20 feet high and 6 or 8 feet thick at the base, tapering to 2 feet at the top. The cells were about 4 feet to 5 feet in width and about 10 feet long. Each had a heavy wooden door about 4 inches thick with a slot in the centre about 8 inches by 4 inches through which a bowl of food was passed.

"The cells were about 12 feet high with a small barred window in the wall opposite the door and situated near the ceiling. The walls were of heavy masonry about 2 feet thick. However, by pressing your ear against the wall and tapping with a button it was possible to communicate in Morse with your neighbour, provided he could read Morse. This worked quite well until the Japs woke up and removed all our buttons. The Japanese sentries patrolled in stockinged feet, and there was absolute silence at all times except for occasional yells or moans."

The other description, by Sir Robert Scott, Commissioner General for the United Kingdom in South-east Asia, was sent to me by Mr M. C.ff. Sheppard (who organized the "Expedition to Singkep"), of the Prime Minister's Department of the Federation of Malaya.

"I was taken out of Outram Road at the end of February 1945. It is possible that they [the Rimau men] were already there [they were], but if so they were rigidly kept away from all the prisoners.

"The system at Outram Road was that the prison was divided into two parts. The upper block contained about 400 prisoners of whom about 300 were Japanese. Of the remainder there were about 20 to 30 each Australian, British, Dutch, and some Indians. They were all military p.o.w.'s who had been convicted, usually for attempts to escape.

"I was one of the very few civilians kept in this part of the prison. Others were W. C. Curtis and Lionel Earle. I do not know their addresses, but they might perhaps be able to throw some light on the fate of the Rimau people. At least they might be able to pinpoint the date of execution as the Japanese custom was, when there was an execution, to borrow some garden tools from the prison to dig the graves and these tools were returned with blood stains on them the next morning to be cleaned up by the prisoners.

"The other section of the prison contained a large number of civilians, mostly Chinese (including, for example, the Choys), but they were kept completely apart from those in the military section, and it is therefore very unlikely that anyone in the lower block of Outram Road should know anything about it."

The Rimau men, I was able to discover after receiving this letter, were kept in cells—two to a cell—in the military section of Outram Road and were well treated and well fed. There is no suggestion anywhere that their treatment was any different from that received at Water Kempeitai—proof again, if proof is needed, that their status was extremely high.

But although treatment did not alter, the emphasis and direction of the new examination was completely different from the day they entered Outram Road, and although some of the prisoners did not seem to be aware of this, at least at the start, Ingleton, Page and the other officers realized immediately that their examination had reached a critical stage, and that their fate—life or death—was being decided.

As Colonel Wild says, "The officers had little doubt what their fate was likely to be, but the whole party remained in excellent spirits and good health until the end."

Hiroyuki Furuta acted as interpreter for Major Kamiya, though he says he was "reluctant" to take part in the new examination.

"It was painful to face my friends under the different circumstances," he explained. "But I was ordered to interpret for Major Kamiya and an order is an order. I had some consolation in feeling, however, that I was the best man to protect their interests, as I knew them all so well."

I feel this is true, not only because of his kindly attitude to the prisoners throughout their imprisonment, and his strong personal feelings for Page, but because of other circumstances which will be described later.

Major Kamiya's investigation took a long time. He personally questioned each man many times, and over more than two months built up a thick file of evidence. He eventually summarized his findings into what he called his three main criminal charges.

The first was that the Rimau men had infiltrated Japanese-occupied territory wearing jungle greens without emblems or insignia, and as the men were members of three services, Army, Navy and Marines (the Japanese regarded Navy and Marines as separate), and all wore jungle green, this was not a uniform, in the correct interpretation of the word, and their action was therefore a violation of international law. (The Japanese, of course, conveniently forgot that many of their own troops, in the campaign in Malaya, dressed as Chinese or Malay civilians, or wore cotton singlets and shorts, without insignia.)

The second charge was a corollary of the first—that in passing through the Rhio Archipelago the Rimau men made sketches of naval ships and, as they were not in uniform, this was an act of espionage.

The third charge was that, while disguised as natives and flying the Rising Sun flag on their junk, they attacked and killed members of a Malay police patrol who were serving under Japanese command, and that, though flying an enemy flag was recognized as a legal "ruse", they did not strike the Japanese flag and raise their own to reveal their true identity when they attacked.

Major Kamiya's conclusion was that, because of all these illegal acts, which were violations of the rules of war, the prisoners could not be regarded as prisoners of war.

"When I knew the finding," Furuta says, "I also knew that the penalty for violation of the Regulations of Land Warfare was death.

"But I could not bear the thought of death for the heroes. I talked to several high-ranking officers I knew and asked them if there was any chance of saving the heroes. Some privately thought they should be made prisoners of war, but not one volunteered to stick his nose out now the investigation had reached this stage. I was merely a despised civilian and it was risky work trying to save an enemy life."

But while Major Kamiya was writing his report, a strange thing happened. It concerns Bob Page, and I describe it just as Furuta told it to me:

"Apart from my official duties with the prisoners, I made a habit of chatting to them, and particularly to Captain Page. One day I casually mentioned to him that the Rimau raid was not the first on Singapore. I told him I had heard that in 1943, long before I was sent to Singapore, a group of twenty local Chinese had destroyed ships in Singapore Harbour with explosives, and that the Chinese when caught had admitted having been trained in the use of explosives by an English captain before the fall of Singapore. I also mentioned that the men, who were still in prison, were to be executed shortly.

"Captain Page was very silent for the rest of our talk, which was about other things, and I paid little attention to his silence, but next day when I saw him he said he wanted to talk to me confidentially. He said he had been a member of the party which had sunk the ships in Singapore in September 1943, and added: 'Because I felt that raid had no bearing on the present case, I have kept the secret until now. But I can't remain silent knowing that twenty innocent men are to be killed.'

"When I heard this I was tremendously surprised and confused, and even a little frightened, because I knew nothing of this other raid, except the little I had heard since coming to Singapore. I did not know what to do. I certainly did not want to add any more black marks against the heroes at a time when their fate would depend on the thin string of a court-martial decision.

"I hurried back to headquarters and checked the records of the Judicial Affairs Section for that period. I found that the time of the explosions and the location of the vessels, as Captain Page had given them to me, were correct, except for one important point. A confession by one of the Chinese, which was attached to the records, said: 'At the time of the British surrender in Singapore a British captain gathered a group of us spies. With explosives from a secret hiding place we later stole into the harbour in the moonlight and demolished five transports."

"After reading this I was even more bewildered. I sought out and found the young Japanese who had interpreted for the Chinese at their examination and trial, and asked him about this confession. He admitted that at the time his knowledge of the Malay language was so limited that he had not understood a word they said, but because the record submitted at the trial by the Kempeitai was so complete, and because he dared not admit to the court that he could not understand Malay, he faked the whole thing by pretending that the natives' confession was accurate.

"I went back to Captain Page and told him what I had found. This I said, 'If this secret of yours becomes known it will decide your fate. No decision has yet been made, as you know.'

"'I realize that,' he said, 'but as a Christian I can't allow innocent people to be killed for something I was responsible for. The Chinese must be released.'

"I didn't know what to do. I was in a serious position. I was really frightened now. I realized that if the information I had from Captain Page became known, through someone else, I would be punished—and punishment would be serious because I would be accused of protecting enemy personnel.

"I finally decided on a method to protect myself. I went to the head of my division, Colonel Nagaaki Yoshida, Chief of G-2, and told him the whole story, and with me he investigated and checked Captain Page's confession about the other raid. He decided that Captain Page was telling the truth, for every detail of his story checked. Finally he said to me, 'Furuta, this matter must be kept secret.'

"After this the execution of the Chinese was postponed on the basis of a procedural fault in their trial, and at the end of the war they were released. They never knew their death was imminent."

I have no way of testing this story, but Page's confession was such an honourable and chivalrous act, and so much in character, that I believe Furuta's account.

Page at this time did not know conclusively what his fate, and the fate of the other Rimau men, would me, although he almost certainly suspected that his chance of survival was slim; but he was ready to prejudice his own life—knowing that his part in Operation Jaywick would probably destroy any chance of life—to save innocent men who were about to die.

Few acts of gallantry, in a war of great personal gallantry, can surpass this confession by Robert Page.

When Major Kamiya completed his long investigation, he wrote a report in which he recommended as Prosecutor that the Rimau men be tried, though strong evidence from all sources suggests that the Japanese did not want to execute the prisoners. Furuta, for example, says that Major Kamiya, "genuinely admired the Rimau men, and was reluctant to prosecute them", but did so only because, as an Army lawyer, he felt that the evidence against them was too strong to be ignored.

This is supported in general terms by Colonel Wild, who says, "There is evidence that the Japanese were anxious to avoid the death sentence. It was in fact suggested to the prisoners before their trial that they should adopt a humble attitude and plead for mercy. Instead, down to the last corporal and able seaman, they remained resolute and defiant to the last."

Major Kamiya handed his report to Major-General Misao Otsuka, Chief of the Judicial Affairs Section, who approved it and sent it on to General Seishiro Itagaki, Commander-in-Chief, 7th Area Army, who had only recently taken over from General Kenji Dohihara. General Itagaki was a ruthless officer of the old school and a protagonist of Japan's "New Order". While a colonel on the staff of the Kwantung Army he had played a leading part in the notorious "Mukden Incident" in 1931 and the establishment of the Japanese puppet state of Manchukuo, and had been Minister for War in the Konoye Cabinet in 1938. Although he believed in the samurai code and admired the heroes as warriors, he was "full of Nippon seichin", the militaristic nationalist spirit of the expansionist warlike 1930s, and had no sympathy with any sentimentalism, any modern ideas, among his officers, any decline in samurai standards, particularly at a time when Japanese armies were retreating everywhere and their morale was dropping.

General Itagaki conferred with his chief of staff, Lieutenant-General Ayabe, and towards the end of May 1945 decided that the Rimau men would be court-martialled and ordered the prosecutor, Major Kamiya, to recommend to the court sentence of death.

(Major-General Otsuka was hanged in Singapore for war crimes—but crimes not connected with Operation Rimau. General Itagaki and General Dohihara were hanged after sittings of the International Military Tribunal for the Far East at Tokyo, for war crimes—again not connected with Rimau. Hiroyuki Furuta was an interpreter at that Tribunal, and also at the trials in Singapore.)

5th July 1945 was the day set down for the court-martial, but so strong, even at this late stage, was the feeling among some Japanese officers against the trial of the Rimau "heroes", that the Judicial Affairs Section had difficulty in getting an officer of standing to act as president of the court.

The president could not be what the Japanese regarded as a non-combatant—anyone from judicial, pay, supply or even medical sections of the Army—but had to be an officer-of-the-line and a lieutenant-colonel or colonel—at least one rank higher than Major Ingleton, the most senior man amongst the Rimau men.

When Colonel Yoshida, chief of G-2, was asked to sit as president he scornfully refused. "I can't accept this position," he said. "If I could be really chief judge and make my own decisions I would find the prisoners not guilty and send them to a prisoner-of-war camp. You don't see such heroes nowadays. I should hate to be used as a tool of the Judicial Department just to read the death sentence prepared by that department."

Eventually, Colonel Towatari, from Singapore Garrison Headquarters, agreed to act, and Major Mitsuo Jifuku, of Judicial Affairs, and Major K. Hisada, of G-2 Section, were appointed his assisting judges.

Technically, this was not a court-martial in the true Japanese sense, but a military court which the Japanese, who did not recognize the Rimau men as prisoners of war, used to try civilians. There was, however, no difference between the two courts. They were identical and followed the same procedure. I therefore use the term "court-martial", which is generally well known and understood.

Under the Japanese military system the prosecutor in a court-martial is really part of the court, and the president, or chief judge as he is also called, accepts the evidence and opinions of the prosecutor as correct. Once the prosecutor recommends a court-martial, and this is approved by the highest authority, the accused is already guilty before the court-martial even begins. And, as the accused is not allowed counsel for his defence, he has no chance at the court-martial to defend himself.

It is therefore self-evident that the court-martial of the

Rimau men was nothing more than a formal hearing to pronounce the sentence already ordered by the Japanese Commander-in-Chief, General Itagaki. It is also clear that this sentence was known in advance, not only by senior men like Colonel Yoshida, but by Japanese officers outside 7th Area Army Headquarters well before the court-martial, as this statement by Colonel Desmond Duffy, an Australian prisoner of war in Malaya, shows:

"Japanese officers told us that a raid on Singapore had been frustrated by the marvellous vigilance of the Imperial Japanese Navy, and that men had been captured.

"They said the men were true heroes and were being treated as such because of the treatment of the Japanese submarine crews in Sydney. They had great admiration for the prisoners who, they said, were in Outram Road Jail and were to be given a heroes' death—execution.

"They told us this well before July 1945, so that execution had obviously been decided before the trial."

A ceiling fan stirred the hot air in the main room of one of the residential buildings at 7th Area Army Headquarters as Colonel Towatari entered with the other two judges for the Rimau court-martial on 5th July 1945.

They unclipped their long swords, placed them in the sword rack on the wall near the door, and took their seats on a dais at one end of the long room, Major Jifuku on the president's right, Major Hisada on his left. They wore full dress uniforms with ribbons, and the metal on their gold tabs and their highly polished top boots snatched at the light, held it and flung it back.

The prosecutor, Major Kamiya, also on the dais, his desk heaped with folders and documents, sat to the right of the judges and an Army shorthand reporter was at the extreme left. Interpreter Furuta sat in front of Major Kamiya below the dais. Generally he wore civilian clothes, but this morning he was in uniform.

At the other end of the long room on four rows of chairs reserved for officers were Major-General Otsuka and many other senior officers from 7th Area Army and Singapore Garrison.

At 10.30 a.m. Major Kamiya nodded to a warrant officer waiting at the door at the gallery end, and a few minutes later the ten Rimau prisoners marched in between two sentries with fixed bayonets.

Furuta pointed to the two wooden forms in the body of the court, and the prisoners, with the guards standing behind them, sat facing the judges. They wore fresh khaki shorts and shirts and Japanese Army boots without socks. They were clean and shaven, and their heads had been newly cropped.

Major Kamiya rose, bowed first to the president, then to the assisting judges. He was a small man—only five feet two inches and little more than seven stone—and in civilian life had been a lawyer—a graduate in law from Tohoku Imperial University. Under his chin he had cultivated a few long hairs because, as he once told Furuta, jokingly, "I am so short-haired that when the enemy catches me and cuts off my head it will be easier for my family to pick up my head by these hairs."

Addressing the judges, Major Kamiya briefly described the Rimau raid and the capture of the prisoners and his own examination of them, and then read the main charge.

"Cho-ho Boryaku Satsujin."

It meant "Espionage and Murder".

Then he handed his report, a thick black volume, to the president.

Colonel Towatari glanced through the report before conferring with the other judges. Then he turned to the prisoners and questioned them on the charges.

Was it true, he asked, that they had worn jungle green without insignia? ... Yes.

Was it true they had penetrated the Rhio Archipelago and sketched naval vessels? ... Yes.

Was it true they had flown the Rising Sun flag on their junk and had fired on a Malay police patrol? ... Yes.

He talked to the other judges again, then directly addressed Captain Page.

"Did you yourself kill any Japanese soldiers?" he asked.

Page stood and came to attention. "I am an officer of the British Army," he said proudly, "and I know that my aim was good." As Furuta translated a murmur of admiration rippled among the senior officers in the gallery.

The president waited for the whispers, the scrape of boots, to cease. Then he closed the report in front of him and nodded to the prosecutor.

Major Kamiya, half facing the judges, half facing the prisoners, outlined the complete case, dividing it into four parts: "Facts, evidence, legal interpretation, and extenuating circumstances." He talked for more than an hour before he had covered every point. Then he clicked his heels and faced the prisoners.

"It has been proved to the court beyond any doubt," he began, speaking quietly, so that the senior officers at the other end of the room had to bend forward to hear, "that the accused are guilty of the charges, and when guilt is so clear it would be a disgrace to the fine spirit of these heroes if we thought of saving their lives.

"We all remember the names of two heroes, Teisuke Oki and Shozo Yokogawa.* These two brave men died gloriously and won immortality only because they were executed by the Russians with full military honours.

"The Forty-seven Ronin of Ako† were also sentenced to death because their violation of the law had to be punished although their spirit was sublime and they willingly killed themselves. This is why their fame will remain undying in our history.

"If you compare these heroes of ours with the heroes of the Rimau Operation you will see that they are identical in their action and their patriotism.

"With such fine determination they infiltrated into the Japanese area. We do not hesitate to call them the real heroes of a forlorn hope. It has been fortunate for us that their intention was frustrated halfway, but when we fathom their intention and share their feelings, we cannot but spare a tear for them. The valorous spirit of these men remind us of the daring enterprise of our heroes of the Naval Special Attack Corps who died in May 1942 in their attack on Sydney Harbour. The same admiration and respect that the Australian Government, headed by the Premier and all the Australian people, showed to those heroes of ours we must return to these heroes in our presence. When the deed is so heroic, its sublime spirit must be respected, and its success or failure becomes a secondary matter. These heroes must have left Australia with sublime patriotism flaming in their breasts, and with the confident expectation of all the Australian people on their shoulders. The last moment of a hero must be historic and it must be dramatic. Heroes have more regard for their reputation than for anything else. As we respect them, so we feel our duty of glorifying their last moments as they deserve, and by doing so the names of these heroes will remain in the hearts of the British and Australian people for evermore. In these circumstances, I consider that a death sentence should be given to each of the accused."

Major Kamiya bowed low to the prisoners and sat.

Then Colonel Towatari and the other judges rose, waited for an orderly to bring their swords, and clipped them on.

What happened next was unusual, for the president was about to break a rule at Japanese courts-martial—to proclaim sentence at the court itself instead of at the execution ground

---

* Teisuka Oki and Shozo Yokogawa were Japanese heroes in the Russo-Japanese War. While wearing civilian clothes they blew up a bridge, and were caught, tried and executed by the Russians.

† In 1702 the Forty-seven Ronin of Ako, who are among Japan's favourite heroes, murdered their dead lord's enemy, Kotsuke-no-Suke, and were ordered to commit hara-kiri as punishment for the deed. They all disembowelled themselves. Ronin were samurai retainers who had in this case lost their feudal lord.

—in Japanese eyes a high "compliment", and yet another illustration of the standing of the Rimau men.

To the prisoners the president said: "You have heard what the prosecutor has said, and we agree with every word. You are heroic men who will die like heroes. You are sentenced to be executed."

Major Ingleton stepped forward.

"We thank you," he said, firmly, "for referring to us as patriotic heroes."

As the court-martial ended and the prisoners were marched out to wait for transport to their prison, Colonel Towatari did something that had never been done before.

Beckoning Furuta to follow him, he went to the guardroom and there shook hands with the ten prisoners and called them "yushi"—heroes.

A letter from the then Australian Minister for the Army (Mr Josiah Francis) to the mother of Lieutenant Carey, one of the prisoners, in 1950, says that "opportunity was given them for their defence" at their court-martial. This, on Japanese admission, was not correct. They were examined, court-martialled, and given the death sentence which General Itagaki had already ordered before their trial, but they were not defended in any way.

Here is the Minister's letter, with the relevant information:

"The Party disguised themselves as natives and concealed all outward appearance of being soldiers or members of the armed forces, and when they were sighted by Japanese aircraft or naval patrol they hoisted the Japanese flag.

"By these means they penetrated the guarded areas and reached the outlying area of the port of Singapore where they were sighted by a Japanese patrol vessel and an engagement took place.

"None had uniform or badges of rank.

"Ultimately, the Japanese captured your son and nine others and they were taken to Singapore where, after full investigation and with fairness to the prisoners, the prisoners, including your son, were charged with engaging in espionage activities, regard being paid particularly to the fact of their disguise and their waging warlike activities in non-military attire, thus depriving themselves of the normal rights and privileges of prisoners of war.

"At their trial, all the men admitted the truth of the charges against them, and opportunity was given them for their defence.

"The most careful consideration has been given to all the facts and I have to inform you that it is considered the Japanese who took part in the trial and execution of our men did not commit a war crime. No action could be taken against the Japanese concerned."

In the forty-eight hours after the death sentence the behaviour and bearing of the prisoners, who were all together in the last hours of their lives, amazed the Japanese.

As Colonel Wild says, quoting direct from the official records of the Judicial Affairs Section:

"After the trial all members of the party were given extra rations and, in accordance with their request, were kept together in one room so that they could freely converse with one another. Their attitude was really admirable. They were always clear and bright, and not a single shadow of dismal or melancholy mood did they show. All who saw them were profoundly impressed."

During this time Furuta says he believed that, because of the magnificent behaviour of the Rimau men before, during and after their trial, General Itagaki would probably cancel the death sentence if he received a special recommendation from Major-General Otsuka. I find this reasoning difficult to understand, particularly as General Itagaki had originally ordered Major Kamiya to recommend death, but Furuta says he even went to Otsuka and pleaded with him.

"I tried to move him the best way I could. I even begged him to make a recommendation to the Commander-in-Chief for mitigation of the sentence.

"He looked scornfully at me and said: 'You are a civilian —not a soldier. You do not understand the psychology of the warrior. Your request only makes you look ridiculous.'

"I talked to two other senior officers whom I knew well enough through my work to approach. They did not see the Rimau men as I saw them. They were soldiers who only thought as soldiers—not as human beings.

"In the end I gave up. I had tried—perhaps not hard enough. But I did not have the personal courage to make another petition."

On the evening of 6th July Furuta visited the prisoners for the last time and brought them cigarettes which they were allowed to smoke in their cell.

"The heroes were calm and cheerful," he wrote. "I have never seen men to equal them.

"I spoke last of all to Captain Page who talked of his love for all his family—of his mother, his wife and his father whom he believed to be a Japanese prisoner. He asked me to search for him. I promised I would and I tried to find him afterwards —but in vain."

10

THE HEAVY DOOR SLOWLY OPENED and the captain of the escort guard entered. He bowed deeply.

"It is time, gentlemen," he said, in English.

The prisoners, who were sitting in groups, some of them smoking, got to their feet and carefully folded their blankets and placed them in a neat row along one wall.

"We are ready," Bob Page said.

Then the captain called an order and soldiers came in and handcuffed each man, and when this was done the officer bowed again.

Flanked by guards with fixed bayonets the prisoners marched out, walking stiffly because of their clamped hands, marched down the long corridor and into the morning sunlight and through the gate in the high yellow wall to where the trucks were waiting.

It was 9.30 a.m. on 7th July 1945—their last day.

A Korean prisoner, among a group of Koreans in Outram Road that morning, watched the Rimau men move out to die.

"They all knew they were going to be executed," he wrote. "When they left the prison to enter the two trucks in which their executioners were waiting, they were in high spirits, laughing and talking and shaking hands with one another. All of us prisoners were amazed."

The trucks, with the guard escort in front and behind, drove round the circular lawn in front of the prison and down the short entrance road below the high long white jail buildings to Outram Road itself, and then along and up the hill past the whitewashed shops in Cantonment Road to Keppel Road and the docks and out along the coast.

None can know what these men felt on this final journey—what Page and Falls particularly felt as they looked out to Blakang Mati and across the Examination Anchorage to Bukum and out further across the low green islands on the sparkling sea to Subar and the night of 26th-27th September 1943, and the triumph of Operation Jaywick.

At Pasir Panjang the trucks left the sea and turned into Reformatory (now Clementi) Road, and growled inland through a wasteland of lonely hills covered in rank grass and low scrub with palms and the black-green of thick growth filling the hollows. Then, at Bukit Timah, they swung west and near Ulu Pandan, on the slope of a low hill where the grass had been heavily trampled and reddish tracks snaked among the scrub which trailed the spotted velvet flowers of Dutchman's Pipe, they stopped.

The ten prisoners climbed out and stood in a group talking and joking. They were bare-headed. They wore clean khaki, and their boots had been taken away that morning at Outram Road and cleaned.

"It is here," the captain of the escort guard said.

He opened a fresh packet of cigarettes and offered them to the prisoners and lit the cigarettes, striking a new match for each man who smoked.

Then he turned and marched along the slope to where Colonel Towatari, the president of the court-martial, Major Kamiya, the prosecutor, and other officers from Judicial Affairs and Intelligence waited.

Hiroyuki Furuta, who had been ordered to attend the execution to interpret, was not present when the prisoners reached the execution ground, but he was soon to arrive.

"On the day of the execution," he explained, "I did not have the courage to see the last hour of the heroes.

"I asked Yoshimura, a member of the Interpreter Section, if he would take my place and interpret the last orders. He agreed and I stayed in my quarters in Nassim Road and prayed to God for their happy rest.

"But as the time of execution approached I could not remain calm. I did not want to go, but I had to go. I drove to the execution ground, but there I found I was still a coward. I just could not face the heroes. I stood just in the background among the bushes and watched.

"My eyes were on Captain Page who was sitting on the ground talking to Major Ingleton, Lieutenant Carey and Able Seaman Falls. I saw them all smile, as though one of them had said something amusing—as though they did not have a care in the world. But my heart was sad."

When the prisoners had finished their cigarettes, Colonel Towatari advanced with Major Kamiya. The prisoners stood.

"Gentlemen," the colonel said, "you are now to be executed."

"We would like to be able to shake hands properly before we die," Major Ingleton replied. "It is our last request."

Interpreter Yoshimura again translated and the colonel nodded and spoke to the captain of the guard. The handcuffs were removed.

Colonel Wild, quoting from the official records of the Judicial Affairs Section, says they "shook hands merrily and even laughingly in a very harmonious manner and bade each other farewell".

And the report adds, with curious Japanese irrelevance:

"The sky was clear and the scenery was beautiful."

But Furuta, who was watching, and who could hear clearly what the prisoners said, is emphatic on one point.

"None said good-bye, but each man said good luck."

Then he adds that he nearly cried when Major Ingleton moved forward and thanked him in his absence for his kindness to the prisoners—a final speech which Colonel Wild confirms with this quotation from the official records of the execution:

"Major Ingleton, on behalf of the whole party, requested the commandant of the prison [Major Kobayashi] and the prosecuting officer [Major Kamiya] to tell the Japanese interpreter [Furuta] that they were all most grateful for the courtesy and kindness which he had shown them for a long time past. He said again that they must not forget to give the interpreter this message. All who heard him were deeply moved."

Then Colonel Towatari called an order to the captain of the guard and the ten prisoners were lined up, officers first. They were again handcuffed, this time with their hands behind their backs, and were blindfolded with white cloths.

Then the executioners—ten of them so that there was one for each prisoner, for this was a ceremonial execution—formed up facing the prisoners and ten yards from them. They were in full uniform, with ribbons, and, holding their sheathed swords in their right hands they came to attention, bowed to the prisoners, then turned and marched off in single file along a track which led through the bushes to the execution place.

They were all officers or warrant officers from 7th Area Army Headquarters, all men who had seen battle, and all expert swordsmen. They were under the command of Major Hisada, of G-2 Section, who had been one of the assistant judges at the court-martial.

At 11 a.m. Major Hisada saluted Colonel Towatari and came to attention in front of the prisoners.

"Ki-o-tsuke," he shouted.

The escort guard, drawn up behind the prisoners, snapped to attention.

"Ichi-ni-tsuke (Take your position)," came the command.

The first guard in the line stepped forward, took Major Ingleton by the arm and led him down the path to the execution place where an officer, his jacket off, his sword drawn ready, waited in a levelled clearing in the bush near a large hole dug in the reddish soil.

"Kneel," Major Ingleton was ordered by interpreter Yoshimura.

Awkwardly, because his hands were manacled behind his back, he went down on one knee, and at this moment the executioner raised his sword high with both hands and swept it down.

Fifty yards away, facing the prisoners, Major Hisada came to attention again.

"Ichi-ni-tsuke."

The second man of the guard took Captain Page's arm. . . .

"I could not bear the sight," Furuta says. "I left my hiding place and ran down the hill. I did not look back. And as I ran I thought, 'Was it right to execute these brave men? Have I done everything I could to help them?'

"These thoughts tortured me for a long time. They still torture me."

There is little more to tell.

"The execution was over by noon," Colonel Wild quotes from the official records.

"Every member of the party went to his death calmly and composedly, and there was not a single person who was not inspired by their fine attitude."

Later, Major-General Otsuka reported to a staff conference of 7th Area Army on the "patriotism, fearless enterprise, heroic behaviour and sublime end of all members of this party", praising them as "the flower of chivalry, which should be taken as a model by the Japanese".

He concluded by saying that "all Japanese soldiers should be inspired by their fine attitude, and on reflection must feel the necessity of bracing up their own spirits in emulation, if they hoped to win the war."

A week later, the Commander-in-Chief, General Itagaki, addressing the full staff of 7th Area Army, referred to the men of Operation Rimau and said: "We Japanese have been proud of our bravery and courage in action, but those heroes showed us a fine example of what true bravery should be.

"Unless we try much harder to make ourselves better soldiers, we ought to feel ashamed of ourselves before these heroes."

On 6th August 1945, one month after the execution, the atom bomb burst above Hiroshima, and nine days later Japan surrendered.

AUTHOR'S NOTES

I.A.S.D.

DURING THE PACIFIC WAR Jaywick and Rimau were only two of many special intelligence-sabotage operations which pierced the Japanese lines from Australia and carried out invaluable work in the wide island-arc from Singapore to New Guinea.

These secret operations, launched from ships, submarines and aircraft, were planned and directed from headquarters in Melbourne, and other places, by an organization which started the war with one meaningless cover-name and acquired two more, equally meaningless, before the war ended. The founding of this organization goes back to before the surrender of Singapore in February 1942, when Britain's Special Operations Executive, which was responsible for subversive operations and the organization of the European resistance movements, sent one of its skilled operatives from Singapore to Australia.

This man was Colonel E. G. Mott. He was not a regular soldier, but a businessman—a director of the big Asia-wide mercantile house of Maclaine, Watson & Co. Ltd.—who had spent years in Java.

S.O.E. had suggested starting a subversive-sabotage organization in Australia, and Colonel Mott, after consulting the Australian Government and Services, and after some opposition to the scheme, but with the strong support of the Australian Commander-in-Chief, General Sir Thomas Blamey, formed the Inter-Allied Services Department in Melbourne in March 1942, with original headquarters at 260 Domain Road, South Yarra.

Colonel Mott, the businessman-specialist in secret warfare whose I.A.S.D. was merely an innocent cover-name for what was to become the Australian carbon copy of the British S.O.E., was advised by Commander R. B. M. Long, the brilliant Director of Naval Intelligence who was also responsible for extending that long-established and superb organization, the Royal Australian Navy's Coast Watchers, and by Colonel A. Gordon Oldham, who was detailed by General Blamey.

The nucleus of Colonel Mott's staff was a small group of British officers who had escaped from Malaya and who had been trained in S.O.E. methods at No. 101 Special Training School, Singapore, and some Australians, including civilians.

The first unit formed by I.A.S.D. was Z Special Unit—the name suggested by General Blamey. Z was not directly a spy-commando force, but an administrative unit for men who performed "secret and unorthodox" tasks. Personnel ranged from saboteurs to Intelligence clerks.

On 26th June 1942, I.A.S.D. came under the control of General Douglas MacArthur, and on 6th July 1942, the Allied

Intelligence Bureau—A.I.B., as it was known—was formed to direct all special units, including I.A.S.D. and its offshoots.

An Australian, Colonel C. G. Roberts, who was the first Controller of A.I.B., was responsible to Major-General Charles A. Willoughby, General MacArthur's Chief of Intelligence. Colonel Allison W. Ind was A.I.B. finance officer. Another Australian, Colonel Kenneth Wills, was Controller towards the end of the war.

In April 1943, the cover-name I.A.S.D. was abolished and Colonel Mott returned to England, and in its place emerged a new cover-name, Special Operations Australia, which soon afterwards was changed to the Services Reconnaissance Department, under another Englishman, Colonel J. Chapman-Walker, S.R.D. though under A.I.B., remained a British unit financed entirely by English-Australian money.

From the formation of I.A.S.D. in March 1942 until the closing-down of S.R.D. after the war, the success of the organization was due to its cell-like structure and rigid secrecy. Not more than a few key men ever knew the full story of I.A.S.D., S.O.A., S.R.D., or how this organization under innocuous names worked. Others knew a little. Most never knew more than fragments of the whole.

The organization's structure was designed to maintain secrecy at all levels, to make impossible the building up of any composite picture from isolated information, to make sure, among other things, that a man who was captured would know so little that, even if he talked, he could not endanger the lives of the many and destroy the total organization.

WHY?

AN INTELLIGENT FRENCH WOMAN married to an aristocratic Western-educated Japanese was once asked if she really understood her husband.

"We get on extremely well," she replied, "except that every now and then his mind slips back a thousand years."

That penetrating observation may help us a little to understand the Japanese, to explain to Western man, who has a tradition of logic, and who at least tries to think logically, the contradiction in the Japanese treatment of the ten men of Operation Rimau.

The Japanese in Singapore called the ten heroes and regarded them almost with reverence—and yet they killed them. Why?

As I was not qualified to answer this question, I went to a man who knows Japan and the Japanese, who lived there for ten years, who speaks the language fluently, and who understands something of the thought processes, emotionalism and traditions of this people still emerging from feudalism.

This man was George Caiger, a Queensland-born Oxford University graduate who, between 1930 and 1940, was Lecturer in English at the Peers' College in Tokyo, and who, during the Pacific war, was head of the Information Department of General Douglas MacArthur's Allied Translator and Interpreter Section.

"This question can't be answered logically," he told me, "for Western logic, which does not appeal to the Japanese, is intellectual, whereas Japanese logic, which is intuitive, almost feminine, is emotional. Western and Japanese logic are poles apart because they start from different premises, different concepts of history and of time.

"We try to distinguish between history and legend, but the Japanese don't even try. We have a sense of time, the Japanese mind moves in time. We fear death, the Japanese don't. We think in terms of a lifetime, the Japanese think in terms of eternity. To most of us the Middle Ages are remote, shadowy, but to the Japanese the Middle Ages are as close as yesterday.

"To the Japanese, who venerate courage and disregard death, the Rimau men were true warrior-heroes in the feudal-samurai tradition, and comparable in every way to their own heroes, ancient and modern. And even when given the chance to plead for mercy before their trial, the heroes acted as true warriors, in the Japanese view, and correctly and scornfully rejected the chance of life.

"According to their traditions, beliefs, feelings, the Japanese in Singapore acted logically in executing the prisoners, for the spirit of a hero is more powerful when he is dead, and only through death can his spirit be set free from his body. The Japanese regarded these men not as ordinary prisoners, but as special men, unique men, real heroes to whom deference and reverence were due by right.

"Execution—ceremonial execution—was therefore the only way to give them the highest honour the Japanese could confer. That honour was immortality for, dead and their spirits liberated, and their execution officially recorded, the heroes were even greater heroes than when they were alive."

That is the interpretation of a man who knows the Japanese, not superficially but after long association and study.

But it still does not answer one most important question: was immortality also conferred on those thousands of defenceless men and women who, in every theatre of the Pacific war, were brutally murdered by Japanese who even bayonetted helpless patients in hospitals and even used prisoners for target practice?

"Logically, it was," George Caiger says, "for death by any means liberates the spirit and makes it immortal. But, as it has already been explained, the Japanese are not logical people in the Western sense, and the slaughter of soldier prisoners and civilians was ruthless killing by a conditioned soldiery, and without a thought given to the spirits of the butchered.

"And to understand the behaviour of the Japanese soldiery you have to go back to 1877 when a revolt in Japan—a very serious one which started largely because of the introduction of conscription—nearly overthrew the Government.

"When this revolt was smashed, the Japanese military caste realized for the first time that an efficient rifle in the hands of a despised peasant could be just as deadly as a rifle held by the proud descendant of a distinguished samurai. And so the military caste deliberately set out to infuse something of the warlike samurai tradition into the conscripts who were mostly peasants, and this policy was continued from then on, reaching its peak in the war with China and the preparations for the war with the West.

"The Japanese conscript Army which fought the Pacific war had been conditioned to the samurai tradition of personal courage, endurance, lack of pity, and, as members of the divine Yamato race, to hate anyone who opposed the divine mission of national expansion, and to despise prisoners.

"With this mental background, consciously produced by a professional officer caste, they killed, as well as tortured, bashed and starved—though much depended on the attitude of individual commanders—with the casual brutality of a primitive conqueror, and without the slightest thought of giving immortality to their victims. Certain of their own divine mission, conditioned to hate and despise, and without even a glimpse of the West's Christian concept of pity, of sympathy, they treated these people as useless despised cattle. Theirs was a conqueror's brutality without a glimmer of compassion.

"But the treatment of the Rimau men was completely different, for these were men who, in the eyes of the Japanese officer caste, had exhibited the highest qualities of the samurai—courage, stoicism in adversity, fearlessness of death. As they revered them as heroes, like the heroes of their own military tradition—and particularly at a time when the morale of their own soldiers was beginning to crack—they looked at them not as Australians or Englishmen, not even as members of enemy nationalities, but as warriors whose spirits must be set free and given, with full and traditional ceremonial, immortality."

So perhaps what that Frenchwoman said was true when she attempted to analyse her Japanese husband.

"Every now and then his mind slips back a thousand years."

LORD LOUIS MOUNTBATTEN

MAJOR-GENERAL CHARLES A. WILLOUGHBY, General Douglas MacArthur's Intelligence Chief, and John Chamberlain in their *MacArthur—Victory in the Pacific*, give another version of the origin of Ivan Lyon's Operation Jaywick. This version is one hundred per cent wrong.

The authors claim that after the fall of Singapore, Admiral Lord Louis Mountbatten cabled General MacArthur from Ceylon suggesting a diversion, a "one-way" suicide attack, in the "direction" of Singapore.

"He [Lord Louis] wanted the Japanese Southern Fleet, based on Singapore, to be frightened into immobility; the sinking of Japanese transports, tankers or freighters at Singapore docks would do the trick. As usual, the 'buck was passed' to G2 [Major-General Willoughby], the whipping boy of the staff, the garbage can for all spurious or half-baked ideas. Everything was against the Mountbatten demand, for submarines were not available and fast seagoing craft were equally scarce. Luckily G2 was more fortunate with personnel. If the Singapore diversion was to be made a reality, the leader of the party had to be someone who knew the harbor of Singapore, preferably a local yachtsman familiar not only with bays, inlets and channels but with native boatmen. Such a specialist was found in the person of a British officer, Lieut.-Col. I. Lyon of the Gordon Highlanders, who, after some high-level negotiations, had to be 'imported' from England to do the job."

This story is so inaccurate that a Senior Intelligence officer of General Willoughby's experience should never have published it.

Here is Admiral Lord Louis Mountbatten's reply to it—the reply is in my possession—dated 12th February 1957:

"My attention has already been drawn to the inaccuracy on Page 151 of Major-General Willoughby's book on General MacArthur and I am hoping that a correction will be made in subsequent editions.

"The point is that I did not take up my appointment as Supreme Allied Commander, South-east Asia, until November, 1943, and my headquarters were in Delhi until April, 1944, when they moved to Kandy in Ceylon.

"I note that your admirable expedition in the M.V. *Krait* sailed on September 2, 1943, which was some two months before I arrived in South-east Asia. You will appreciate that I can, therefore, have had no choice in the leader of the operation, as I knew nothing of it."

THE *KRAIT*

WHAT HAPPENED to the *Krait*—Paddy McDowell's "bloody crate"—after she brought the men of Operation Jaywick back to Australia from Singapore in October 1943?

From Exmouth Gulf she was sailed to Darwin and handed over to Captain Jack Chipper, then commanding the Lugger Maintenance Unit—another harmless cover-name for another S.R.D. secret group.

After the *Krait* was refitted, Sub-Lieutenant Harry Williams captained her on an agent-pick-up trip to Timor, and her name was given to a small bay on Browse Island, in the Timor Sea west of Cape Londonderry in the northern Kimberleys. This island was used by S.R.D. men operating between Darwin and Timor.

Later Williams took her to Morotai and then to the occupation of Amboina, where she was used for reconnaissance and cargo-carrying.

At the end of the Pacific war he handed her over to the occupying authorities at Labuan, British North Borneo.

The last time I was able to trace the *Krait* she was operating as a timber carrier out of Jesselton in Borneo—still moving through those island seas where she made her most historic voyage, and where her story began for this book when she was still the Japanese fishing boat *Kofuku Maru*.

Postscript: January 1964

In June 1963 "Z" Special Unit Association formed the Krait Committee to raise money to bring the *Krait* back to Australia as a national memorial, and Sydney's Lord Mayor, Alderman Harry Jensen, and the Sydney *Sun* opened an appeal.

The *Krait* then was owned by the River Estates Limited, of Sandakan, Sabah (North Borneo), where, twenty years after Operation Jaywick, she was being used as a timber tug. This company generously offered to sell her cheaply for £6,000 (later reduced to £4,500); the Government of Sabah contributed £1,500 to the appeal; P. and O.-Orient offered to bring her south—free as deck cargo; the R. W. Millers Group gave a major guarantee; and many others contributed and helped.

As 1964 opened, plans were being prepared to bring the *Krait* from Sandakan and for Ted Carse, captain and navigator of the *Krait* during Operation Jaywick, to bring her into Sydney Harbour on Anzac Day, 25 April 1964, to be handed over to the Volunteer Coastal Patrol for use as a training and sea rescue vessel.

Members of the Krait Committee: Patron, the Lord Mayor of Sydney (Alderman Harry Jensen); chairman, Major-General Denzil Macarthur Onslow; members, Major-General Ivan Dougherty, W. A. Chaffey, M.L.A., Angus McWilliams, Richard Cardew, Desmond Foster, Harold Nobbs, Ronald McKie, Louis d'Alpuget, Rupert Herps, Roderick Pegg, Raymond Irish, Roy L. Pegler and Co., John Trew, of Parish Patience and McIntyre.

1946

ALTHOUGH AUSTRALIAN NEWSPAPERS first reported the raids on Singapore in August 1945, the first official statement about them was not made until 1st August 1946.

On that day the Minister for the Army (Mr Forde) briefly described the first raid (Jaywick) to members of the House of Representatives in Canberra, and mentioned the second (Rimau).

He said the story was one of the best kept secrets of the war, and announced gallantry awards, which the King had approved in 1944, to the men who took part in the first raid. Nine of the men of Jaywick were decorated and the other five were mentioned in dispatches.

But because of military secrecy about the raids and the awards, Captain Robert Page, who was executed on 7th July 1945, never knew that he had won the D.S.O.

The Melbourne *Herald* published this report from Canberra on 1st August 1946:

> Members wishing to ask election propaganda questions protested in the House of Representatives today when the Minister for the Army (Mr Forde) rose to make a statement on the Singapore raid.
>
> Proceedings in the House were then being broadcast.
>
> The Speaker (Mr Rosevear) ruled that he should proceed on the ground that the first 35 minutes of broadcasting of questions had elapsed.
>
> In deference to members still anxious to reach their electors by radio, Mr Forde shortened his statement by omitting the names of the troops concerned in the exploit, but proposed that they be incorporated in the Hansard report.
>
> Dame Enid Lyons interjected urgently and with great feeling and insisted that the names should be read publicly in the House.
>
> The Minister complied.

THANK YOU

I AM MOST GRATEFUL to the following people for much help or advice during my long search:

Captain J. McL. Adams and members of the R.A.N. Archives Branch, Donald K. Baldwin, Norman Bartlett, A. C. Berryman, Walter Brooksbank, Colin Ednie-Brown, A. E. Brown, G. M. Bunning, J. S. Burns, R. H. C. Cardew, Mrs H. E. Carey, Spencer H. Carey, Professor S. W. Carey, George Caiger, Patricia Carse, Spencer Coleman, Colonel N. L. Currie, Major-General Sir Maurice Dowse, Colonel Desmond Duffy, Captain R. Fogg Elliot, C. H. Fone, Des Foster, Helen Frizell, Brigadier F. G. Galleghan, John Gowing, Major W. H. Grant and Warrant Officer E. C. Tarr and men of the 1st Infantry Battalion (Commando), Leslie Grinham, Cyril Hankinson, Red Harrison, Mrs C. Howell, Mrs V. Huston, Dr R. L. James, E. L. S. Jennings, R. Kirke, C. H. Locke, R. B. M. Long, Rowland Lyne, Colonel T. F. B. MacAdie, N. G. Macauley, Jack Macalister, the staff of the Australian War Memorial, Admiral Lord Louis Mountbatten, James Mudie, Mrs Yoko Murai, A. Gordon Oldham, R. M. Pegler, Hall Richardson, C. G. Roberts, Austin R. Samut, Sir Robert Scott, M. C. ff. Sheppard, Colin Simpson, Field Marshal Sir William Slim, E. C. Smith, O. K. Snowball and Betty Snowball, C. C. Spry, Harry Standish, Don Tait, M. J. Uren, J. N. Watt, Harry Williams, K. A. Wills, J. W. C. Wyett.

William Blackwood and Sons for kind permission to quote from "Expedition to Singkep" which first appeared in *Blackwood's Magazine*.

A very special thank you to Mrs Celia Wild, Mrs J. Heath, Mrs H. H. Page, Mrs K. C. Elvy, and Mrs. R. P. Greenish, and to Ronald Monson, H. E. Carse, Arthur Jones, Horace Young and Hiroyuki Furuta.

And, finally, to my wife for her enduring patience and encouragement—and all those cups of tea.

MORE REAL-LIFE ADVENTURE FROM ANGUS & ROBERTSON PUBLISHERS

WHEEL TRACKS
W.W. Ammon

THE BLACKBIRDERS
Edward Wybergh Docker

THE WRECK ON THE HALF MOON REEF
Hugh Edwards

SQUATTER'S CASTLE
George Farwell

THE TERRITORY
Ernestine Hill

WATER INTO GOLD
Ernestine Hill

GYMPIE GOLD
Hector Holthouse

RIVER OF GOLD
Hector Holthouse

S'POSE I DIE
Hector Holthouse

UP RODE THE SQUATTER
Hector Holthouse

BACK O' CAIRNS
Ion L. Idriess

CORAL SEA CALLING
Ion L. Idriess

FORTY FATHOMS DEEP
Ion L. Idriess

ONE WET SEASON
Ion L. Idriess

THE TIN SCRATCHERS
Ion L. Idriess

KILLERS OF EDEN
Tom Mead

TOM PETRIE'S REMINISCENCES OF EARLY QUEENSLAND
Constance Campbell Petrie

SAILORMEN'S GHOSTS
Malcolm Uren

UP RODE THE SQUATTER
Hector Holthouse

The story of the early settlement of western Queensland is a savage one. When the best land around the established settlements was taken, squatters pushed their way relentlessly beyond settlement boundaries to graze their cattle and sheep on the rich pastures of the Darling Downs. Consequently, violent clashes broke out between the squatters and Aborigines, leaving many a squatter's settlement the scene of a bloody massacre and irreparably disrupting the age-old pattern of Aboriginal life. In this powerful book Hector Holthouse evokes with vivid accuracy all the pathos, humour and savagery surrounding the people who struggled to win a living from a harsh and reluctant land.

BACK O' CAIRNS
Ion L. Idriess

Ion Idriess went to north Queensland prospecting at a time when the fabulous country "back o' Cairns" was being opened up. It was a time when a young man could hear round a campfire the stories of the great pathfinders — men like Mulligan, Doyle, Atherton and Palmerston — and of the search for a route from the coast to the hinterland. Ion Idriess found more than gold in the North, he found the true beauty and fascination of that country, and makes it come alive in his stories of the unforgettable men and women who were its pioneers.

CORAL SEA CALLING
Ion L. Idriess

The treacherous and beautiful Coral Sea is the background for this story of the nineteenth-century adventurers on perilous voyages into its waters in search of bêche-de-mer and pearlshell, of the savage chiefs who ruled its islands, of the explorers struggling up its mainland coast and of the Queen's representatives whose task it was to tame the wilderness and its people. Ion L. Idriess vividly weaves his own experiences into this story to produce a rich and fascinating saga of the Coral Sea.

WHEEL TRACKS
W. W. Ammon

Wheel Tracks is the tale of the first transport drivers who crossed the tough desert lands of north-west Western Australia. The drivers were the lifeline of the north-west settlers, as they carried wool crops to Carnarvon and returned with mail and vital supplies. Told by one of those drivers, the story follows the trucks along hundreds of miles of rutted wheel tracks, over endless loose sandhills, through raging floods and across treacherous, washed-out river beds. In this vivid portrayal of humour, endurance and adventure W. W. Ammon has created a memorable and authentic piece of outback literature.

THE WRECK ON THE HALF MOON REEF
Hugh Edwards

On 26 March 1728 the first ship ever built in Australia put crankily out to sea. She was the little *Sloepie*, built and crewed by survivors from the Dutch East Indiaman *Zeewyk*. Months before, the *Zeewyk* had impaled herself on the savage reefs around the Abrolhos Islands and had been broken up by the huge seas thundering in from the Indian Ocean. The result was a quick death for some, a slow death for others, and the torture and execution of two youths for the "stupid sin" of sodomy. The rest of the survivors wrangled themselves to the verge of mutiny and cast greedy eyes on the chests of treasure salvaged from the wreck. At last they realised that rescue would never come and built the *Sloepie*.

THE TERRITORY
Ernestine Hill

Timeless because it is history, timelessly popular because it is so full of life, colour and adventure, Ernestine Hill's *The Territory* is the story of the first hundred years of exploring, pioneering and settlement in Australia's tropic north. Cattle droving over unknown wildernesses, tragic encounters — for both races — with Aborigines, efforts to establish settlements that were cut off from the world, the building of the Overland Telegraph Line and the incredible lives of the men and women of three generations — these are the stuff of the book. Every character, incident and scene comes vividly to life.

SQUATTER'S CASTLE
George Farwell

In this magnificent chronicle of the life of a New England squatter, George Farwell describes how Edward Ogilvie and his family arrived in Australia and trekked to the Hunter River, where eventually they prospered. Then, in 1840, Edward and his brother Fred decided to go farther afield — over the New England Ranges to the banks of the Clarence River. But Edward's ambition to create a dynasty split his family and soured its relationships . Finally, the castle he had constructed as a symbol of his prestige and power became the focus of wranglings caused by his obstinate pride.

ONE WET SEASON
Ion L. Idriess

One Wet Season is the story of the yearly meeting of men from the Kimberleys at the tiny port of Derby, there to be isolated for some three months throughout every wet season, just waiting for "the Wet" to end and "the Dry" to come. When these men congregate some of the monotony of the long three months is relieved by the yarning of mates and by the telling of incidents in their own lives . . . Of such material is this book made, with close-ups of localities as they are and events as they actually happened.

TOM PETRIE'S REMINISCENCES OF EARLY QUEENSLAND
Constance Campbell Petrie

What did Queensland's shining bays, fantastic Glasshouse Mountains and rich valleys mean to the white settlers who first came upon them? What did they mean to the Aboriginal tribes whose vast home they had once been? The memories of Tom Petrie, recorded by his daughter, answer these questions. They range from life in the penal settlement of Brisbane in the 1840s to scenes of the countryside around his homestead at North Pine. Most importantly, he describes his contact with Aboriginal customs, myths and folklore, for he was closely associated with the Aborigines from his early boyhood days.

GYMPIE GOLD
Hector Holthouse

For fifty years after James Nash discovered gold in 1867 at the spot on the Mary River in Queensland where Gympie now stands, gold was the town's main source of income. And in that period the lure of a fortune made from gold was responsible for many dramatic events — the sensational Escort Murder, hold-ups by bushrangers, battles between Chinese and European prospectors — which Hector Holthouse vividly describes against a background of life in a frontier town with all its hardships. *Gympie Gold* is popular history at its most readable.

RIVER OF GOLD
Hector Holthouse

"The goldrush at Palmer River on Cape York lasted about seven years in the 1870s, but with 35,000 diggers it was this country's wildest while it lasted. Holthouse has researched the story of those days well to make a lively and very readable book." *The Bulletin*

Hector Holthouse spent several years in the north Queensland sugar belt, during which time he became interested in the colourful history of the North. In *River of Gold* he gives an account of the Palmer River goldrush — sparked off in 1873 by a find of 102 ounces of gold in a few weeks.

WATER INTO GOLD
Ernestine Hill

Here is the dramatic and colourful story of how a waterless wasteland was transformed into Australia's most fertile garden. It is the story of the Murray Valley, now a sparkling land jewelled with orchards and vineyards, growing everything from asparagus to walnuts. This was made possible by the faith and courage of a few hopeful men and women, by new scientific methods which developed cultivation and by a miracle of yesterday — irrigation. Ernestine Hill's *Water into Gold* is not only a fine piece of Australian literature, but also a true story of human endeavour, a part of our heritage which every Australian should read.